# Location and Competition



The 'new economic geography' is one of the most significant developments to have occurred in economics in recent years. The new insights gained from this approach have been successfully applied to issues such as globalisation, international integration and policy competition.

*Location and Competition* brings together leading academics to analyse the research inspired by the 'new economic geography' and examines the ensuing policy implications. Issues that are germane to this approach such as core–periphery patterns, transportation costs and economic modelling are explored in depth.

**Steven Brakman** is Professor of Economics at the University of Groningen, the Netherlands.

**Harry Garretsen** is Professor of International Economics at the Utrecht School of Economics, Utrecht University, the Netherlands.

**Studies in Global Competition**

*A series of books edited by John Cantwell, The University of Reading, UK and David Mowery, University of California, Berkeley, USA*

**Volume 1**
Japanese Firms in Europe
*Edited by Frédérique Sachwald*

**Volume 2**
Technological Innovation, Multinational Corporations and New International Competitiveness
The case of intermediate countries
*Edited by José Molero*

**Volume 3**
Global Competition and the Labour Market
*By Nigel Driffield*

**Volume 4**
The Source of Capital Goods Innovation
The role of user firms in Japan and Korea
*By Kong-Rae Lee*

**Volume 5**
Climates of Global Competition
*By Maria Bengtsson*

**Volume 6**
Multinational Enterprises and Technological Spillovers
*By Tommaso Perez*

**Volume 7**
Governance of International Strategic Alliances
Technology and transaction costs
*By Joanne E. Oxley*

**Volume 8**
Strategy in Emerging Markets
Telecommunications establishments in Europe
*By Anders Pehrsson*

**Volume 9**
Going Multinational
The Korean experience of direct investment
*Edited by Frédérique Sachwald*

**Volume 10**
Multinational Firms and Impacts on Employment, Trade and Technology
New perspectives for a new century
*Edited by Robert E. Lipsey and Jean-Louis Mucchielli*

**Volume 11**
Multinational Firms
The global–local dilemma
*Edited by John H. Dunning and Jean-Louis Mucchielli*

**Volume 12**
MIT and the Rise of Entrepreneurial Science
*Henry Etzkowitz*

**Volume 13**
Technological Resources and the Logic of Corporate Diversification
*Brian Silverman*

**Volume 14**
The Economics of Innovation, New Technologies and Structural Change
*Cristiano Antonelli*

**Volume 15**
European Union Direct Investment in China
Characteristics, challenges and perspectives
*Daniel Van Den Bulcke, Haiyan Zhang and Maria do Céu Esteves*

**Volume 16**
Biotechnology in Comparative Perspective
*Edited by Gerhard Fuchs*

**Volume 17**
Technological Change and Economic Performance
*Albert L. Link and Donald S. Siegel*

**Volume 18**
Multinational Corporations and European Regional Systems of Innovation
*John Cantwell and Simona Iammarino*

**Volume 19**
Knowledge and Innovation in Regional Industry
An entrepreneurial coalition
*Roel Rutten*

**Volume 20**
Local Industrial Clusters
Existence, emergence and evolution
*Thomas Brenner*

**Volume 21**
The Emerging Industrial Structure of the Wider Europe
*Edited by Francis McGowen, Slavo Radosevic and Nick Von Tunzelmann*

**Volume 22**
Entrepreneurship
A new perspective
*Thomas Grebel*

**Volume 23**
Evaluating Public Research Institutions
The U.S. Advanced Technology Program's Intramural Research Initiative
*Albert N. Link and John T. Scott*

**Volume 24**
Location and Competition
*Edited by Steven Brakman and Harry Garretsen*

# Location and Competition

**Edited by Steven Brakman and Harry Garretsen**

Routledge
Taylor & Francis Group
LONDON AND NEW YORK

First published 2005
by Routledge
2 Park Square, Milton Park, Abingdon, Oxon OX14 4RN

Simultaneously published in the USA and Canada
by Routledge
711 Third Avenue, New York, NY 10017

*Routledge is an imprint of the Taylor & Francis Group, an informa business*

First issued in paperback 2012



Typeset in Times New Roman by Keyword Group Ltd



*British Library Cataloguing in Publication Data*
A catalogue record for this book is available from the British Library

*Library of Congress Cataloging in Publication Data*
Location and competition/editors, Steven Brakman and Harry Garretsen.

p. cm.

Includes bibliographical references and index.

1. Economic geography. 2. Competition. 3. Industrial concentration.
4. Economic policy. I. Brakman, Steven. II. Garretsen, Harry.

HF1025.L593 2005

338.6′048--dc22

2004030383

ISBN13: 978-0-415-36547-5 hardback

ISBN13: 978-0-415-65547-7 paperback

# Contents

# Figures

# Tables

# Contributors

**Roel Beetsma** is Professor of Macroeconomics at the Faculty of Economics and Econometrics of the University of Amsterdam.

**Steven Brakman** is Professor of Economics at the Faculty of Economics of the University of Groningen.

**Harry Garretsen** is Professor of International Economics at the Utrecht School of Economics, Utrecht University.

**Joeri Gorter** is Policy Adviser and Researcher at the Netherlands' Bureau for Economic Policy Analysis (CPB) in The Hague.

**Jeroen Hinloopen** is Associate Professor of Industrial Organisation at the Faculty of Economics and Econometrics of the University of Amsterdam and also Scientific Director of the Economics Network for Competition and Regulation (ENCORE).

**Jan Lambooy** is Honorary Professor of Spatial Economics at Utrecht University and Professor Emeritus of Economic Geography of the University of Amsterdam.

**Charles van Marrewijk** is Professor of Economics at Erasmus University Rotterdam and Chairman of International Bachelor Economics and Business at the Faculty of Economics of Erasmus University.

**Ruud de Mooij** is Professor of Public Economics at the Faculty of Economics of Erasmus University Rotterdam and Program Manager, Welfare State at the Netherlands' Bureau for Economic Policy Analysis (CPB) in The Hague.

**Richard Nahuis** is Program Manager, Public Organisations at the Netherlands' Bureau for Economic Policy Analysis (CPB) in The Hague. He is also Researcher at the Utrecht School of Economics, Utrecht University.

**Frank van Oort** is Senior and Coordinating Researcher of Spatial Economics at the Ruimtelijk Planbureau (RPB) in The Hague and Assistant Professor of Spatial and Urban Economics at the Faculty of Geosciences of Utrecht University.

**Jan Oosterhaven** is Professor of Spatial Economics at the Faculty of Economics of the University of Groningen.

**Piet Rietveld** is Professor of Transport Economics at the Faculty of Economics and Business of the Free University of Amsterdam.

**Koen Vermeylen** is Assistant Professor at the Faculty of Economics and Econometrics of the University of Amsterdam.

# Location and competition: an introduction

*Steven Brakman and Harry Garretsen*

## INTRODUCTION

'Location and competition' was the theme of the papers presented at the 2003 annual meeting of the Royal Netherlands Economic Association (Brakman and Garretsen 2003). Based on deduction, increasing integration of the world economy, and for that matter the European Union (EU), may be expected to influence concentration and specialisation patterns in the economy. For the EU, two issues stand out. First, the completion of economic and monetary union (EMU) with the introduction of the euro. Second, the unprecedented enlargement of the EU with the 12 new accession countries, which almost doubled the membership of the EU and increased its population to 500 million. These events reduced trade barriers within the largest trading block of the world. Moreover, one of the principal aims of the EU is to allow and stimulate cross-border mobility. In combination, these factors imply that relocation of factors of production is likely and will change concentration and specialisation patterns in the EU.

This raises the question of what the most likely outcome of this process will be. In a neoclassical world, removal of trade barriers will make the world more equal. The neoclassical Heckscher-Ohlin model, for example, predicts that in the absence of trade barriers the final trading-equilibrium is characterised by factor price equalisation. Factors of production no longer have an incentive to relocate to other regions or countries. This is basically the reason why trade theory treats countries as dimensionless points, with no geographical features whatsoever. For this reason, international trade theory does not have to deal with the relocation decision of factors of production. Factor price equalisation makes such analyses redundant. Also, the neoclassical growth models predict that countries will converge with respect to their per capita incomes. This implies that in the final growth-equilibrium there is no need to consider the relocation decision of factors of production as they have no incentive to migrate. The general conclusion is that in a neoclassical world more integration implies that the world becomes more equal.

What happens if the neoclassical model is not valid? Suppose production is characterised by economies of scale, rather than by constant returns to scale as in the neoclassical world. In the presence of transportation costs, firms have an incentive to think about their location.[1] This follows from the so-called 'spatial impossibility theorem', which states that when economic activity is not perfectly divisible, as is the case with increasing returns to scale, transportation of goods is unavoidable (Fujita and Thisse 2002). In autarky, production and consumption take place within a single region. But when regions are not in autarky, firms have an incentive to concentrate production in a smaller number of sites to exploit economies of scale. The preferred site is the site where firms have access to the largest market. In a core market customers can avoid paying transportation costs and thus have a higher real disposable income. This makes it attractive for both customers and firms to locate at the same site. In a world characterised by increasing returns to scale, the ongoing process of economic and monetary unification within the EU could lead to more concentration and agglomeration. This could start a process of cumulative causation in the sense that agglomeration of economic activity also leads to agglomeration of spending power. Factor rewards in core regions will be (much) higher than in peripheral regions. This makes the core region attractive to newcomers and stimulates further agglomeration of economic activity and spending power. In contrast to the conclusion of neo-classical models, the world becomes more unequal with increased integration. In this sense, inequality is an equilibrium outcome. Recently, Krugman (1991a; 1991b) extended well-known trade models in order to deal with the (re)location decisions of firms and workers. This work has initiated a whole new branch of international trade models, the so-called 'new economic geography' (NEG), that include the location decisions of factors of production and explicitly explains core–periphery patterns.

The five chapters in this volume, which are based on the papers presented at the Royal Netherlands Economic Association 2003 annual meeting, are focused on the presence and analysis of core–periphery patterns in the world economy. In Chapter 1, Hinloopen and Van Marrewijk show that core–periphery patterns are scale invariant: at all levels of regional aggregation, core–periphery patterns can be distinguished. They implicitly show that the world is probably best characterised by increasing returns to scale and imperfect markets. In Chapter 2, Oosterhaven and Rietveld take a closer look at the single most important variable of NEG: transportation costs. They show that transportation costs have declined considerably over the past centuries, but that in contrast to popular opinion it is too early to conclude that 'distance is dead'. Transport costs are still a dominant factor in explaining concentration and agglomeration patterns. In Chapter 3, Lambooy and Van Oort welcome the renewed attention of geography in NEG, but also point out that these models are too stylised to be useful for empirical analyses of core–periphery structures. Standard models from spatial economics tell us what is missing from NEG. The final two chapters, by De Mooij, Gorter and Nahuis, and Beetsma and Vermeylen, introduce policy issues in the discussion of core–periphery patterns. In Chapter 4, De Mooij, Gorter and Nahuis explain that the effects of, for example, international tax competition in a neoclassical world is completely different from those in NEG. In a neoclassical world, tax competition might result in a 'race to the bottom', in the sense that the country with the lowest tax rate has the best competitive position and forces other countries to reduce taxes.

In NEG, agglomeration rents make high taxes possible and prevent a race to the bottom. In Chapter 5, Beetsma and Vermeylen analyse the likelihood of asymmetric shocks between countries in the presence of economic agglomeration, and how this affects the rationale of the euro. NEG predicts that the likelihood of asymmetric shocks might increase, but Beetsma and Vermeylen show that in the case of EMU all relevant factors combine to most likely reduce this possibility.

In the next section, we briefly discuss and introduce NEG and its policy implications. This is then followed by summaries of the chapters and their ensuing policy recommendations.

## LESSONS FROM THEORY

What is the main contribution of NEG? In our view, it is that this theory serves as a foothold for gaining a better insight into agglomeration effects through a model-based approach. While it is true that the basic elements of the modern theory are anything but new, we have only recently been able to bring together fruitfully in a single model aspects such as economies of scale, imperfect competition and the associated choice of location, and the possibilities of multiple equilibria. This not only shows that core–periphery equilibria are possible, but also generally demonstrates why that is the case. The theoretical developments discussed in this introduction provide an important contribution to integrating international and regional economics. With respect to policy implications, the new theory shows that, regardless of the spatial aggregation level, economic inequality, in the sense of spatially unequal distribution or growth of economic activity, can be persistent even if a freely operating price mechanism is in place. Where equilibria are (in part) historically determined and where self-reinforcing processes are at play, only an extensive change in the economic environment, whether policy-induced or not, will lead to different equilibria of growth, trade and the location of enterprises and employees, etc.

For policymakers, the difficulty is how to succeed in generating enough critical mass, as it were, to bring this change about. Conversely, in the case of structural changes in the economy (arising, for example, from the process of economic integration in Europe), it is unwise from a policy perspective to ignore the policy implications of the modern NEG theory. In terms of this theory, economic integration can be seen as a systematic lowering of transportation costs, or of the transaction costs of trade more generally. For the enlargement of the EU towards the east, this could mean that Eastern Europe might not necessarily profit from inclusion in the EU but that, for the reasons outlined above, the head-start enjoyed by Western Europe at the moment of this inclusion could have a self-reinforcing effect.

Another example in the European context is EMU. If economic integration, via the reduction of transaction costs and stimulated by economies of scale, leads to greater spatial concentration of economic activity in the EU (e.g. the European car industry entirely in Germany, the financial sector fully concentrated in London or Frankfurt, etc.), the rationale behind monetary union could be partly undermined because such a concentration process would increase the likelihood of asymmetric shocks. In terms of the time-honoured theory on optimum currency areas, this would make the shift to a currency union in Europe as a whole less desirable.

The main lesson that NEG theory holds for policymakers, as the above examples show, is the need to refine the ultimate neoclassical message that where a price mechanism operates unhindered, economic convergence arises automatically. In a world such as that of NEG theory, in which agglomeration and equalisation forces influence each other and the choice of location is crucial, economic divergence or inequality can (but need not!) be the equilibrium outcome. Whether and how policy could influence such results is a complex matter. Clearly, the new perspective on the relationship between economy and geography offers policy insights that cannot be found in the more common (traditional) views on regional or location policy. Baldwin *et al.* (2003) provide a very clear summary of the additional policy insights, the most important of which have been mentioned in this section.

## SUMMARY OF THE CHAPTERS

This section gives an extensive summary of each of the five chapters.

### Spatial distribution of economic activity – empiricism

Chapter 1, by Hinloopen and Van Marrewijk, identifies – for different variables, aggregation levels and periods – the spatial distribution of economic activity and whether any regularity can be discerned in that distribution. In their contribution, the authors deliberately do not give a possible explanation for the stylised facts that they present but confine themselves to a description of the facts, thus launching the discussion of location and competition. Given the multitude of possible analyses and approaches regarding the spatial distribution of economic activity in terms of 'what' (population, GNP, sectors), 'where' (groups of countries, individual countries, regions and cities) and 'how' (the structure in the distribution), there are striking similarities in the results of the various analyses performed. In summary, the following stylised facts are brought to the fore in their paper.

- There is an uneven distribution regardless of the *type* of economic activity.
- There is an uneven distribution regardless of the spatial or *geographical* aggregation level.
- There is an uneven distribution regardless of the *economic* aggregation level.
- There is a clear regularity in the distribution of economic *activity*.
- There is a clear regularity in the interaction between economic *centres*.

The conclusions on the distribution of economic activity are based, first and foremost, on the World Bank's classification of all individual countries into seven groups. For this classification, the spatial distribution of the population density and GNP density appears to be extremely uneven. A subsequent review of individual countries at global level yields the same conclusion. Further spatial disaggregation yields the same picture. Within the Netherlands, and at the regional level in Europe, calculation of a core–periphery (CP) index reveals a very uneven distribution.

In the second part of the chapter, the authors illustrate the regularity of the distribution of economic activity with the help of estimates of Zipf's law for urban agglomerations. Zipf's law states that the largest city will be exactly *x* times as large as the *x*th largest city. This empirical law is shown to apply at the levels of the world as a whole, parts of the world and individual countries. The regularity also emerges from estimates of a gravity equation for bilateral trade flows, according to which the greater the size of two countries' separate 'economic masses' (i.e. income) and the smaller the distance between them, the more trade they will engage in with each other. The estimates performed by the authors confirm the significance of the gravity relationship.

## Transport costs, location and economy

Transportation costs play a crucial role in all theoretical explanations for the spatial concentration of economic activities. In the absence of transportation costs, location is not an essential consideration. If the movement of goods and production factors through space does not entail costs, location decisions by enterprises and employees are no longer relevant (Fujita and Thisse 2002: 35). Accordingly, a closer insight into the development and determinants of transportation costs is desirable. This is the subject of Chapter 2, by Oosterhaven and Rietveld. First and foremost, the authors demonstrate that transportation costs have vastly decreased in the past centuries. This decrease is evident in the transportation of both goods and passengers. The lower cost of goods transport has clearly had a positive influence on international trade. This finding is in line with the analysis on the basis of the gravity comparison in Chapter 1.

Oosterhaven and Rietveld emphasise that in assessing transportation costs, we should not only look at monetary transportation costs and transportation speeds, but also at aspects such as the frequency and reliability of transport. In addition, as regards spatial economic interactions, not only are transportation costs, narrowly defined, relevant, but so too is the wider concept of transaction costs. Notably, empirical research shows that the relatively high transaction costs of cross-border transactions explain why the spatial interaction between regions within a country is two to twenty times as large as the interaction between comparable regions at a comparable distance, but located in different countries. The authors conclude that despite the decrease that has occurred, transportation costs will be no less important in the future and there is no guarantee that these costs will continue to decline (consider congestion problems).

Following the discussion of the long-term development of transportation costs, the authors deal more closely with the accessibility of the Netherlands in Europe. Again in accordance with their first finding, they state that the Netherlands, and particularly the urban conglomerate of the Randstad in the western part of the country, basically has a central position in Europe. However, when taking several accessibility aspects into account, such as the quality of the transportation network, the scores of the Dutch regions are close to the Western European average. Owing to the trade-off between (market) proximity and congestion problems, the differences between the Western European regions are generally small. Only in the case of the highly urbanised European regions do the advantages of (market) proximity and the density of the transportation network clearly outweigh the disadvantages of congestion.

Against the backdrop of the actual development of transportation costs and the determination of accessibility, the authors focus in the second part of their chapter on the importance of transportation costs, and thus of the infrastructure, for decisions on location at urban and regional levels. The literature on agglomeration at the urban level traditionally concentrates on the location decisions of households. In the early nineteenth century, high transportation costs of agricultural products limited the size of cities. The introduction of railways changed this situation and stimulated rapid growth of (specialised) cities. Transportation of people was, however, still very costly. This led to densely built cities. The introduction of tram systems lowered the commuting costs of people, which stimulated cities to grow in area (but not necessary grow in economic size). This growth was further stimulated by the car. In modern approaches to location decisions, such as NEG, the emphasis lies more on location decisions by enterprises. The tension between the forces of agglomeration and distribution is, according to NEG, the determining factor for the location of enterprises (and the mobile production factors). The effect of a reduction in transportation costs on the degree of agglomeration is largely dependent on the initial level of these costs. In respect of the intermediary values of these costs, a reduction will generally stimulate agglomeration – unless transportation costs were already very low at the outset, in which case distribution occurs (Puga 1999; Brakman *et al.* 2001).

At the regional level, the influence of transportation costs is analysed in the second finding by identifying the spatial economic consequences of investments in infrastructure. In this context, Oosterhaven and Rietveld discuss six methods for estimating these effects. In assessing the suitability of these various methods, it must always be considered whether an answer should be obtained to the *ex post* question regarding the historical influence or the *ex ante* question regarding the future influence of specific new infrastructure.

Following a discussion on the advantages and disadvantages of each of these methods, the authors provide a thorough review of the recently developed spatial computable general equilibrium (SCGE) models. In the context of their findings, this type of model is of interest primarily because the model structure is explicitly based on the basic ingredients of the NEG approach. The first SCGE model for the Netherlands, developed by Knaap and Oosterhaven (2001), has three features that can be directly traced back to the basic NEG model of the Krugman type (1991a):

- enterprises enjoy economies of scale
- enterprises and consumers have a preference for (product) variety, and
- there are positive transportation costs between regions.

Furthermore, in comparison with other methods, SCGE models allow for a more realistic analysis of the consequences of investment in infrastructure for location decisions by enterprises, and also facilitate estimation of the indirect gains – on account of the reduction in market imperfections – from such investment.

The SCGE-type model also has disadvantages: so far, it can only be used for comparative static analyses. Oosterhaven and Rietveld argue that, in part by including indirect costs, it is possible to make improved social cost–benefit analyses of large-scale infrastructure projects. To illustrate the working of an SCGE model, the model developed by Knaap and Oosterhaven (2001) is used to investigate the employment benefits arising from four options for a magnetic-levitation railway. Depending on the chosen option, the employment effects are considerable. The same applies to the calculated increase of the consumer surplus (the net cash value of the increase of this surplus varies from €141 million to €724 million).

The authors conclude that, through a decline of the transportation costs, the relative importance of other kinds of transaction costs has increased. Spatial interaction and location patterns cannot be understood properly unless the influence of these costs is taken into account. The authors emphasise that while transportation costs have indeed sharply declined, there is certainly no question yet that a 'death of distance' occurs.

## Agglomeration(s) in equilibrium?

Following the discussion in the first two chapters of the stylised facts on the spatial distribution of economic activity and, subsequently, the role of transportation costs, Chapter 3 focuses on possible explanations for the concentration or agglomeration of economic activities. The contribution by Lambooy and Van Oort first gives a brief review of the various location or agglomeration theories. While the authors see NEG as a welcome attempt within mainstream economic theory to (once again) devote attention to the role of location in economic analyses, they find (for several reasons) that NEG has significant limitations. Lambooy and Van Oort argue that alternative contributions to the agglomeration theories, stemming notably from economic geography, evolutionary economics and complexity theory, are essential for a good understanding of the formation of economic agglomerations. More specifically, they assert that the use of these alternative theoretical insights facilitates a deeper understanding of the following four aspects, which play important roles in actual agglomeration effects:

- life-cycle phases of enterprises and sectors
- structuring effect of spatial scale or aggregation levels
- differentiation for various types of firms of the factors underlying agglomeration, and
- disequilibria aspects such as population selection and path dependence.

The importance of the first three aspects is illustrated in the chapter by reference to an empirical study of agglomeration factors in the Dutch ICT sector (Van Oort and Atzema, 2004). Before turning to empiricism, the authors briefly further explain why it is difficult to incorporate the above-mentioned four aspects into NEG, which follows the neoclassical pattern. By putting too much emphasis on the representative firm and the representative space, in other words by presenting both firms and the geography in an overly one-dimensional light, it is difficult to take account of the first three of the aspects listed above. The main reason for this, according to Lambooy and Van Oort, is that NEG gives too much prominence to the equilibrium school of thought. This makes the work of Krugman *et al.* (1991a; 1991b) less suitable for the analysis of the location choices and formation of agglomerations in new and growing sectors (such as the ICT sector), where a more evolutionary or Schumpeterian perspective would be of greater value.

Before the nature of the main determinants of cluster formation in the ICT sector is more closely examined in respect of the Dutch ICT sector, two other factors are explored. To begin with, it is briefly explained that the recent empirical literature on the testing of agglomeration hypotheses at the urban level highlights three determinants (see Glaeser *et al.* 1992). Firstly, in the case of the ICT sector, agglomeration is said to be stimulated by positive sector-specific externalities: ICT enterprises benefit from the proximity of similar kinds of enterprises through research and development spillover or the creation of a local pool of specialised labour. Such benefits are known in literature as localisation economies and they predict strong specialisation in cities. Secondly, following the work of Jane Jacobs (1969), some researchers find that it is not so much the concentration of similar firms but, on the contrary, a varied range of enterprises that is beneficial to the region or city in question. The advantages attached to urban diversity are known as urbanisation economies. Thirdly, the literature indicates that the degree of competition between firms is important for agglomeration formation. Hence these three determinants play a pivotal role in the empirical research.

Having described these determinants, the authors show that the spatial level at which the analysis is made (municipal or higher) has a strong bearing on the dependent variable: the intensity with which new ICT enterprises were set up in the period 1996–2000. This is taken into account in the estimates.

In the period under review, measurement of employment showed that ICT enterprises were strongly concentrated in the Randstad, with pockets in south-west

Brabant and the municipalities in the Gelderland valley. As regards the creation of employment, it is striking that the north axis of the Randstad (Amsterdam–Utrecht) and the Gelderland valley has a high score.

In the first instance, the estimates show that all three listed determinants have a significant influence on the number of new ICT firms at municipal level. If the positioning of the municipality and its new ICT firms relative to other municipalities (i.e. whether or not it is close to other municipalities with many new enterprises) is taken into account, the diversity variable no longer appears significant.

Finally, it is shown that the spatial level does indeed have a bearing on the impact of the three determinants. Both the theoretical review and the empirical research lead to the conclusion that the relationship between location and competition and the relevant variables should be able to vary in terms of time, sectors and space. To be able to do this, both economists and geographers should pay more attention to these aspects in their research. This would also enhance the relevance of their work for policy.

## Location competition

The main message of the first three chapters is that location matters. The key follow-up question is: what are the policy implications of this conclusion? The fourth chapter deals with location competition, and in their contribution De Mooij, Gorter and Nahuis examine in detail the manner in which governments might be able to influence the location choices of mobile production factors through their policies. More specifically, the authors look at the question of whether or not competition between governments on this point is desirable. For example, is the fear that location competition would lead to a race to the bottom justified? Or, on the contrary, should location competition be welcomed because market discipline would force governments to pursue more efficient policies? And, in answering these and other questions, what difference does it make whether the role of location is explicitly mentioned in the underlying analysis or not?

De Mooij, Gorter and Nahuis begin their analysis by noting that location competition exists where various (regional or national) governments compete with each other for the same mobile production factors (capital or labour). In their contribution, they do not discuss either the classical or traditional literature, in which neither location nor distance form separate objects of analysis. Location competition is, according to Tiebout's (1956) well-known metaphor, 'voting by feet'. It is efficient if mobile households are free to locate in the particular jurisdiction where the mix of local taxes and expenditure best matches their preferences. Moreover, according to the proponents of location competition, an additional advantage would be the stimulating effect of the decentralised policy, which is also seen as efficiency enhancing. However, what happens if the assumptions on which this rosy vision of policy competition is based are not met? If households or part of the production factors are not fully mobile, it can be demonstrated that location competition is damaging and that the feared 'race to the bottom', in which all governments offer too low a level of public goods, could indeed come about. In this view, location competition puts pressure on the welfare state, leading to calls, both within the EU and at other levels, for policy coordination or harmonisation.

Who is right? Empirical work yields a varied picture. The authors first show that, measured by the effective tax rates on capital and labour in the EU, there is no question of tax competition. However, countries have begun to take more account of changes in each other's tax burden. Evidence for 'social dumping', a systematic reduction in social spending in the areas of social security, health care and labour market policy, is not very strong. Something similar applies to 'environmental dumping'; at most, location competition forms an obstacle for the introduction (as against maintenance or even increase) of taxes on industrial users. However, there is evidence within the EU that some convergence of institutions has occurred, which ties in with location competition. Finally, it emerges that the EU countries do not all hold the same preferences with respect to the question whether or not, stimulated by location competition, social Europe is best served by policy decentralisation.

For De Mooij, Gorter, and Nahuis, the fact that the empirical picture is anything but clear is a reason to question the relevancy of theories on location competition in which location or space does not play an explicit role. When asked, managers of multinational firms also state that location factors are important when making their location decision. Notably, proximity to the (sales) market scores high on the list. If location, and hence distance, are relevant, a spatial concentration of activity has positive effects. Such agglomeration effects can result in all mobile economic activity being concentrated in one location, the centre. The benefits of being located in the centre are denoted by the term 'agglomeration gains'. On the basis of this extreme core–periphery result, the authors show that, assuming that the centre has a higher tax rate on mobile capital than the periphery, capital does not leave the centre as long as the tax differential remains smaller than the agglomeration gains associated with the centre. In this case, tax competition will not occur and there will be no race to the bottom in relation to the tax rates. This result is reasonably consistent with the empirical findings. However, if the centre increases the tax burden to such an extent that the tax differential is less than the agglomeration gains, or if the spatial distribution of the economic activity is more even than in the core–periphery example, there can indeed be tax competition, and tax harmonisation may be a suitable policy reaction.

Besides tax competition, location competition can also take place through competition as regards government spending. Notably, infrastructure competition is relevant in this context. This competition not only relates to physical infrastructure, but also to matters such as quality of life and standard of education. The authors point to the difference between investment in regional and interregional infrastructure. As far as investment made within one region is concerned, this form of location competition can be seen as the opposite of tax competition. This investment only results in the reallocation of mobile production factors if its effects match the existing agglomeration rents. Looking at interregional investment, it can be said that the positions of both core and peripheral regions are influenced. In the authors' opinion, such investments usually benefit the core regions.

What are the policy implications of the classical and the spatial analysis of location competition? The key assumption in a non-spatial analysis of location competition is that economic integration and location competition go hand in hand. Closer integration within the EU would hence imply more location competition. As the authors neatly sum up, in political terms, those tending to the right welcome more competition while those leaning to the left emphasise the negative consequences for the welfare state. The analysis of this issue on the basis of NEG leads to a more balanced conclusion. Within certain margins, more integration will not lead to more location competition. Nonetheless, this does not mean that national governments are free to raise taxes or increase social expenditure. If tax rates are higher than those in other countries, the mobile part of production factors can still decide to leave the country and locate elsewhere. For the Netherlands, this means that in several policy areas the country must operate in an environment of location competition. This makes some institutions vulnerable, notably the Netherlands' extensive welfare state. It is hence desirable to agree on European rules within which the process of location competition can run its course. Within this context, the Netherlands, as a small open economy at the core of Europe, mainly stands to benefit from location competition.

## Clustering, optimum currency areas and macroeconomic policy

The spatial distribution of economic activity is also relevant for stabilisation, or macroeconomic policy. In the context of EMU, the geographical concentration of economic activity increases the likelihood of country- or region-specific shocks, and these asymmetric shocks not only make it more difficult to pursue a common monetary policy but also have consequences for fiscal policy.

In the fifth and final chapter, Beetsma and Vermeylen first address the question as to how EMU will itself influence the geographic concentration or clustering of economic activity and so influence the importance of clustering as a determinant of asymmetric shocks. It is difficult to draw definitive conclusions only five years after the launch of EMU, but the available empirical research suggests that economic and monetary integration in the EU is coupled with greater synchronisation of national economic cycles. However, according to the theoretical literature (notably Puga 1999), the impact of economic and monetary integration on the degree of clustering is non-linear and it is not clear whether the reduction in the importance of clustering will persist as EU integration continues to advance.

The spatial clustering of economic activity offers only one possible explanation for the existence of asymmetric shocks. Empirical research into the importance of such shocks for the EU member states shows, first and foremost, that the correlation of demand and supply shocks is strongest between a core group roughly comprising Germany, France, Denmark, the Benelux and Austria. At the regional level also, significant differences emerge between the various EU regions as regards vulnerability to certain economic shocks. Finally, research into the degree of industrial specialisation shows that, at the national level, specialisation is increasing. This suggests greater vulnerability to asymmetric shocks. It should be noted that at the regional level the tendency for greater specialisation is not yet visible (Gorter 2002).

All in all, the literature discussed by Beetsma and Vermeylen indicates that asymmetric shocks cannot be disregarded. In his analysis of optimum currency areas, Mundell (1961) showed that in the case of country-specific shocks the shift to monetary integration should only be made if, in the absence of national monetary policy, effective alternative adjustment mechanisms are in place. Factor mobility is potentially a suitable answer to asymmetric shocks, but the actual mobility both of labour and capital is still too limited to adequately absorb these shocks. This means that within EMU both monetary and fiscal policy have to contend with asymmetric shocks. For the common monetary policy, the asymmetric shocks, which stem in part from geographical concentration, form a potential source of differences of opinion regarding the policy to be pursued. Beetsma and Vermeylen argue that this will not necessarily lead to a suboptimal monetary policy for EMU, provided that, in the 16-member policy-determining committee of the European System of Central Banks, the president, vice-president and four executive board members of the European Central Bank base their voting pattern on what is, on average, best for the euro area.

The existence of asymmetric shocks and limited factor mobility should lead to the conclusion that the euro area is not an optimum currency area. However, that is not necessarily a correct conclusion because many asymmetric shocks are specific to regions rather than to countries. In the case of region-specific shocks, the effectiveness of national monetary policy is moderate and the costs of the changeover from a national to a common monetary policy are lower in comparison with a situation in which asymmetric shocks are mainly country-specific. All the same, the problem of asymmetric shocks is important, and in the absence of effective alternatives in EMU for absorbing these shocks, fiscal policy has a key role to play.

Beetsma and Vermeylen also discuss the roles of automatic stabilisers, a centralised fiscal system and a so-called international fiscal insurance scheme. Even under the Stability and Growth Pact, the tempering effect arising from the fluctuations in government expenditure and revenue, which are sensitive to economic cycles, should be significant enough to allow the automatic stabilisers to operate adequately. In a centralised fiscal system, the regions transfer taxes to the federal government, and they also receive payments from the federal government. In principle, this mechanism can ensure that asymmetric shocks are absorbed: a positive shock leads to more transfers to the federal government and a negative shock to more payments from the federal government to the region affected. This system is effectively a simple insurance mechanism and operates as such in federations such as the USA, Canada and Germany, where it is in part able to absorb the asymmetric shocks.

An alternative insurance mechanism is a system of direct fiscal transfers between countries, whereby countries that are relatively thriving transfer funds to countries that are temporarily performing below par. Given that economic shocks cannot be precisely observed, the problem of moral hazard arises. As shown by Beetsma and Bovenberg (2001), this is a considerable problem in the euro area and the introduction of an international fiscal insurance scheme would therefore not be a good idea. The only scheme that should be considered is one in which the transfers are based on variables that fall outside government influence.

When looking at the whole picture, Beetsma and Vermeylen conclude that they expect that geographic concentration or clustering in EMU at the national level might decrease, which, all things being equal, would also mean a reduction in the likelihood of asymmetric shocks at the national level. Given the increase in factor mobility, which is expected in the long term, this means that EMU will even more closely resemble an optimum currency area. However, these changes will proceed slowly, and in the medium term, fiscal policy will remain a very important adjustment mechanism for asymmetric shocks. Automatic stabilisers should be sufficient, but if a switch to a central tax or transfer system were to be considered in the EU, the adequate institutional formation of such a system would be essential.

## CONCLUSIONS

The 2003 annual meeting of the Royal Netherlands Economic Association highlighted a very important aspect of location and competition: core–periphery patterns are here to stay. The recently developed 'new economic geography' shows that such patterns might be equilibrium outcomes of migration decisions of footloose firms and workers. The submissions discussed the relevance and implications of these patterns, and in a general sense they permit us to draw the following conclusions.

- Core–periphery patterns are prevalent in the world economy. At all levels of aggregation, economic activity seems to be concentrated in a few specific places. According to NEG, this points to the relevance of increasing returns to scale and imperfect markets. NEG therefore applies the so-called 'spatial impossibility theorem' to specific models, notably the Dixit-Stiglitz model of monopolistic competition (Fujita and Thisse, 2002). Basically this theorem states that if economic activity is not perfectly divisible, as in the case of increasing returns to scale, transportation of goods becomes unavoidable and transportation costs become important. Therefore, in case of increasing returns to scale, the location decision is always important. Although NEG does not include all the relevant variables that determine the location decision in practice, it stresses that location is important in a more abstract sense.
- The most important variable in core–periphery models is transportation cost. Despite the fact that transportation costs have decreased enormously over

the past centuries, they still affect location decisions in important ways. Other barriers to trade have the same effect. Therefore, all transaction costs are potentially important in determining core–periphery patterns and migration decisions. Distance is certainly not dead.

- If increasing returns to scale and imperfect market forms give a better description of the world than constant returns to scale and perfect market forms, this has important policy implications. Firstly, policies that try to stimulate peripheral regions are doomed to failure. It is not that peripheral regions are 'bad' locations as such, they simply had bad luck. These regions are peripheral because other regions became core regions. The German unification illustrates this. Massive income transfers towards eastern Germany did not turn eastern Germany into a core region. The investments into the infrastructure, for example, simply reduced transportation costs and made the core position of western Germany stronger (it became less expensive to export from western to eastern Germany). This example illustrates why regional stimulation policies often fail: core regions become core by change, and once the process of cumulative causation starts working it is difficult to change the resulting core–periphery pattern. Secondly, in a world that is characterised by increasing returns to scale and imperfect market forms, policy competition does not imply a 'race to the bottom'. Sometimes, it is feared that in an increasingly globalised and integrated world, competition results in low taxes, a poor social security system, etc. NEG explains that agglomeration rents are present in core regions, allowing relatively high taxes and relatively generous social security systems.

## ACKNOWLEDGEMENTS

We would like to thank Peter van Els for his advice and encouragement, two anonymous referees for their suggestions, and Herma van Vleuten for her very professional help in preparing the manuscript for this book.

## NOTES

1 Transportation cost is a moniker for all sorts of barriers to trade.

## REFERENCES

Baldwin, R., Forslid, R., Martin, P., Ottaviano, G. and Robert-Nicoud, F. (2003) *Economic Geography and Public Policy*, Princeton, NJ: Princeton University Press.

Beetsma, R. and Bovenberg, L. (2001) 'The optimality of a monetary union without a fiscal union', *Journal of Money, Credit and Banking*, 33/2, Part 1: 179–204.

Brakman, S. and Garretsen, H. (2003) *Locatie en Concurrentie* [Location and Competition], Preadviezen van de Koninklijke Vereniging voor de Staathuishoudkunde, Amsterdam: KVS.

Brakman, S., Garretsen, H. and van Marrewijk, C. (2001) *An Introduction to Geographical Economics*, Cambridge: Cambridge University Press.

Fujita, M. and Thisse, J.-F. (2002) *Economics of Agglomeration: Cities, industrial location and regional growth*, Cambridge: Cambridge University Press.

Glaeser, E.L., Kallal, H., Scheinkman, J. and Shleifer, A. (1992) 'Growth in cities', *Journal of Political Economy*, 100/6: 1126–52.

Gorter, J. (2002) 'The Economic Geography of Europe', *CPB Report, Quarterly Review of Netherlands Bureau for Economic Policy Analysis*, 2002/4: 22–29.

Hirschman, A. (1958) *Strategy of Economic Development*, New Haven, CT: Yale University Press.

Jacobs, J. (1969) *The Economy of Cities*, New York: Random House.

Knaap, T. and Oosterhaven, J. (2001) 'Het eerste ruimtelijke algemene evenwichtsmodel voor Nederland, met resultaten voor de magneetzweefbaan Schiphol-Groningen', *Maandschrift Economie*, 65/2: 89–107.

Krugman, P.R. (1991a) 'Increasing returns and economic geography', *Journal of Political Economy*, 99: 483–99.

Krugman, P.R. (1991b) *Geography and Trade*, Leuven/Cambridge, MA: MIT Press.

Mundell, R. (1961) 'A theory of optimum currency areas', *American Economic Review*, 51: 657–65.

Myrdal, G. (1957) *Economic Theory and Underdeveloped Regions*, London: Duckworth.

Oort, F.G. van and Atzema, O. (2004) 'On the conceptualization of agglomeration economies: the case of new firm formation in the Dutch ICT-sector', *Annals of Regional Science* 38: 1–28.

Puga, D. (1999) 'The rise and fall of regional inequalities', *European Economic Review*, 43/2: 303–35.

Tiebout, C.M. (1956) 'A pure theory of local expenditure', *Journal of Political Economy*, 64: 416–24.

# 1 Locating economic concentration

*Jeroen Hinloopen and Charles van Marrewijk*

## INTRODUCTION

We were asked by Steven Brakman and Harry Garretsen for a contribution to this volume with the primary objective 'to show that economic activity is not uniformly distributed across space'. Although the editors also asked us several other research questions, which we will address in the sequel, the reader's first reaction to the primary objective may be 'but of course economic activity is not homogenously distributed across space, everyone knows that!' An Australian walkabout in the bush will give an entirely different picture of economic activity than an attempt to cross the centre of Manila during rush hour. Evidently, the distribution of economic activity is uneven. Nonetheless, the reader's potential first reaction regarding the obviously uneven distribution of economic activity is unjustified for at least three reasons.

First, we have to be precise in what we mean by 'economic activity'. Obviously, this is activity that involves people, so a first indication of the distribution of economic activity would be the distribution of people across the globe. As a result of differences in education, available capital, quality of infrastructure and communication, however, there are enormous differences in productivity between people, leading to huge differences in value added per capita, which is to be taken into consideration in analysing the distribution of economic activity. In turn, this correction for productivity differences should not be pushed too far as it is positively correlated with the local price level, for which we then should also correct. This brings us to purchasing power corrected value added as probably the most suitable empirical measure of economic activity.

Second, we have to take the level of aggregation into consideration, both in terms of geography and economic activity. The geographic level of aggregation may focus on global regions as defined by the World Bank (see below), on countries, on regions within countries, on cities, and even on areas within cities. The economic level of aggregation focuses on a specific type of economic activity. This might be all produced goods and services,[1] a specific category (such as agriculture or services), or an analysis of just one or only a few types of goods (such as the flower or the movie industry).

Third, we can analyse if there are regularities in the distribution (whether even or uneven) of economic activity or in the interaction between centres of economic activity. We then go beyond the affirmation that economic activity is not evenly distributed across space, to try to find a pattern in this distribution. If there is such a pattern, we would of course like an explanation for it. This explanation, in turn, can be of the 'first-nature' type (exogenous in character: the wood industry is usually located in areas with lots of trees; large harbours are usually at the mouths of navigable rivers) or the 'second-nature' type (endogenous in character: computer activity is located in Silicon Valley to benefit from local knowledge spillover; there are many hot dog stands in New York because there are many people). Insights in these explanations can result in proper policy advice. This chapter analyses the structure and distribution of economic activity, but not the possible explanations for this distribution or the concomitant policy recommendations. The latter two issues are addressed in the other chapters in this volume, notably Chapter 2 (transport costs and infrastructure), Chapter 3 (agglomeration powers) and Chapter 4 (location decisions).

As there is an endless series of possible combinations that we could analyse regarding type of economic activity, distribution, economic and geographic aggregation, and interaction, it is remarkable that a few clear and simple conclusions regarding the distribution and interaction of economic activity can be drawn nonetheless, as summarised in the following five stylised facts.

- There is an uneven distribution regardless of the *type* of economic activity.
- There is an uneven distribution regardless of the *geographic level* of aggregation.
- There is an uneven distribution regardless of the *economic level* of aggregation.
- There is a remarkable *regularity* in the *spatial distribution* of economic activity.
- There is a remarkable *regularity* in the *interaction* between economic centres.

## GLOBAL REGIONS[2]

There are many countries in the world. The World Bank distinguishes 207 different countries on its CD-Rom (World Bank 2002), many of which are so small that you may not know them (such as Palau and Kiribati). Because China considers it a province, Taiwan is the only important country not included as a separate entity, although it is included within various groups of countries. In the next section, differences between countries are analysed, however this section characterises groups of countries based on the World Bank's grouping in global regions (see the appendix to this chapter for details):

1. EAP: East Asia and Pacific (includes China and Indonesia)
2. ECA: (Eastern) Europe and Central Asia (includes Turkey and Russia)
3. HIC: High-income countries (includes Western Europe, USA and Japan)
4. LAC: Latin America and Caribbean (includes Brazil and Mexico)

5. MNA: Middle East and North Africa (includes Egypt)
6. SAS: South Asia (includes India)
7. SSA: Sub-Saharan Africa (includes Nigeria and South Africa).

With the exception of the high-income countries (HIC), these are geographically coherent entities, although the World Bank classification is also based on social, political, economic and historical factors.[3] Table 1.1 provides basic information regarding population, area and production for these global regions.

According to the United Nations, the world population reached six billion on 12 October 1999, a doubling in about 40 years. Almost a third of these six billion people live in south-east Asia (EAP; 1.85 billion), more than six times as many as the 295 million people in the Middle East and North Africa (MNA). The other global regions are within these two extremes. Obviously, these absolute numbers give no indication regarding the distribution of the population as the global regions also differ in size, ranging from 30.9 million km$^2$ for the high-income countries (HIC) to 4.8 million km$^2$ for South Asia (SAS). The earth's total area is about 130 million km$^2$, indicating that there are on average about 47 people per km$^2$. As there is a negative correlation at this level of aggregation between size and population, the population density (people per km$^2$) is more unevenly distributed than the absolute population levels. The highest density (283) is reached in South Asia (SAS), more than 14 times higher than the lowest density (20), which is found in (Eastern) Europe and Central Asia (ECA).

*Table 1.1* Basic information for global regions (2000)

| | *EAP* | *ECA* | *HIC* | *LAC* | *MNA* | *SAS* | *SSA* | *World* |
|---|---|---|---|---|---|---|---|---|
| Population (millions) | 1,855 | 474 | 903 | 516 | 295 | 1,355 | 659 | 6,057 |
| Area (million km$^2$) | 16.0 | 23.8 | 30.9 | 20.1 | 11.0 | 4.8 | 23.6 | 130.2 |
| GNP[a] ($ billion) | 2,027 | 927 | 24,945 | 1,922 | 651 | 591 | 303 | 31,351 |
| GNP ppp[b] ($ billion) | 7,609 | 3,140 | 24,793 | 3,624 | 1,545 | 2,984 | 1,044 | 44,459 |
| Population density (people/km$^2$) | 116 | 20 | 29 | 26 | 27 | 283 | 28 | 47 |
| GNP density ($ thousand/km$^2$) | 127 | 39 | 807 | 96 | 59 | 124 | 13 | 241 |
| GNP ppp density ($ thousand/km$^2$) | 476 | 132 | 802 | 181 | 141 | 624 | 44 | 342 |

Notes
a GNP = gross national product
b ppp = purchasing power parity
All data are for 2000

The uneven distribution of people across the global regions provides only a limited view of the distribution of economic activity. One person may be much more productive than another, for example as a result of better schooling, the availability of powerful machinery, good transport links (railways, waterways or roads), efficient communications, a stable and secure system of law, etc. To measure economic activity we have to take three steps. First, a well-functioning statistics office will have to gather accurate information regarding the value of millions of different goods produced by all firms in an area. This occurs, of course, in local currency: the euro in Western Europe, the US dollar in the USA, and the yen in Japan. Second, we have to determine what to compare between different areas: whether it is the production of all goods or of specific types of goods, goods produced in an area (domestic product) or goods produced by factors of production owned by inhabitants of an area (national product), etc. Third, we have to decide how to compare the gathered information for the various areas.

In this section we concentrate on a comparison of gross national product (GNP) as this provides the best indication of all kinds of economic activity in an area.[4] GNP is equal to the market value of all goods produced by factors of production owned by inhabitants of an area. This implies that we are literally comparing apples and oranges, measured in a common domestic currency. For an international comparison, we can then, for example, use the average exchange rate on the currency markets in this period. Measured accordingly, the total world production of goods in 2000 was valued at $31,351 billion, a truly astronomical figure. Obviously, the GNP value is highest for the high-income countries (HIC), with a total of $24,945 billion, more than 82 times the production value of $303 billion in sub-Saharan Africa (SSA). Usually, our attention focuses on differences in income per capita, and it is clear that these differences are substantial. To determine the distribution of economic activity, however, the interaction between population density and productivity differences is important, so it is best to focus on production density per area unit (in this case GNP $ thousand per km$^2$). This turns out to be highest for the high-income countries (HIC; $807 thousand per km$^2$), being more than 62 times higher than for sub-Saharan Africa (SSA; $13 thousand per km$^2$).

Based on the above information, it appears that the distribution of economic activity is more uneven than the distribution of population. Although true in general, we should note that the method of comparison (using the average exchange rate in a given period) leads to an overestimation of the value of production in high-income countries relative to low-income countries. The distinction between tradable and non-tradable goods is important in this respect. Since tradable goods can in principle be shipped to other regions (perhaps at considerable costs), the suppliers of tradable goods more or less compete with each other on a global market based on the exchange rate, which is partly determined by these activities. Non-tradable goods, on the other hand, are produced and consumed locally and do not compete on a global market. Since different sectors in an economy compete for the same worker, such that the wage rate in an economy reflects average productivity and the productivity differences between countries are larger for tradable goods than for non-tradable goods, using the exchange rate as a basis for comparison for non-tradable goods leads to an underestimate of the value of production in low-income countries. Using the exchange rate as a basis for comparison, it may cost for example $15 to get a simple haircut in Chicago and less than $1 to get the same haircut in Tanzania. Similarly, if you go to the latest James Bond movie in Rotterdam it will cost $8, while viewing the same movie in the Philippines will cost $1.50.

To correct for these price difference for non-tradable goods, the United Nations' International Comparison Project gathers information on the prices of goods in virtually all countries of the world. It uses the information to calculate exchange rates that have been corrected for purchasing power parity (ppp). Table 1.1 also provides an overview of GNP ppp for the various global regions using the ppp exchange rates. This gives a better picture of the real economic activity in an area. The total value of world production is then $44,459 billion, ranging from $24,793 billion for the high-income countries to $1,044 billion for sub-Saharan Africa. Using this to calculate production density in $ thousand per km$^2$, the high-income countries are still in the lead, with a value of $802 thousand, more than 18 times higher than the $44 thousand in sub-Saharan Africa. The differences in production density therefore become considerably smaller after correcting for purchasing power, but they do not disappear. The distribution of economic activity is still very uneven across the globe.

In conclusion, there are large differences in the distribution of economic activity between the global regions analysed in this section. The relative density differences (expressed as: highest density ÷ lowest density) are large for population density (more than 14), GNP density (more than 62) and GNP density corrected for purchasing power differences (more than 18).

## CONCENTRATION AT THE COUNTRY LEVEL

Having illustrated the uneven distribution of economic activity at the level of global regions, in this section we focus on differences at the country level. We start with all countries in the world, and then zoom in on the countries of sub-Saharan Africa, one of the global regions analysed above.

The World Bank provides information regarding the population density for 195 countries in the world. On average there are 47 people per km$^2$. At the country level this varies from 6,587 for Singapore (no less than 140 times the world average), to 1.53 for Mongolia, and to 0.16 for Greenland (part of Denmark). The differences between countries are therefore enormous (Figure 1.1). We should note, however, that the city-state of Singapore is an exception as its population density is five times as high as the second-highest density (Bermuda's 1,260 people per km$^2$). Table 1.2 gives an overview of the 15 countries with the highest population densities. These are all countries of small geographic area, with the exception of Bangladesh (ranked 4th), South Korea (ranked 10th) and the

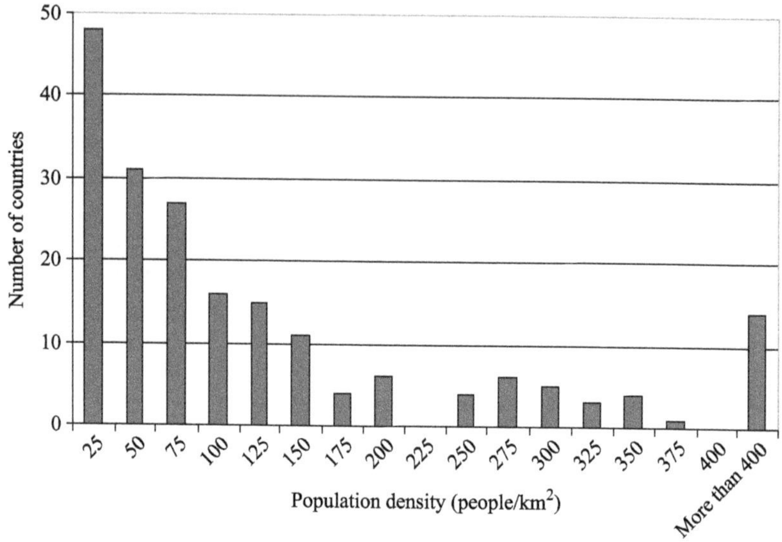


*Figure 1.1* Variation in population density: 195 countries (2000).

Netherlands (ranked 11th). It is therefore no surprise that only a minority of the countries (about 40 per cent) have a population density below the world average. As illustrated in Figure 1.2, the countries with a high population density are geographically concentrated in South-East Asia and Europe, with a few exceptions in Africa and Central America.

*Table 1.2* Top 15 counties by density of economic activity (2000)

| *Rank* | *Population density* | | *GNP ppp density* | |
|---|---|---|---|---|
| | *Country* | *People/km²* | *Country* | *$ million/km²* |
| 1 | Singapore | 6,587 | Singapore | 164.05 |
| 2 | Bermuda | 1,260 | Malta | 20.15 |
| 3 | Malta | 1,219 | Netherlands | 12.15 |
| 4 | Bangladesh | 1,007 | Japan | 9.43 |
| 5 | Bahrain | 1,001 | Barbados | 9.33 |
| 6 | Maldives | 920 | Belgium | 8.58 |
| 7 | Barbados | 621 | South Korea | 8.28 |
| 8 | Mauritius | 584 | Israel | 5.84 |
| 9 | Aruba | 532 | United Kingdom | 5.84 |
| 10 | South Korea | 479 | Mauritius | 5.81 |
| 11 | Netherlands | 470 | Germany | 5.74 |
| 12 | San Marino | 450 | Switzerland | 5.53 |
| 13 | Puerto Rico | 442 | Italy | 4.60 |
| 14 | Lebanon | 423 | Maldives | 3.90 |
| 15 | Virgin Islands | 356 | Denmark | 3.43 |

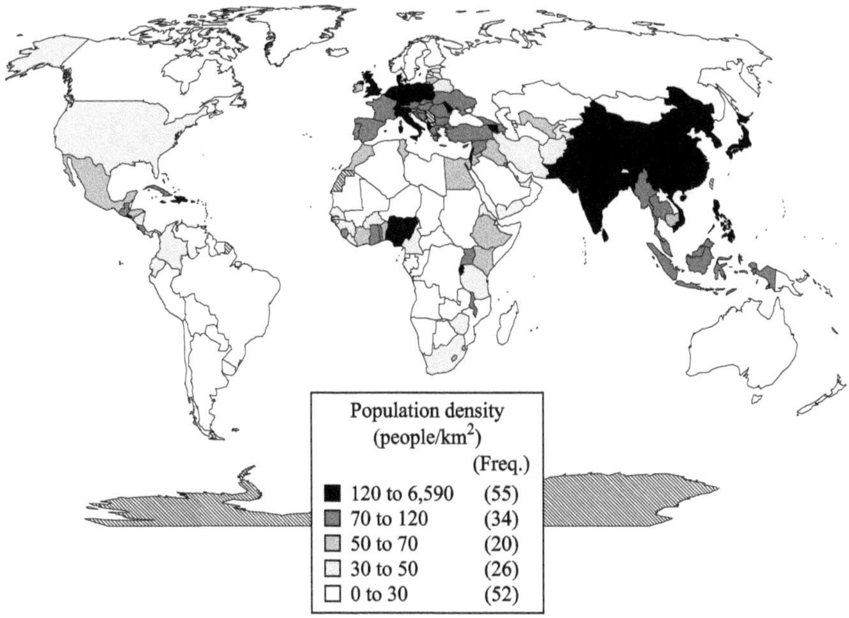


*Figure 1.2* Geographic distribution of population density: 195 countries (2000).

As explained above, to get an adequate picture of the distribution of economic activity it is better to correct for differences in productivity and purchasing power between countries. The World Bank provides the relevant data for 160 countries in the world, with an average ppp-corrected value of production of $342 thousand per km$^2$ in 2000. Table 1.2 also lists the 15 countries with the highest production density. Singapore is again in the lead, with a value of $164.05 million per km$^2$, which is 480 times the world average, eight times higher than the country ranked number two (Malta; $20.15 million) and almost 14 times higher than number three (the Netherlands; $12.5 million). The top 15 countries by production density also include large countries, such as Japan (ranked 4th), South Korea (ranked 7th), the United Kingdom (ranked 9th), Germany (ranked 11th) and Italy (ranked 13th). Consequently, about 57 per cent of all countries have a production density below the world average. Seven countries are in the top 15 in terms of both population density and production density. As suggested by this fact, and by Singapore's solid first place on both lists, there is a positive association between population density and production density at the country level: the correlation coefficient is 0.73. There is also a geographic clustering of production density around the core of rich countries: Europe, Japan and the USA (see Figure 1.3). Of the less-developed countries, the high production densities of Bangladesh (ranked 26th), the Philippines (ranked 39th) and Sri Lanka (ranked 41st) are

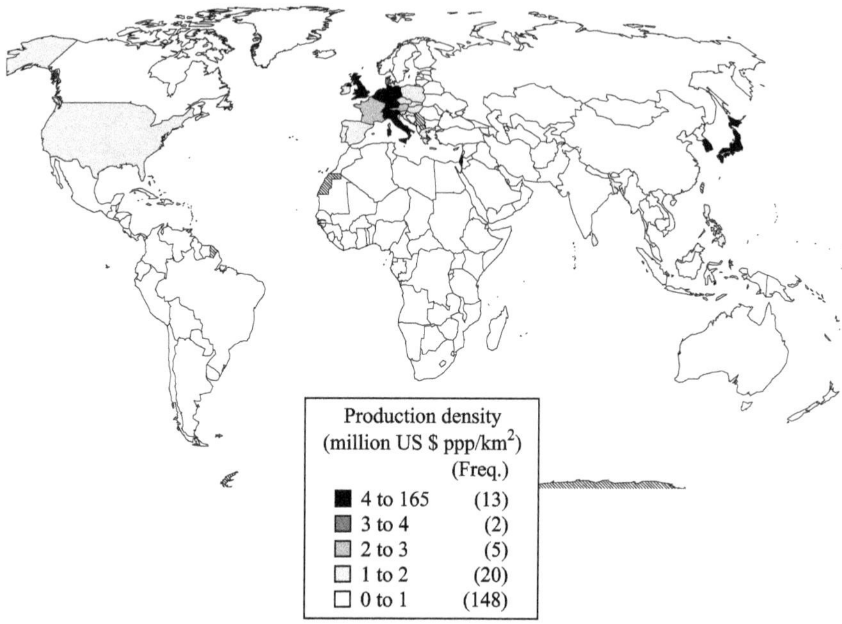


*Figure 1.3* Geographic distribution of production density: 160 countries (2000).

remarkable. These are, indeed, all countries with a high population density, ranked 4th, 32nd and 23rd, respectively.

If we break down the World Bank's global regions into the countries comprising those regions, as we did above, it is not remarkable that the unevenness of the distribution increases. As we saw, however, the extent of this increase is remarkable. We can also disaggregate geographically in a different way. After noting that economic activity is unevenly distributed at the level of global regions, we can 'zoom in' on one of those regions and analyse the distribution of economic activity within that region. As an example, we take sub-Saharan Africa, a relatively coherent geographical region consisting of a fairly large (48) number of individual countries. Table 1.3 gives an overview of the countries in sub-Saharan Africa with the highest and lowest population and production densities, and the averages of these variables for the region as a whole.

The average population density in sub-Saharan Africa is 28 people per km$^2$, varying from 584 for Mauritius (more than 20 times the average) to 2.1 for Namibia (less than 10 per cent of the average). The production density varies in a similar fashion: the average is $44 thousand per km$^2$ in 2000, ranging from $5,809 thousand in Mauritius (more than 130 times the average) to $4.2 thousand in Mauritania (less than 10 per cent of the average). For both density measures the variation within the sub-Saharan Africa region is enormous. Again, there is a clear positive association between population density and production

*Table 1.3* Variation in density within sub-Saharan Africa (2000)

| *Average population density (people/km²)* | | *Average GDP ppp density ($ million per km²)* | |
|---|---|---|---|
| Sub-Saharan Africa | 28 | Sub-Saharan Africa | 44 |
| Highest | | Highest | |
| Mauritius | 584 | Mauritius | 5,809 |
| Rwanda | 345 | Cape Verde | 525 |
| Burundi | 265 | Comoros | 444 |
| Comoros | 250 | South Africa | 321 |
| Seychelles | 181 | Rwanda | 317 |
| Lowest | | Lowest | |
| Central African Rep. | 6.0 | Central African Rep. | 6.9 |
| Gabon | 4.8 | Niger | 6.3 |
| Botswana | 2.8 | Chad | 5.3 |
| Mauritania | 2.6 | Congo, Rep. | 5.1 |
| Namibia | 2.1 | Mauritania | 4.2 |

density: for the 42 countries for which data are available the correlation coefficient is 0.79.

In conclusion, at a lower level of geographic aggregation, in this case at the country level, the uneven distribution of economic activity becomes more pronounced, both for population and production (measured as value added, after correcting for purchasing power).

## DEEPER STILL: REGIONAL PERIPHERY AND URBAN CONCENTRATION

In this section we will first apply the procedure used at the end of the preceding section (where we looked at the countries comprising sub-Saharan Africa), again at the country level (in this case by looking at the different regions of the Netherlands). Second, we will illustrate the core–periphery economic structure of Europe at the regional level using a periphery index. Third, we will illustrate the dynamic tendency of increasing economic concentration at the city level for the world as a whole.

The regional classification used within the European Union (EU) is based on three levels of detail defined within the Nomenclature of Territorial Units for Statistics (NUTS) and therefore referred to as NUTS I, NUTS II and NUTS III. At the NUTS I level, the Netherlands is subdivided into four regions (North, East, West and South). At the NUTS II level, these are subdivided in 12 subregions (the 12 Dutch provinces). Finally, at the NUTS III level, these are subdivided again into 40 sub-subregions, see Table 1.4 (see below for the periphery indices for this table). In 1997, the average population density in the Netherlands was 380 people per km². At the NUTS III (sub-subregion) level, this varied from 86 for South-West Friesland (23 per cent of the average) to 2,815 for the agglomeration of

*Table 1.4* Economic activity in the Netherlands and periphery indices

| | | *Density* [a] | | *Periphery index* [b] | | | |
|---|---|---|---|---|---|---|---|
| | | *Population (people/km²)* | *Production (€ thousand/km²)* | *GDP* | *GDP ppp* | *Population* | *Labour force* |
| Netherlands | | 380 | 7,620 | | | | |
| NL1 | North-Netherlands | 144 | 2,786 | | | | |
| NL11 | Groningen | 188 | 4,725 | | | | |
| NL111 | East Groningen | 168 | 2,083 | 50.4 | 50.9 | 58.8 | 59.8 |
| NL112 | Delfzijl and surr. | 147 | 2,497 | 52.7 | 53.2 | 62.2 | 63.2 |
| NL113 | Misc. Groningen | 208 | 6,619 | 49.9 | 50.2 | 58.4 | 59.5 |
| NL12 | Friesland | 107 | 1,758 | | | | |
| NL121 | North Friesland | 94 | 1,638 | 51.9 | 52.2 | 60.8 | 62.1 |
| NL122 | South-West Friesland | 86 | 1,261 | 50.5 | 50.7 | 58.6 | 60.0 |
| NL123 | South-East Friesland | 168 | 2,599 | 49.7 | 50.0 | 57.7 | 59.0 |
| NL13 | Drenthe | 173 | 2,832 | | | | |
| NL131 | North Drenthe | 183 | 2,888 | 49.4 | 49.7 | 57.3 | 58.5 |
| NL132 | South-East Drenthe | 191 | 3,388 | 48.9 | 49.3 | 56.4 | 57.7 |
| NL133 | South-West Drenthe | 148 | 2,318 | 46.2 | 46.5 | 51.9 | 53.5 |
| NL2 | East-Netherlands | 309 | 5,377 | | | | |
| NL21 | Overijssel | 310 | 5,444 | | | | |
| NL211 | North Overijssel | 214 | 3,857 | 44.2 | 44.5 | 48.5 | 50.2 |
| NL212 | South-West Overijssel | 330 | 6,300 | 40.8 | 41.1 | 42.2 | 44.1 |
| NL213 | Twente | 411 | 6,952 | 42.5 | 43.1 | 46.0 | 47.9 |
| NL22 | Gelderland | 368 | 6,560 | | | | |
| NL221 | Veluwe | 333 | 5,999 | 39.7 | 40.0 | 40.6 | 42.6 |
| NL222 | Achterhoek | 244 | 4,093 | 40.9 | 41.3 | 42.7 | 44.7 |
| NL223 | Arnhem/Nijmegen | 685 | 12,760 | 38.0 | 38.2 | 37.5 | 39.6 |
| NL224 | South-West Gelderland | 287 | 4,812 | 38.9 | 39.0 | 39.4 | 41.6 |
| NL23 | Flevoland | 149 | 2,090 | 45.7 | 45.8 | 51.9 | 53.4 |

| | | | | | | | |
|---|---|---|---|---|---|---|---|
| NL3 | West-Netherlands | 615 | 13,257 | | | | |
| NL31 | Utrecht | 756 | 17,013 | 36.7 | 36.6 | 35.7 | 37.6 |
| NL32 | North-Holland | 614 | 13,883 | | | | |
| NL321 | Top of North-Holland | 163 | 2,395 | 52.4 | 52.6 | 61.9 | 63.3 |
| NL322 | Alkmaar and surr. | 697 | 11,115 | 44.8 | 44.9 | 50.3 | 51.8 |
| NL323 | Ijmond | 983 | 19,482 | 48.8 | 48.9 | 56.9 | 58.5 |
| NL324 | Agglom. Haarlem | 1,363 | 27,291 | 39.5 | 39.4 | 41.7 | 43.2 |
| NL325 | Zaanstreek | 1,164 | 19,606 | 39.7 | 39.7 | 42.0 | 43.2 |
| NL326 | Agglom. Amsterdam | 1,295 | 37,120 | 37.6 | 37.4 | 38.3 | 39.7 |
| NL327 | Gooi and Vechtstreek | 983 | 19,302 | 37.3 | 37.2 | 36.7 | 38.5 |
| NL33 | South-Holland | 973 | 20,179 | | | | |
| NL331 | Agglom. Leiden and bollenst. | 1,375 | 24,658 | 40.7 | 40.6 | 43.4 | 45.0 |
| NL332 | Agglom. The Hague | 2,815 | 63,899 | 39.3 | 39.1 | 41.3 | 43.1 |
| NL333 | Delft and Westland | 1,121 | 28,051 | 37.9 | 37.7 | 38.6 | 40.4 |
| NL334 | East South-Holland | 579 | 9,811 | 39.7 | 39.6 | 41.2 | 43.0 |
| NL335 | Agglom. Rijnmond | 823 | 17,537 | 41.2 | 41.1 | 44.2 | 46.1 |
| NL336 | South-East South-Holland | 713 | 13,385 | 40.1 | 40.0 | 41.9 | 44.2 |
| NL34 | Zeeland | 126 | 2,419 | | | | |
| NL341 | Zeeuwsch-Vlaanderen | 123 | 2,862 | 44.3 | 43.9 | 49.3 | 52.3 |
| NL342 | Misc. Zeeland | 127 | 2,231 | 44.6 | 44.3 | 49.8 | 52.6 |
| NL4 | South-Netherlands | 473 | 9,232 | | | | |
| NL41 | North-Brabant | 455 | 9,141 | | | | |
| NL411 | West North-Brabant | 426 | 8,622 | 37.6 | 37.4 | 37.5 | 40.2 |
| NL412 | Mid North-Brabant | 410 | 7,351 | 37.1 | 37.0 | 36.3 | 38.9 |
| NL413 | North-East North-Brabant | 464 | 9,507 | 37.4 | 37.4 | 36.9 | 39.2 |
| NL414 | South-East North-Brabant | 509 | 10,729 | 35.1 | 35.2 | 32.8 | 35.4 |
| NL42 | Limburg (NL) | 515 | 9,446 | | | | |
| NL421 | North Limburg | 316 | 6,230 | 33.3 | 34.0 | 30.3 | 33.3 |
| NL422 | Mid Limburg | 327 | 6,133 | 34.8 | 35.3 | 32.9 | 35.8 |
| NL423 | South Limburg | 941 | 16,620 | 35.1 | 35.4 | 32.8 | 36.3 |

Notes

a Density calculations based on Eurostat data: population data, 1997; production data, 1996.

b Periphery indices from Copus (1999).

The Hague (740 percent of the average). In 1996, the average production density in the Netherlands was €7,620 per km$^2$, varying from €1,261 for South-West Friesland (17 per cent of the average) to €63,899 for the agglomeration of The Hague (839 per cent of the average). As suggested by the consistent first and last places for both lists (the same regions), the positive association between population density and production density is high: the correlation coefficient is 0.981.

The above descriptive analysis has sufficiently demonstrated that economic activity, measured in various ways at different levels of aggregation, is unevenly distributed across space and that the various measures of density and production are strongly correlated. Regional economists have long since felt a need to measure this unevenness and, subsequently, to identify and analyse core–periphery structures. Harris's (1954) 'market potential' approach is the basis of this procedure; this is applied by calculating an indicator of market potential at the county level, taking into consideration the size of economic markets in the vicinity of this county, corrected for distance to this market. The demand by policymakers for the identification of core–periphery structures and analysis of the economic consequences of such structures led Keeble, Owens and Thompson (1981) to apply Harris's approach to the construction of a periphery index for the regions of the EU at the NUTS I level. Over the years, the methods used for calculating such a periphery index have become more sophisticated, ultimately leading to Andrew Copus's (1999) study of 1,105 European regions (at the NUTS III level for the EU plus 19 European countries). For each region, Copus defines a 'centre' (usually the largest city, but sometimes the geometric centre) and calculates detailed travel times to other centres, taking into consideration the types of roads, ferries, waiting times for ferries and border crossings, driving speeds in mountains and urban areas, rest times for drivers, etc.[5] Copus uses this as the basis for calculating the potential for each region as follows:

$$P_i = \sum_j \frac{M_j}{D_{ij}} \tag{1.1}$$

in which: $P_i$ is the potential for region $i$, $M_j$ is economic mass of region $j$ and $D_{ij}$ is distance between regions $i$ and $j$.

An adequate economic theoretical explanation for the structure of Equation 1.1 is not simple. It is the basis for a substantial body of economic research, culminating in the 'new economic geography' or 'geographical economics' approach (Fujita, Krugman, and Venables 1999; Brakman, Garretsen and Van Marrewijk 2001). For the distances between regions, Copus uses the travel times, as described above. For the economic mass of a region, he uses four indicators:

- gross domestic product (GDP), in euros
- gross domestic product corrected for purchasing power (GDP ppp)
- population size
- labour force size.

Finally, on the basis of this outcome, he calculates a periphery index: from 0 for the most central region (with the highest potential) to 100 for the most peripheral region (with the lowest potential). Exactly which measure is used as an indicator of 'economic mass' for constructing the periphery index hardly matters (see Table 1.5).

Table 1.4 also gives the results of the Copus periphery index calculations (Copus 1999) for the 40 NUTS III regions in the Netherlands. Again, the choice of indicator of economic mass is hardly relevant as even the lowest correlation coefficient is 0.996 (see Table 1.5). In all cases, the most central region is North Limburg. In three out of four cases, Delfzijl and surroundings is the most peripheral region (only on the basis of population is the top of North Holland classified as such). We note, of course, that the region with the highest economic density (The Hague) is not the most central region in the Netherlands (depending on the index used, it is ranked at 14th or 16th). The most important reason for this is that the Copus periphery indices identify core–periphery structures at the European level and thus take into consideration the location of other European regions. In view of their locations, being close to the Dutch Randstad (Amsterdam, Rotterdam, the Hague and Utrecht), the German Ruhrgebiet, and also Brussels in Belgium, the three Limburg regions and South-East North Brabant are always the four most central regions in the Netherlands. The first Randstad region is Utrecht (ranked 5th). The regions in Groningen, Friesland, Drenthe and the top of North Holland constitute the Dutch periphery.

At the European level, none of the Dutch regions is located in the periphery, as even the most peripheral Dutch region is in the top half of the rankings. To illustrate this at a not too-detailed level of analysis, while still using the detailed Copus data, Figure 1.4 depicts the European core–periphery structures at the NUTS I level using the average score of the NUTS III components (GDP ppp). At the European level, the southern half of the Netherlands is part of a large European core, consisting also of Flanders, Brussels, Nordrhein-Westfalen, Hessen, Rheinland-Palts and London. Almost all of the Netherlands, Belgium and West Germany are economically centrally located. Paris is a fairly separate economic entity, although still linked to the European core. Other examples are Lombardy (Milan), Berlin and Madrid. Clearly, some of the new EU members, who entered on 1 May 2004, such as Poland, the Czech Republic and Slovakia, are economically more centrally located than some of the older EU members, such as Greece, Finland, Sweden, Portugal, Ireland, Scotland and parts of Italy.

*Table 1.5* Correlation coefficients for the Copus periphery indices (Copus 1999)

| | *GDP* | *GDP ppp* | *Population* | *Labour force* |
|---|---|---|---|---|
| *GDP* | 1 | 0.996 | 0.978 | 0.977 |
| *GDP ppp* | 0.996 | 1 | 0.980 | 0.975 |
| *Population* | 0.978 | 0.980 | 1 | 0.995 |
| *Labour force* | 0.977 | 0.975 | 0.995 | 1 |

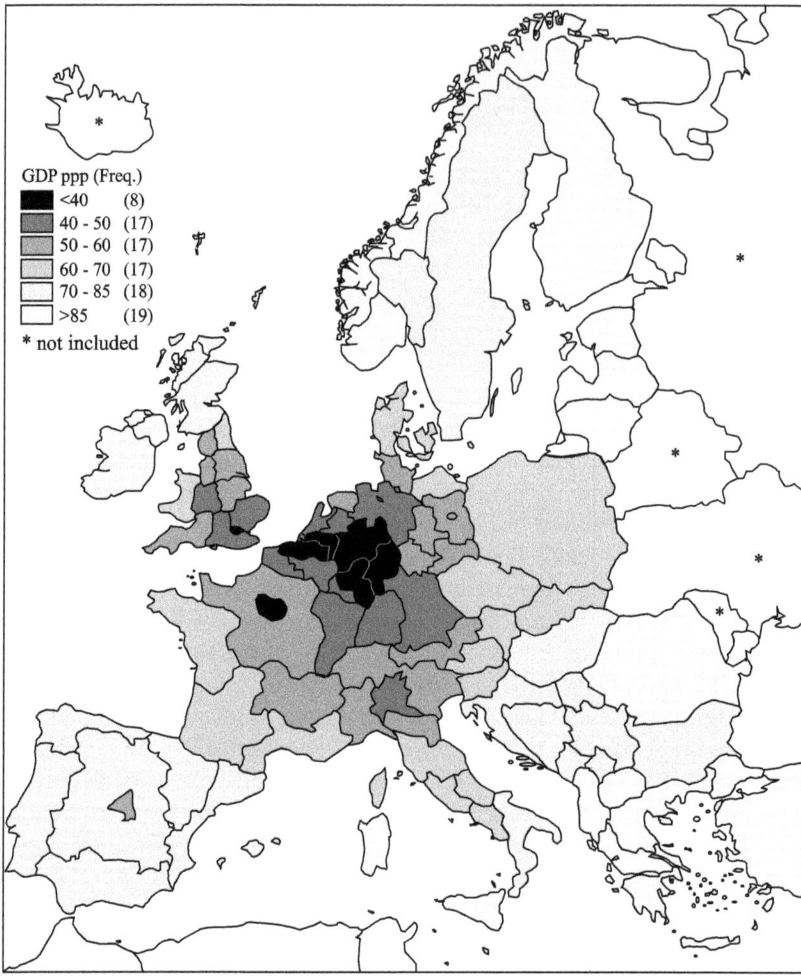


*Figure 1.4* Core–periphery structures in Europe (based on GDP ppp). Source: calculations based on Copus (1999).

If we look in more detail at the spatial distribution of economic activity within a region of a country, we have to investigate the distribution of cities and villages. A process of urbanisation has been noticeable worldwide for a considerable time. Of the 3,021 million people living on our planet in 1960, about 1,017 million (almost 34 per cent) lived in cities.[6] During the following 40 years, the number of people on our planet doubled, to 6,057 million in 2000. The number of people in urban areas rose relatively more rapidly, to 2,848 million (47 per cent of the population). Obviously, this does not mean that the population in the rural areas has fallen (it rose from 2,004 million in 1960 to 3,210 million in 2000), it is rather that the urban population rises more rapidly. At this rate, the urban population will be larger than the rural population by the year 2009. The process of urbanisation has been virtually completed in many countries. In the Netherlands, for example, the urban population rose from 85.0 per cent in 1960 to 89.4 per cent in 2000. Of the global regions identified above, urbanisation in the period 1960–2000 has been highest in percentage terms in Latin America (LAC; from 49.3 to 75.4 per cent) and highest in relative terms in sub-Saharan Africa (SSA; from 14.5 to 34.4 per cent). As the urbanisation process is largely completed in most high-income countries, the increase has been lowest in percentage and relative terms in those countries (HIC; from 67.8 to 78.9 per cent), see Figure 1.5.

According to the World Bank (2000), the majority of the urban population (63.5 per cent) lives in small- and medium-sized cities (population less than 1 million), whereas 21.4 per cent lives in large cities (population between 1 and 5 million) and 'only' 15.1 per cent lives in megacities (population above 5 million). The number of megacities, however, rapidly increased in the twentieth century; in 1900, London (6.5 million inhabitants) was the only megacity, whereas in 2000 there were 16 cities with more than 10 million inhabitants.

In conclusion, a 'fractal dimension' in the distribution of economic activity becomes clear now that we have established that at regional- and city-level economic activities are also unevenly distributed. This enables the identification of core–periphery patterns at the regional level. The degree of urbanisation, which varies from country to country, is still increasing worldwide.

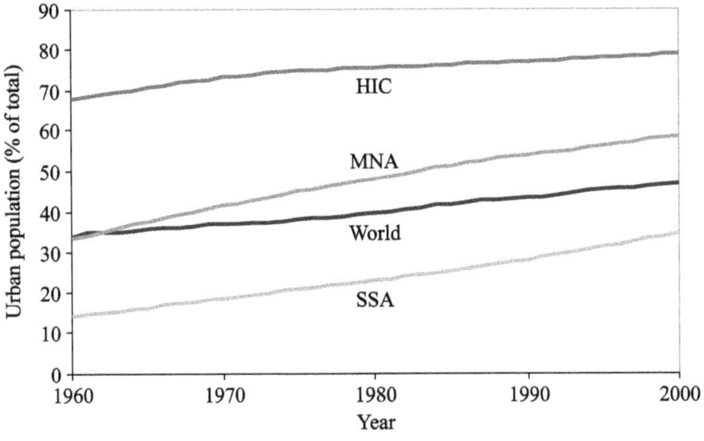


HIC High-income countries
MNA Middle East and North Africa
SSA Sub-Saharan Africa

*Figure 1.5* Urbanisation; global regions and world total (1960–2000).

## THE FRACTAL DIMENSION OF REGULARITY IN CONCENTRATION

Now that we have sufficiently illustrated the uneven distribution of economic activity, it is time to analyse the empirical structure of that distribution. We will do this in two ways. In this section we focus on the spatial distribution of economic activity, known as the 'rank-size rule' (with Zipf's law as a special case). In the next section, we focus on the spatial interaction between economic centres, known as the 'gravity equation'. Both empirical regularities have inspired theorists in geography and economics to try to construct models to improve our understanding of these facts. As noted before, we do not discuss these theoretical contributions.

The regularity in the spatial distribution of economic activity is most easily demonstrated using the size distribution of urban agglomerations. There are cities of many sizes. Most are small or of reasonable size. A few are truly large, with millions of inhabitants. We should note that 'large' has been a relative measure in history. When Christ was born, Rome was considered to be an extremely large city with at least 500,000 inhabitants (some estimates are up to 1 million).[7] Nowadays, however, there are more than 400 cities with more than 1 million inhabitants (see below).

A well-known problem in comparing or measuring the size of cities is the distinction between urban agglomeration and city proper (official boundaries). The latter usually arose in a complex historical process of evolution, annexation and coincidence. A ranking based on city proper sizes therefore usually gives a less-complete picture of the economically relevant size. The city of Rotterdam, for example, had 599,463 inhabitants on 1 November 2002, according to the Dutch Central Bureau of Statistics. Other municipalities in the direct vicinity, such as Schiedam (75,901 inhabitants) and Capelle aan den IJssel (65,304 inhabitants), are effectively part of the same economic entity as the city of Rotterdam. Together with some other municipalities, they constitute the agglomeration of Rotterdam. The data we use here are taken from Thomas Brinkhoff's website,[8] which tries to compare the size of city agglomerations worldwide as much as possible by calculating the central city (or sometimes the central cities, such as for the Ruhrgebiet) together with economically associated surrounding municipalities.

There were 408 agglomerations in the world with more than 1 million inhabitants in 2002, of which Tokyo (including Yokohama and Kawasaki) was the largest (with 35.1 million inhabitants), followed by New York (21.65 million) and Seoul (21.35 million). The largest European agglomeration is Moscow (13.2 million, ranked 15th). The above-mentioned agglomeration of Rotterdam is ranked 350th (1.175 million), preceded in the Netherlands by the agglomeration of Amsterdam (2.1 million, ranked 170th).

To illustrate the regularity in the spatial distribution of economic activity, we rank the cities in size. The largest city (Tokyo) is given rank 1, the second largest city (New York) is given rank 2, etc. We then calculate the natural logarithm of the rank of each city and the natural logarithm of the size of each city. Figure 1.6

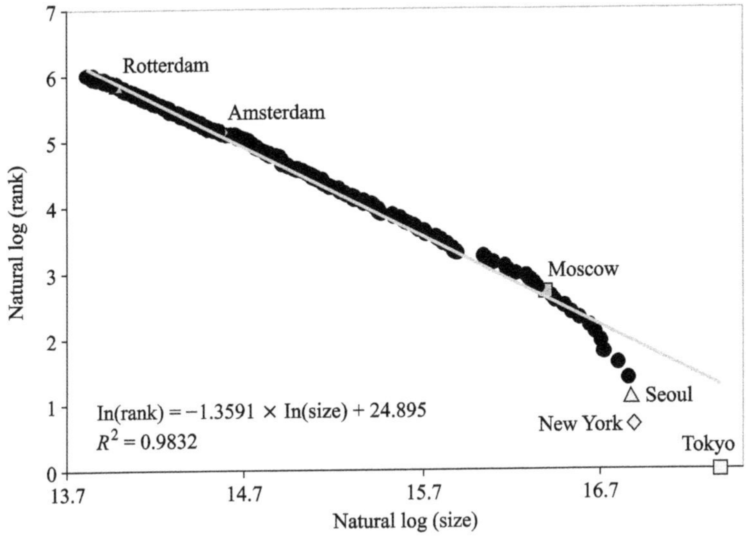


*Figure 1.6* Regularity in the distribution of economic activity: urban agglomerations in the world (2002).

plots the 408 data points calculated accordingly. With the exception of the largest cities (due to a phenomenon well-known in the literature; see Brakman, Garretsen, and Van Marrewijk 2001: Chapter 7), all data points are almost exactly on a straight line. A simple regression analysis explains 98.32 per cent of the variance in the data, see Figure 1.6. Based on its size, the rank number predicted by the regression analysis for the city of Amsterdam (166), for example, is very close to the actual rank number (170). Similarly for the city of Rotterdam (actual rank 350, compared with predicted rank 365). The negative relationship between rank and size follows, obviously, from our way of organising the data. The almost perfect log-linear relationship between rank and size, indicating regularity and predictability in the spreading of economic activity, is highly remarkable. It was first discovered by George Kingsley Zipf (1949) and in general it is referred to as the rank-size rule. If the slope of the estimated regression is equal to one, it is referred to as Zipf's law.

We can illustrate the fractal dimension in the regularity of the distribution of economic activity in a similar way as we did for the unevenness of this distribution; first by showing that the same regularity holds if we limit ourselves to a global region, in this case Europe, and second by repeating this exercise for one of the countries in Europe, in this case Germany. Moscow (13.2 million inhabitants) is the largest agglomeration in Europe, followed by London (11.85 million), Istanbul (10.65 million) and Paris (9.8 million). Within Europe, Amsterdam is ranked 25th and Rotterdam 61st. Similar calculations to those performed for the global level again lead to the rank-size rule, see Figure 1.7 (note that the 'problem'

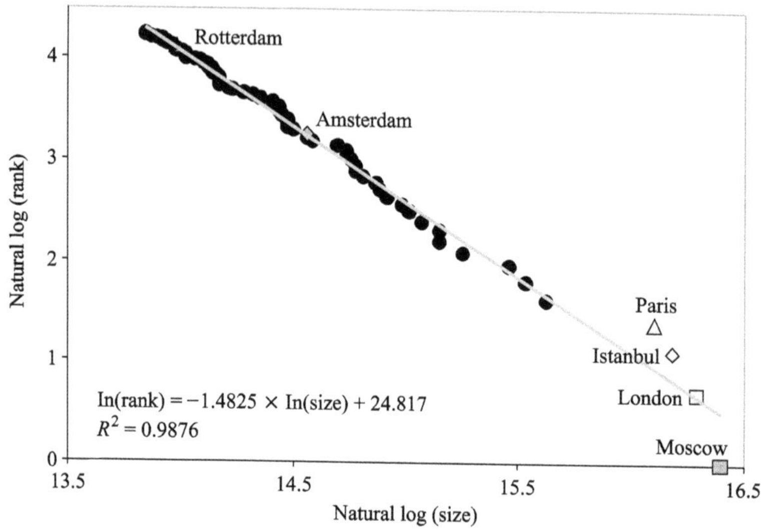


*Figure 1.7* Regularity in the distribution of economic activity: urban agglomerations in Europe (2002).

with the largest cities is less pronounced than in Figure 1.6). A simple regression explains 98.76 per cent of the variance in the data, which are again on an almost perfect log-linear distribution. The economic powers at work at the global level to create order in the distribution chaos are apparently also operative at the European level.

Within Germany, Essen (5.93 million inhabitants) was the largest agglomeration in 1996, followed by Berlin (4.06 million), Stuttgart (2.52 million), Hamburg (2.46 million) and Frankfurt (1.87 million). Similar rankings and calculations as before lead to Figure 1.8, which again shows that the relationship between rank and size creates an almost perfect log-linear distribution. A simple regression explains 97.62 per cent of the variance in the data. At the country level too, therefore, similar regulatory powers in the distribution of economic activity play a role. Brakman, Garretsen and Van Marrewijk (2001: Chapter 7) and Soo (2002) provide a detailed overview of the rank-size rule for all countries in the world for which data are available. In general, this rule holds regardless of the size of a country, its political system, its cultural, social or ethnical background, etc. Indeed, the rank-size rule for the empirical distribution of economic activity holds almost perfectly for such diverse countries as, for example, the USA, Brazil, France, India, Russia and China.

In conclusion, there is a 'fractal dimension' in the regularity of the spatial distribution of economic activity, known as the 'rank-size rule' (with Zipf's law as a special case). This empirical regularity holds globally, at the continent level and at the country level.

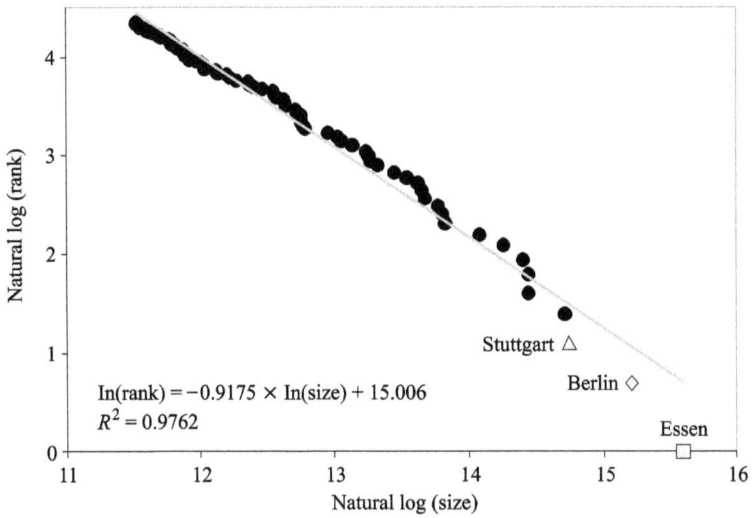


*Figure 1.8* Regularity in the distribution of economic activity: urban agglomerations in Germany (1996).

## REGULARITY IN INTERACTION

As explained in the preceding section, the spatial distribution of economic activity displays a remarkable regularity. In this section we will show that this also holds for the interaction between economic centres in the form of international trade flows. Before investigating the interaction at the country level, we first give an overview of this interaction at the global region level (see also the section Global Regions, above). In this respect it is useful to subdivide the group of high-income countries into three subgroups: Western Europe, North America and Australasia. In combination with the six developing regions, this creates nine global regions. Our overview is based on a combination of the CID-UC-Davis/Feenstra data set (2000), consisting of annual observations on bilateral trade flows for four-digit sectors, 183 countries and 28 years, with a total of slightly less than 18.4 million positive observations.[9] First, we aggregated all data to the country level. Second, we calculated the intraregional trade flows (that is, trade flows between countries within the same global region) and the interregional trade flows (that is, trade flows between countries in two different global regions).

With a combined total of more than 75 per cent of world trade, the three high-income regions are the three largest trade regions. This image is reinforced when we take into consideration the fact that these three regions only contain about 16 per cent of the world population. Western Europe is by far the most important trade region within this group. It is the source of about 42 per cent of world exports, more than twice as much as the other two high-income regions (North America and Australasia), which each are the source of about 17 per cent of world exports. South-East Asia is the most important developing region (10 per cent of world exports), followed by Latin America (5 per cent of world exports). The trade shares of South Asia and sub-Saharan Africa (both about 1 per cent of world exports) are remarkably small.

For the nine global regions identified here, no less than 41.1 per cent of world trade flows are intraregional. There is, however, a large difference between the regions as to the extent of intraregional trade flows. South Asia (SAS; 2 per cent), the Middle East and North Africa (NMA; 3 per cent) and sub-Saharan Africa (SSA; 4 per cent) have very low intraregional trade flows, implying that they depend mostly on other (far away) parts of the world for their export flows. North America (NAM; 35 per cent) and (Eastern) Europe and Central Asia (ECA; 31 per cent) have much higher levels of intraregional trade flows. By far the highest level of intraregional trade flow is reached, however, in Western Europe (two-thirds of its trade flows), making it the only region with above average intraregional trade flows at the world level.

The most important information on international trade flows at the global level is effectively illustrated in Figure 1.9. Since there are nine global regions, there are in principle $9 \times 8 = 72$ interregional and 9 intraregional trade flows. Expressed as a percentage of total world trade flows and rounded to the nearest integer, however, only 30 out of these possible 81 trade flows have a value of 1 per cent or higher – these are shown in Figure 1.9. It is immediately evident that South Asia hardly participates in the global economy: none of its trade flows are large enough to be depicted in Figure 1.9. The central role of Western Europe (partially based on its past as a colonial power) is also evident. Finally, the local character of international trade flows becomes evident: the intraregional trade flows are relatively large and the largest interregional trade flows are usually directed towards neighbouring global regions.

This local character of international trade flows is at the centre of the regularity in interaction between economic centres, known as the 'gravity equation'. Newton's second law states that the attraction between two objects is proportional to their masses and inversely proportional to the distance between them. A similar feature holds in economics if we replace attraction with trade flows and use GDP as a measure of mass. Not surprisingly, it was a physicist, Nobel laureate Jan Tinbergen (1962), who first used Newton's second law to explain international trade flows. Many researchers since then have confirmed this empirical regularity in economics, which yields a solid empirical explanation of bilateral trade flows and thus illustrates the regularity of interaction between economic centres quite effectively.

As an illustration of the regularity of the interaction between countries, Table 1.6 shows estimated results of a basic gravity equation for 96 countries in the world with at least 50 observations in 1996. The income data are from the *World Development Indicators CD-ROM* (World Bank 2002: GNI, current dollars). The distances were determined using longitude and latitude data from the

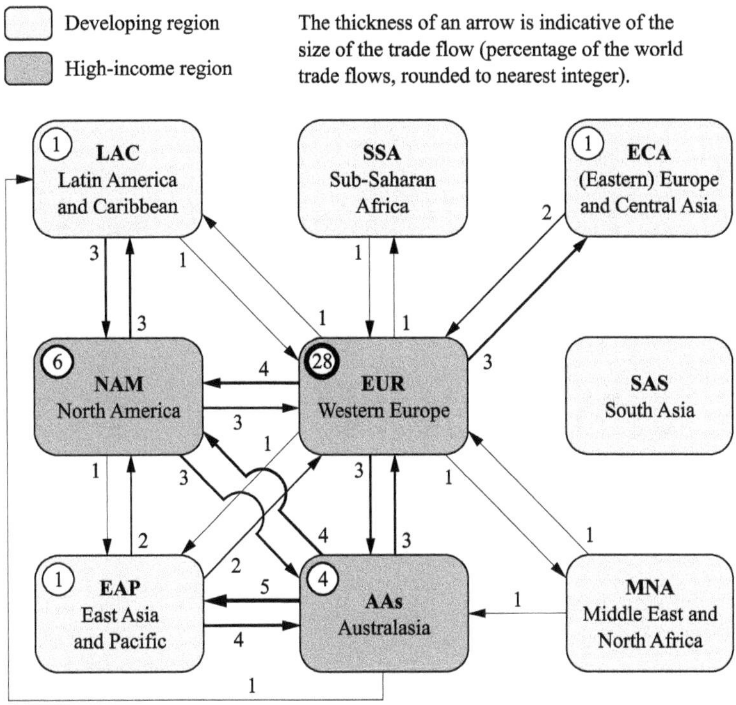


• Of the 81 interregional and intraregional trade flows, 51 are smaller than 0.5 per cent; these are not shown.

• Intraregional trade flows are indicated by a circle in that region.

*Figure 1.9* Interregional and intraregional trade flows: global regions (% of world total, 1996). Source: Based on Van Marrewijk (2002).

*Britannica Atlas* for the most important economic centre in a country (usually the capital city) and by calculating the distance to other economic centres using the assumption that the earth is a perfect sphere.[10] The estimated equation is:

$$\ln(\text{export}) = \text{constant} + [\text{coefficient}_1 \times \ln(\text{GDP})] + [\text{coefficient}_2 \times \ln(\text{distance})] \quad (1.2)$$

Except for Barbados and Jamaica, the estimated income coefficient has the right sign (i.e. is positive) and is highly significant.[11] The estimated significant coefficients are fairly close together, ranging from 0.194 for Algeria to 0.957 for South Africa, with an average of 0.545, a median of 0.544 and a variance of only 0.027. For all countries except Taiwan, the distance variable has the correct sign (i.e. negative). The estimated coefficient is usually statistically (highly)

*Table 1.6* Results from estimated gravity equation (1996 data)

| *Country* | *Income* | t-*stat* | *Distance* | t-*stat* | *Adjusted* $R^2$ | *Number of observations* |
|---|---|---|---|---|---|---|
| Africa | | | | | | |
| 1 South Africa | 0.957 | 11.87 | −2.886 | −7.39 | 0.67 | 129 |
| 2 Algeria | 0.194 | 1.35 | −1.256 | −3.57 | 0.16 | 53 |
| 3 Morocco | 0.552 | 6.63 | −1.860 | −6.48 | 0.40 | 99 |
| 4 Tunisia | 0.471 | 5.43 | −1.698 | −6.84 | 0.39 | 93 |
| 5 Egypt | 0.519 | 6.41 | −1.771 | −8.02 | 0.51 | 104 |
| 6 Cameroon | 0.600 | 4.67 | −2.873 | −8.34 | 0.41 | 70 |
| 7 Gabon | 0.680 | 4.40 | −2.009 | −4.96 | 0.28 | 64 |
| 8 Congo (Zaire) | 0.500 | 2.05 | −1.171 | −1.77 | 0.12 | 53 |
| 9 Ethiopia | 0.483 | 2.86 | −1.047 | −2.12 | 0.17 | 55 |
| 10 Ghana | 0.824 | 4.04 | −1.399 | −3.18 | 0.30 | 57 |
| 11 Cote d'Ivoire | 0.528 | 4.43 | −2.167 | −5.31 | 0.38 | 58 |
| 12 Kenya | 0.497 | 4.78 | −2.199 | −7.24 | 0.29 | 94 |
| 13 Madagascar | 0.529 | 3.51 | −0.792 | −1.10 | 0.16 | 73 |
| 14 Malawi | 0.516 | 4.99 | −1.490 | −4.18 | 0.28 | 58 |
| 15 Mauritius | 0.500 | 4.50 | −1.448 | −2.44 | 0.17 | 80 |
| 16 Nigeria | 0.666 | 4.27 | −1.325 | −2.68 | 0.27 | 67 |
| 17 Senegal | 0.559 | 4.26 | −1.647 | −2.64 | 0.23 | 50 |
| 18 Zimbabwe | 0.820 | 6.41 | −2.239 | −6.44 | 0.42 | 90 |
| 19 Tanzania | 0.618 | 3.47 | −1.221 | −2.08 | 0.22 | 59 |
| North America | | | | | | |
| 20 Canada | 0.673 | 9.60 | −0.946 | −2.44 | 0.58 | 132 |
| 21 USA | 0.345 | 6.79 | −0.749 | −3.42 | 0.39 | 133 |
| South America | | | | | | |
| 22 Argentina | 0.821 | 11.12 | −1.612 | −5.90 | 0.51 | 119 |
| 23 Bolivia | 0.785 | 3.64 | −2.341 | −7.01 | 0.45 | 60 |
| 24 Brazil | 0.564 | 9.02 | −2.037 | −7.74 | 0.47 | 125 |
| 25 Chile | 0.761 | 10.44 | −2.394 | −7.81 | 0.55 | 111 |

| | | | | | | | |
|---|---|---|---|---|---|---|---|
| 26 | Colombia | 0.661 | 7.71 | −1.901 | −10.43 | 0.51 | 101 |
| 27 | Ecuador | 0.553 | 4.53 | −1.608 | −7.04 | 0.37 | 80 |
| 28 | Mexico | 0.609 | 8.83 | −1.892 | −10.53 | 0.56 | 113 |
| 29 | Peru | 0.955 | 7.95 | −1.935 | −6.28 | 0.50 | 97 |
| 30 | Uruguay | 0.831 | 7.11 | −1.560 | −4.62 | 0.49 | 88 |
| 31 | Venezuela | 0.615 | 4.85 | −2.744 | −9.81 | 0.46 | 77 |
| 32 | Costa Rica | 0.491 | 5.12 | −2.155 | −11.11 | 0.51 | 88 |
| 33 | El Salvador | 0.595 | 5.52 | −1.992 | −9.96 | 0.52 | 50 |
| 34 | Guatemala | 0.414 | 3.24 | −1.828 | −8.77 | 0.41 | 78 |
| 35 | Honduras | 0.579 | 6.08 | −1.756 | −10.58 | 0.47 | 60 |
| 36 | Nicaragua | 0.518 | 3.00 | −1.732 | −5.74 | 0.32 | 51 |
| 37 | Bahamas | 0.519 | 3.14 | −0.340 | −1.01 | 0.18 | 62 |
| 38 | Barbados | −0.000 | −0.00 | −1.165 | −3.12 | 0.12 | 51 |
| 39 | Dominican Republic | 0.368 | 2.39 | −1.608 | −5.28 | 0.27 | 65 |
| 40 | Jamaica | −0.007 | −0.04 | −1.217 | −2.99 | 0.15 | 58 |
| 41 | Neth. Antilles | 0.343 | 1.75 | −1.701 | −5.97 | 0.28 | 65 |
| 42 | Trinidad and Tobago | 0.380 | 2.15 | −2.146 | −7.47 | 0.31 | 68 |
| 43 | Panama | 0.319 | 3.04 | −1.433 | −6.61 | 0.32 | 61 |
| Middle East | | | | | | | |
| 44 | Israel | 0.657 | 10.72 | −0.531 | −3.10 | 0.53 | 111 |
| 45 | Japan | 0.398 | 8.40 | −0.276 | −1.34 | 0.42 | 133 |
| 46 | Bahrain | 0.522 | 5.88 | −1.565 | −7.66 | 0.36 | 68 |
| 47 | Cyprus | 0.667 | 9.28 | −1.613 | −8.56 | 0.59 | 103 |
| 48 | Iran | 0.508 | 3.27 | −1.651 | −5.24 | 0.41 | 71 |
| 49 | Jordan | 0.588 | 4.52 | −1.224 | −3.36 | 0.36 | 62 |
| 50 | Kuwait | 0.645 | 7.20 | −1.980 | −7.97 | 0.49 | 78 |
| 51 | Lebanon | 0.489 | 4.16 | −1.264 | −6.10 | 0.36 | 66 |
| 52 | Oman | 0.205 | 1.81 | −1.498 | −4.11 | 0.15 | 81 |
| 53 | Saudi Arabia | 0.636 | 4.49 | −1.579 | −5.40 | 0.43 | 70 |
| 54 | Syria | 0.481 | 4.69 | −1.734 | −6.51 | 0.45 | 67 |
| 55 | United Arab Emirates | 0.508 | 3.68 | −2.218 | −4.36 | 0.33 | 73 |
| 56 | Turkey | 0.578 | 9.21 | −1.214 | −9.52 | 0.62 | 125 |

*Continued*

*Table 1.6* Results from estimated gravity equation (1996 data) (continued)

| *Country* | *Income* | *t-stat* | *Distance* | *t-stat* | *Adjusted* $R^2$ | *Number of observations* |
|---|---|---|---|---|---|---|
| Asia | | | | | | |
| 57 Afghanistan | 0.366 | 2.77 | −0.508 | −1.45 | 0.12 | 53 |
| 58 Bangladesh | 0.771 | 8.79 | −0.234 | −0.96 | 0.44 | 102 |
| 59 Myanmar (Burma) | 0.599 | 2.86 | −1.824 | −3.48 | 0.32 | 52 |
| 60 Sri Lanka | 0.597 | 6.08 | −1.843 | −5.18 | 0.50 | 79 |
| 61 Hong Kong | 0.199 | 5.01 | −0.078 | −0.44 | 0.17 | 131 |
| 62 India | 0.381 | 7.22 | −0.756 | −4.24 | 0.34 | 132 |
| 63 Indonesia | 0.439 | 8.61 | −1.119 | −4.75 | 0.44 | 114 |
| 64 Malaysia | 0.406 | 7.27 | −1.083 | −6.80 | 0.39 | 129 |
| 65 Pakistan | 0.444 | 6.83 | −1.079 | −4.24 | 0.38 | 128 |
| 66 Philippines | 0.723 | 8.05 | −1.568 | −6.49 | 0.52 | 109 |
| 67 Singapore | 0.306 | 4.86 | −1.118 | −3.91 | 0.38 | 107 |
| 68 Taiwan | 0.308 | 3.55 | 0.041 | 0.22 | 0.17 | 83 |
| 69 China | 0.402 | 7.49 | −0.413 | −1.31 | 0.39 | 133 |
| 70 Vietnam | 0.829 | 5.25 | −1.062 | −2.40 | 0.46 | 72 |
| Western Europe | | | | | | |
| 71 Belgium-Luxembourg | 0.383 | 7.05 | −0.371 | −2.83 | 0.41 | 133 |
| 72 Denmark | 0.447 | 7.74 | −0.723 | −5.40 | 0.56 | 133 |
| 73 France | 0.263 | 5.22 | −0.228 | −2.19 | 0.27 | 133 |
| 74 Germany | 0.274 | 6.99 | −0.367 | −3.76 | 0.47 | 133 |
| 75 Greece | 0.706 | 10.14 | −1.278 | −6.35 | 0.53 | 127 |
| 76 Ireland | 0.539 | 10.03 | −0.495 | −3.13 | 0.58 | 131 |

| | | | | | | | |
|---|---|---|---|---|---|---|---|
| 77 | Italy | 0.280 | 7.29 | −0.305 | −3.70 | 0.44 | 133 |
| 78 | Netherlands | 0.406 | 6.97 | −0.373 | −2.48 | 0.46 | 133 |
| 79 | Portugal | 0.599 | 9.03 | −0.960 | −4.76 | 0.51 | 128 |
| 80 | Spain | 0.419 | 7.99 | −0.269 | −2.24 | 0.40 | 129 |
| 81 | United Kingdom | 0.227 | 5.90 | −0.175 | −2.18 | 0.24 | 133 |
| 82 | Austria | 0.705 | 10.63 | −0.806 | −6.53 | 0.68 | 129 |
| 83 | Finland | 0.609 | 10.24 | −0.933 | −5.28 | 0.61 | 126 |
| 84 | Iceland | 0.547 | 4.10 | −1.708 | −3.82 | 0.40 | 63 |
| 85 | Norway | 0.655 | 8.73 | −0.615 | −3.34 | 0.54 | 131 |
| 86 | Sweden | 0.477 | 7.43 | −0.402 | −3.31 | 0.47 | 133 |
| 87 | Switzerland | 0.541 | 8.15 | −0.239 | −1.49 | 0.48 | 133 |
| 88 | Malta | 0.499 | 5.83 | −1.019 | −4.34 | 0.33 | 88 |
| Eastern Europe | | | | | | | |
| 89 | Bulgaria | 0.639 | 5.95 | −1.366 | −8.17 | 0.60 | 74 |
| 90 | Czechoslovakia | 0.592 | 8.43 | −0.938 | −5.73 | 0.54 | 128 |
| 91 | Hungary | 0.686 | 9.25 | −1.164 | −6.98 | 0.60 | 119 |
| 92 | Poland | 0.782 | 9.20 | −0.932 | −4.61 | 0.66 | 115 |
| 93 | Romania | 0.606 | 7.82 | −1.584 | −8.62 | 0.51 | 120 |
| 94 | Former USSR | 0.598 | 6.35 | −1.563 | −7.50 | 0.52 | 109 |
| Oceania | | | | | | | |
| 95 | Australia | 0.727 | 10.07 | −2.802 | −7.20 | 0.56 | 132 |
| 96 | New Zealand | 0.631 | 6.54 | −2.696 | −5.66 | 0.40 | 109 |

significant, ranging from –2.886 for South Africa to –0.078 for Hong Kong. The average distance estimate is –1.354, the median is –1.399 and the variance is 0.486.

In conclusion, there is a remarkable regularity in the interaction between economic centres. As it is proportional to the (economic) mass of a country and inversely related to the distance between countries, this is known as the 'gravity equation'.

## SUMMARY AND CONCLUSIONS

There is an enormous array of possibilities to analyse regarding economic concentration in terms of 'what' (population, value added, specific sectors), 'where' (global regions, countries, regions, districts, cities), and 'how' (structure in spreading and interaction). At the global regional level, as identified by the World Bank, economic activity is unevenly distributed. The relative density differences (highest density compared with lowest density) are large for population density (more than 14 times), GNP density (more than 62 times) and GNP density corrected for purchasing power differences (more than 18 times). At a lower level of geographic aggregation (the country level) the uneven distribution of economic activity becomes more pronounced, both for population and production (measured as value added, after correcting for purchasing power). A 'fractal dimension' in the distribution of economic activity becomes evident after establishing that at the regional and city level economic activity is also unevenly distributed. This enables the identification of core–periphery patterns at the regional level.

There are remarkable regularities in the distribution of economic activity, both with respect to the spatial distribution itself and regarding the interaction between economic centres. The degree of urbanisation, which varies from country to country, is still increasing worldwide. There is a fractal dimension in the regularity of the spatial distribution of economic activity, known as the rank-size rule (with Zipf's law as a special case), since this empirical regularity holds globally, at the continent level and at the country level. The regularity in the interaction between economic centres, which is proportional to the (economic) mass of a country and inversely related to the distance between countries, is known as the gravity equation.

We can summarise the distribution of economic activity in five stylised facts.

- There is an uneven distribution regardless of the *type* of economic activity.
- There is an uneven distribution regardless of the *geographic* level of aggregation.
- There is an uneven distribution regardless of the *economic* level of aggregation.
- There is a remarkable *regularity* in the *spatial distribution* of economic activity.

- There is a remarkable *regularity* in the *interaction* between economic centres.

## ACKNOWLEDGEMENTS

We would like to thank Steven Brakman, Harry Garretsen and the participants at the 2003 annual meeting of the Royal Netherlands Economic Association for useful comments and suggestions. The usual disclaimer applies.

## NOTES

1 The term 'goods' also refers to services.
2 Unless otherwise indicated, all data in the following three sections are for the year 2000 and are taken from the *World Development Indicators CD-ROM 2002*. Rural population density data are for the year 1999.
3 A subgrouping of high-income countries is sometimes warranted, see the section Regularity in Interaction.
4 At this level of aggregation there is virtually no difference between GNP and GDP.
5 The distance of a region to itself equals one-third of the axis of the smallest rectangle containing the region.
6 This is the population identified as living in an urban area. Note that the definition of an urban area may vary from country to country, which leads to an underestimate of the urban population, e.g. in China and India.
7 See www.Lamp.ac.uk/~Noy/rome1.htm.
8 All data in this section are taken from that website (dated 12 November 2002), see Th. Brinkhoff: *Principal Agglomerations and Cities of the World*, www.citypopulation.de.
9 See the Empirical Trade Analysis Centre website for details: www.few.eur.nl/few/people/vanmarrewijk/eta. We focus on the data for 1996 in view of missing observations for the year 1997.
10 For the USA, the shortest distance to either New York or Los Angeles was taken.
11 The calculated *t*-values are consistent under heteroscedasticity (White 1980).

## REFERENCES

Brakman, S., Garretsen, H. and Marrewijk, C. van (2001) *An Introduction to Geographical Economics*, Cambridge: Cambridge University Press.

Copus, A.K. (1999) *A new peripherality index for the NUTS III regions of the European Union*, ERDF/FEDER Study 98/00/27/130, A Report for the European Commission, Directorate General XVI.A.4 (Regional Policy and Cohesion).

Fujita, M., Krugman, P.R. and Venables, A.J. (1999) *The Spatial Economy: Cities, regions, and international trade*, Cambridge, MA: MIT Press.

Harris, C.D. (1954) 'The market as a factor in the localization of industry in the United States', *Annals of the Association of American Geographers*, 64: 315–48.

Keeble, D., Owens, P.L. and Thompson, C. (1981) *The Influence of Peripheral and Central Locations on the Relative Development of Regions*, Department of Geography, Cambridge University.

Marrewijk, C. van (2002) *International Trade and the World Economy*, Oxford: Oxford University Press.

Soo, Kwok Tong (2002) ‘Zipf’s Law for Cities: A cross country investigation’, mimeo: London School of Economics.

Tinbergen, J. (1962) *Shaping the World Economy*, New York: Twentieth Century Fund.

White, H. (1980) ‘Nonlinear regression on cross-section data’, *Econometrica,* 48/3, 721–46.

World Bank (2000) *World Development Report 1999*, Washington, DC: World Bank.

World Bank (2002) *World Development Indicators 2002 CD-ROM*, Washington, DC: World Bank.

Zipf, G.K. (1949) *Human Behavior and the Principle of Least Effort*, New York: Addison-Wesley.

## APPENDIX: WORLD BANK GLOBAL REGIONS, 2002

### EAP: East Asia and Pacific, excluding high-income economies

- American Samoa
- Cambodia
- China
- Fiji
- Indonesia
- Kiribati
- Korea, Dem. Rep.
- Korea, Rep.
- Lao PDR
- Malaysia
- Marshall Islands
- Micronesia, Fed. Sts.
- Mongolia
- Myanmar
- Palau
- Papua New Guinea
- Philippines
- Samoa
- Solomon Islands
- Thailand
- Tonga
- Vanuatu
- Vietnam

### ECA: Europe and Central Asia, excluding high-income economies

- Albania
- Armenia
- Azerbaijan
- Belarus
- Bosnia and Herzegovina
- Bulgaria
- Croatia
- Czech Republic
- Estonia
- Georgia
- Hungary
- Isle of Man
- Kazakhstan
- Kyrgyz Republic
- Latvia
- Lithuania
- Macedonia, FYR
- Moldova
- Poland
- Romania
- Russian Federation
- Slovak Republic
- Tajikistan
- Turkey
- Turkmenistan
- Ukraine
- Uzbekistan
- Yugoslavia, Fed. Rep.

### HIC: High-income countries, group aggregate (GNI per capita in 2000 of $9,266 or more)

- Andorra
- Aruba
- Australia
- Austria
- Bahamas, The
- Barbados
- Belgium
- Bermuda
- Brunei
- Canada
- Cayman Islands
- Channel Islands
- Cyprus
- Denmark
- Faroe Islands
- Finland
- France
- French Polynesia

- Germany
- Greece
- Greenland
- Guam
- Hong Kong, China
- Iceland
- Ireland
- Israel
- Italy
- Japan
- Kuwait
- Liechtenstein
- Luxembourg
- Macao, China
- Malta
- Monaco
- Netherlands
- Netherlands Antilles
- New Caledonia
- New Zealand
- North Mariana Islands
- Norway
- Portugal
- Qatar
- San Marino
- Singapore
- Slovenia
- Spain
- Sweden
- Switzerland
- United Arab Emirates
- United Kingdom
- United States
- Virgin Islands (US)

**LAC: Latin America and Caribbean, excluding high-income economies**

- Antigua and Barbuda
- Argentina
- Belize
- Bolivia
- Brazil
- Chile
- Colombia
- Costa Rica
- Cuba
- Dominica
- Dominican Republic
- Ecuador
- El Salvador
- Grenada
- Guadeloupe
- Guatemala
- Guyana
- Haiti
- Honduras
- Jamaica
- Mexico
- Nicaragua
- Panama
- Paraguay
- Peru
- Puerto Rico
- St Kitts and Nevis
- St Lucia
- St Vincent and Grenada
- Suriname
- Trinidad and Tobago
- Uruguay
- Venezuela, RB

**MNA: Middle East and North Africa, excluding high-income economies**

- Algeria
- Bahrain
- Djibouti
- Egypt, Arab Rep.
- Iran, Islamic Rep.
- Iraq

- Jordan
- Lebanon
- Libya
- Morocco
- Oman
- Saudi Arabia
- Syrian Arab Republic
- Tunisia
- West Bank and Gaza
- Yemen, Rep.

## SAS: South Asia

- Afghanistan
- Bangladesh
- Bhutan
- India
- Maldives
- Nepal
- Pakistan
- Sri Lanka

## SSA: Sub-Saharan Africa

- Angola
- Benin
- Botswana
- Burkina Faso
- Burundi
- Cameroon
- Cape Verde
- Central African Rep.
- Chad
- Comoros
- Congo, Dem. Rep.
- Congo, Rep.
- Côte d'Ivoire
- Equatorial Guinea
- Eritrea
- Ethiopia
- Gabon
- Gambia, The
- Ghana
- Guinea
- Guinea-Bissau
- Kenya
- Lesotho
- Liberia
- Madagascar
- Malawi
- Mali
- Mauritania
- Mauritius
- Mayotte
- Mozambique
- Namibia
- Niger
- Nigeria
- Rwanda
- São Tomé and Principe
- Senegal
- Seychelles
- Sierra Leone
- Somalia
- South Africa
- Sudan
- Swaziland
- Tanzania
- Togo
- Uganda
- Zambia
- Zimbabwe

# 2 Transport costs, location and the economy

*Jan Oosterhaven and Piet Rietveld*

## INTRODUCTION

Economic activities and welfare are distributed anything but evenly in space. The explanation of the spatial pattern of dispersion and concentration rests on a combination of physical-geographical factors and the systematic impact of transport costs (Von Thünen 1826; Weber 1909; Lösch 1940). Historically, transport costs have put their stamp on the spatial economic structure of cities, countries and continents. But in real terms, transport costs have been falling for a long time. Some authors (for example Cairncross 1997) even claim that the role of transport costs has come to an end, resulting in the 'death of distance'. Economic activities should have become footloose, implying the emergence of widely dispersed location patterns. However, many economic activities are characterised by strongly concentrated patterns, and that means that this conclusion is premature. Besides, there is no guarantee that the constant decrease in transport costs will continue. Systems of roads, railways and airports are experiencing bottlenecks in various parts of the world and this may well lead to an increase of transport costs in the future. Investments to overcome the bottlenecks are huge, and this calls for a critical analysis of the various effects of these investments.

The aim of this chapter is to clarify the role of transport costs in the economy generally, and in spatial patterns of economic activities in particular. We start with a review of long-term developments in transport costs. We then discuss the contribution of transport costs to the accessibility of regions, after which we focus on the impact of transport on spatial patterns within metropolitan regions. We then review methods available for assessing the impact of transport infrastructure investments on regional and interregional economic performance and conclude that spatial general equilibrium models represent the best tool. Finally, an application of this type of modelling to a series of rail infrastructure proposals in the Netherlands is shown to provide relevant information.

## LONG-TERM DEVELOPMENTS IN TRANSPORT COSTS

During the past centuries, transport costs have decreased drastically. This holds true for both freight and passenger transport, as we will demonstrate below.

## Freight transport

Crafts and Venables (2001) demonstrate that for maritime transport, real costs decreased by about 83 per cent during the period between 1770 and 1990 (see Table 2.1). This decrease did not occur in an even way; during the period between 1830 and 1910 the price decrease was extremely fast, whereas it was clearly slower during the other periods. The decrease during the 1830–70 period resulted from substantial improvements that took place in the technology of sailing boats, which still dominated maritime transport at that time. The arrival of the steamship had a main impact on developments between 1870 and 1910. A remarkable feature in Table 2.1 is that the costs of maritime transport did not decrease after 1960, despite the rapid increase of container traffic during this period.

The generalised costs of transport depend not only on the monetary costs, but also on time costs, including the costs of keeping appropriate stores (capital costs, which depend on the interest rate) and depreciation. One might expect that for most types of products the time-related costs are limited: small for bulk products and higher for high-value products. However, Hummels (2001) finds that for international freight flows to the USA the duration of transport has a much larger role than one might expect on the basis of pure costs of stores. This implies that there is a higher willingness to pay for reducing transport times than one might expect on the basis of the capital costs. This might imply a high estimate of depreciation costs. Indeed, Hummels arrives at a high estimate for specialised capital goods, such as office equipment: for every day that such goods are in transit, their value would decrease by 2.2 per cent. This underlines the importance of speed increases in maritime transport. This result also implies that although the large-scale development of container traffic during the past decades did not lead to cheaper traffic, the effect on generalised costs must have been favourable: it led to a speeding up of transport and hence to a decrease of the time-related costs.

Compared with airfreight, maritime traffic remains slow. The high importance of time costs led to a shift in international freight transport towards airfreight.

*Table 2.1* Real costs of maritime transport

| *Year* | *Cost index (1910 = 100)* |
|---|---|
| 1750 | 298 |
| 1790 | 376 |
| 1830 | 287 |
| 1870 | 196 |
| 1910 | 100 |
| 1930 | 107 |
| 1960 | 47 |
| 1990 | 51 |

Sources: Crafts and Venables (2001); Dollar (2001); Harley (1988); Isserlis (1938).

This was reinforced by the trend that speeds and frequencies strongly increased in air transport. Also, the real costs of airfreight have decreased by 60 per cent between 1940 and 1980, which must be considered substantial. It is therefore no surprise that, in terms of value, the share of airfreight of total international trade from the USA to other countries – except its direct neighbours Canada and Mexico, where surface transport is important – has increased to more than 50 per cent.

A similar estimate for the costs of surface transport indicates that these decreased even more strongly: by 90 per cent between 1800 and 1910 (Bairoch 1990; Crafts and Venables 2001). This was mainly due to two important breakthroughs during this period: the development of extensive canal systems in important parts of Europe and the USA, followed by the formation of extensive railway systems in almost all countries in the world. The development of the road system during the twentieth century led to further decreases in the costs of freight traffic. MuConsult (2001) estimates, for example, that the real costs per tonne-km decreased by about 80 per cent during the past century. This means that the initial advantage of maritime transport over surface transport has become smaller.

MuConsult (2001) gives a detailed set of estimates of the development of costs per tonne-km for various modalities during the past century (see Table 2.2). It appears that the costs of rail, inland navigation and road traffic all decreased rapidly, of which road traffic scored the largest decrease. Cost decreases in aviation were even larger, with a reduction of about 6 per cent per year. This underlines the importance of aviation as an attractive transport mode for exports of high-value goods.

In addition to the direct monetary costs in these transport modes, the changes in transport speeds also deserve attention. Here, the changes during the past decades have been less impressive, although the overall trend still shows improvements. In road transport, the proportion of expressways has increased, more powerful motors induced slightly higher speeds for barges, and cruising speeds in aviation have increased somewhat. In addition, the increase in volumes transported led to an increase in frequencies of service, implying a decrease in scheduling costs. Since congestion mainly occurs in and near the large metropolitan areas, one may safely assume that it has a much larger impact on local and regional traffic than it has on long-distance traffic.

*Table 2.2* International transport costs, in 1990 prices

| | *Transport costs (euro cents/tonne-km)* | | |
|---|---|---|---|
| | *1900* | *1950* | *1998* |
| Rail | 40 | 18 | 9 |
| Inland navigation | 15 | 7.5 | 6 |
| Road | 110 | 40 | 20 |
| Aviation | – | 750 | 44 |

Source: MuConsult (2001).

These improvements in costs and speeds of freight transport had a substantial impact on international trade. Maddison (2001) shows, for example, that exports have grown much faster than national economies during the past centuries (Table 2.3). Increasing trade barriers between 1929 and 1950 caused the decrease in world trade during that period. It is important to note that the rapid increase in exports since 1950 cannot be explained by the decrease in the costs of maritime traffic (see Table 2.1). The decrease in trade barriers, increase in the quality of transport (speed, frequency and reliability) and a decrease of the maritime share must have played an important role here.

In a spatial sense, the decrease of transport costs in international and interregional trade has led to ongoing concentration processes in central regions, or conversely, the shift of activities to peripheral regions (Krugman 1991). It is important to note that in the long term the progress of maritime transport and inland navigation has been faster than for surface transport and air transport. Water transport has been the dominant transport mode in Europe for many centuries and this has put its stamp on urbanisation patterns. Many of the large cities of Europe are located at or near the sea, or near to a navigable river. But we demonstrated that the initial transport-cost advantage of these cities has shrunk. It is therefore remarkable that relatively little change occurred in the urban hierarchies in Europe during the past century. Apparently, the cities concerned have achieved sufficient economic mass that they have become less dependent on the initial advantage. This is a clear example of path dependence and 'lock-in'.

## Passenger transport

Speeds have increased in all important transport modes of passenger traffic during the past century. The speeds given in Table 2.4 relate to average speed of all trips, based on total travel time (including time for access and egress). Since access and egress is usually slow, the mean speed increases when travel distances increase. In addition, speeds increase with distance because a larger share of trips can be made via expressways and intercity trains, therefore part of the speed

*Table 2.3* Exports as a percentage of GDP at world level

| *Year* | *Exports (% of GDP)* |
|---|---|
| 1820 | 1.0 |
| 1870 | 4.6 |
| 1913 | 7.9 |
| 1929 | 9.0 |
| 1950 | 5.5 |
| 1973 | 10.5 |
| 1998 | 17.2 |

Source: Maddison (2001).

*Table 2.4* Average passenger transport travel speeds in the Netherlands

| | *Average travel speed*[a] *(km/hr)* | | |
|---|---|---|---|
| | *1900* | *1950* | *1990* |
| Car | 15 | 33 | 43 |
| Rail | 18 | 26 | 40 |
| Bus/tram/subway | 9.5 | 15 | 20 |
| Motorcycle | – | 20 | 23 |
| Air | – | 75 | 200 |

Source: MuConsult (2001).

Notes
a Including access and egress times.

increase can be attributed to increases in distances. However, most of the speed increase can probably be explained by improved infrastructure, network design, power of vehicles and frequencies. This reasoning makes it clear that as the quality of a transport system improves, leading to an increase in speeds, people will travel longer distances, having a secondary effect on speeds (Rietveld *et al.* 1999). Of course there is also negative feedback when quality improvement leads to an increase in demand and hence to congestion, but during the period considered the positive effects seem to dominate the negative ones.

The monetary costs of passenger transport are described in Table 2.5. Real transport costs per km decreased for all travel modes during the past century, with the car having the largest decrease. The decrease for public transport can partly be explained by the introduction of subsidies after the 1960s. Without these subsidies the prices would have been considerably higher.

The concept of generalised costs can be used to integrate the outcomes for travel times and monetary costs. It appears that monetary costs decreased at a faster rate than the time costs, aviation being an exception. While weighing the

*Table 2.5* Average monetary costs of passenger transport, in 1990 prices

| | *Average monetary costs*[a] *(euro cents/km)* | | |
|---|---|---|---|
| | *1900* | *1950* | *1990* |
| Car | 575 | 95 | 59 |
| Rail | 37 | 18 | 13 |
| Bus/tram/subway | 132 | 40 | 14 |
| Air | – | 110 | 90 |

Source: MuConsult (2001).

Notes
a Including access and egress times.

two elements, one has to take into account the value of time, which most probably increases with income. This underlines the increasing importance of travel times in generalised costs. Not only do travel times decrease at a slower rate than monetary costs, they may be expected to get a higher weight. Another implication is that the decrease of generalised costs per km has not been as fast as the two tables above suggest.

## Other costs of spatial interaction

It is important to realise that spatial interactions such as trade, commuting and migration depend not only on monetary costs and speeds, but also on several other factors, such as frequencies and reliability, the latter being an indicator of the variability in transport performance. For frequencies, we expect that these increase as a response to increases in transport volumes. Also, the introduction of hub-and-spoke networks, for example in aviation, leads to an increase in frequency. Conversely, increases in the size of transport vehicles, such as aircraft and container ships, may have reduced frequencies. But in general, during the past decades total volumes have increased more than vehicle size, and so as a result frequencies have increased.

In the field of reliability, a less favourable development has taken place in transport systems during the past decade in many countries. On roads and railways, bottlenecks slow down traffic and lead to unpredictability. This leads to extra costs for users in the form of preventive measures, such as departing earlier in order to reduce the risk of late arrival. This theme of unreliability of transport systems and the valuation of unreliability certainly deserves more attention than it has achieved in the past.

In addition to the components of generalised costs, as mentioned above, there are still other elements that play essential roles in spatial interactions. These become visible when, for example, one compares interregional flows within a country with international flows. For activities such as freight transport, passenger transport, telephone traffic and migration, the level of spatial interaction between regions within a country appears to be 2–20 times larger than the interaction between regions in different countries at comparable distances (Rietveld 2001). This also holds true for countries that are both within the European Union (EU).[1] This indicates that there must be other types of costs involved.

The theory of transaction costs, with its focus on search, negotiation and enforcement to comply with agreements, sheds light on this. As long as these costs are strongly associated with passing borders, one may expect that spatial interaction patterns have a strong domestic orientation, which will not simply disappear when large improvements take place in international infrastructures, such as the Channel Tunnel and the Öresund fixed link. It is important to note that transaction costs in international interactions do not only concern such costs as time losses when passing borders, formal trade barriers and the costs of complying with formalities. The point is that national borders still delimitate territories with different cultures, formal and informal procedures and often also languages. Therefore, transactions between actors at different sides of borders have to overcome extra impediments.

This emphasis on transaction costs in relation to national borders does not imply that their role is unimportant within countries. It is with good reason that Storper and Venables (2004) call attention to the lasting relevance of face-to-face contact for location choices of entrepreneurs. This obviously reinforces agglomeration tendencies in locational patterns of, for example, headquarters of large companies and their research and development activities. It also leads to a spatial orientation in the direction of regions with good air connections.

## ACCESSIBILITY OF REGIONS

After considering the long-term changes in transport costs, we now discuss the implications for location patterns. This section focuses on the interregional level, whereas in the subsequent section the consequences within metropolitan regions will be discussed.

Accessibility is a term that has been given much attention in the literature. In an intuitive sense it can be described as the ease of interaction from a certain point with all relevant destinations. Two elements are important in the definition: the transport costs between origins and destinations and the level of the relevant activities at these destinations. Since the relevant activities and transport modes taken into consideration may vary according to the aim of the analysis, it is no surprise that many different definitions and operationalisations of the accessibility concept exist.

As an example we consider a study of Perrels and Hilbers (2000). In this study, five factors are listed as contributing to accessibility of a region:

1 centrality
2 network density, in combination with detour factors
3 quality of the network in terms of speed, reliability, frequencies
4 density of activities in the own region
5 density of activities in the regions nearby.

Within Europe one usually finds that regions with a high density (factor 4) are also surrounded by regions with high density (factor 5) and are often centrally located (factor 1). Examples are metropolitan areas such as London, Paris, The Randstad, Brussels–Antwerp, and the Ruhr area. Network densities (factor 2) are also high there, so detour factors are limited. The only disadvantages these regions face concern the quality of the network in terms of congestion and reliability. Considering generalised costs per km as the crow flies, passenger traffic via roads at shorter distances (50 km) within core regions has a disadvantage of about 5–10 per cent above the Western European average (see Table 2.6). Conversely, rural regions may have scores up to 15 per cent below this average. As soon as these costs are considered at somewhat longer distances, the differences

*Table 2.6* Generalised costs of passenger transport by road and maximum costs necessary to reach a given market share

| *Region* | *Generalised costs of road transport up to 50 km (Western Europe = 100)* | *Maximum cost to reach 10 million customers (Western Europe = 100)* |
|---|---|---|
| Mecklenburg | 85 | 150 |
| West Nederland | 100 | 60 |
| Ile de France | 108 | 45 |

Source: Perrels and Hilbers (2000).

between Western European regions are very modest because the weight of congestion problems in specific regions is much lower in that case.

In the context of the Perrels and Hilbers (2000) study, accessibility is operationalised as the maximum distance one has to travel from a region for it to have a certain value of employment (for example 10 million workers) within its reach. It appears that in regions with low generalised costs of traffic – which happen to coincide with peripheral regions in Europe – the distances to be travelled are substantially higher. In a similar way, one may consider the maximum costs (an index is given in Table 2.6). In rural regions, the maximum cost of reaching 10 million customers is 50 per cent above the Western European average. The centrally located European cities have the disadvantage of higher transport costs per km within their areas, but this is more than compensated for by the high densities within these regions and the regions nearby. The positions are presented in Figure 2.1.

We conclude that regions close to other regions with high levels of economic activity have a natural accessibility advantage. Conversely, peripheral regions

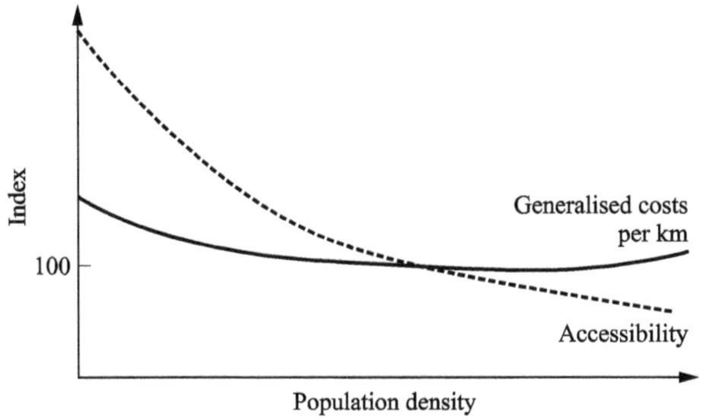


*Figure 2.1* Accessibility and generalised transport costs in Western European regions, as a function of population density.

with long distances to other regions will have low accessibility. Even if large investments were to be made, their accessibility would remain low. As a consequence, the accessibility landscape of European regions is rather stable. Even large investments in missing links, such as the construction of the Channel Tunnel and the Öresund fixed link, have relatively small impacts on accessibility maps. Concerning future developments, it is imaginable that the regions close to the large existing centres, such as Paris and London, will eventually push these centres from their top positions. Much depends on the value of time applied. For business traffic this is higher than for other purposes, and this will make the accessibility outcomes sensitive to delays due to congestion.

## TRANSPORT AND THE INTERNAL DEVELOPMENT OF CITIES

Having discussed the relevance of transport costs for the accessibility of regions within a large system, we now turn to the impacts transport has on the cities themselves. In his interesting contribution, Colin Clark (1958) indicates how changes in transport costs have always played a role in urban dynamics. Up until the nineteenth century the costs of transport of agricultural products were so high that they put a limit on the size of the urban centres. With the rise of the railways, this situation came to an end. It then became feasible to exploit economies of scale in manufacturing production, which led to a period of urban growth. This then led to new bottlenecks: railways had mainly been constructed for long-distance freight transport and so passenger transport (for the increasing number of workers to their work places) became problematic. Cities therefore remained compact and limited in size. The emergence of tramways in the second part of the nineteenth century finally enabled a process of spatial expansion of cities (Hall 1994), and this was further reinforced by the introduction of the electric tram in the beginning of the twentieth century. The coming of busses and cars led to a further growth of urban agglomerations, but now this was mainly an increase of surface area, not of population size. Gradients of density and rents started to level off. An extreme example is Los Angeles, where the centre-supporting role of rail was broken down and a large area with almost homogeneous densities of workplaces and residences emerged.

Clark in 1958 expected a similar development for the large European agglomerations: suburbanisation not only of residences, but also of work. However, this expectation did not come true. Examples of cities where there is still a strong concentration of employment in the centre and where public transport plays a dominant role in commuting are London and New York. Although a certain trend can indeed be observed of work places moving towards the city fringes, this tendency has remained limited in many cases. In addition, it appears that in those cases where jobs moved towards the fringes of the cities, this often led again to concentrations of employment. For this phenomenon, Garreau (1988) introduced the concept of edge cities. Researchers such as Henderson and Mitra (1996) and Glaeser and Kahn (2004) developed new models for this purpose, in which explicit attention is paid to agglomeration advantages for firms. The centre is ultimately restricted in its growth by high costs of transport from the residential areas located further away. The formation of subcentres allows the further growth of urban economies. The underlying trade-off concerns the advantages of a reduction of total transport costs of employed persons and the lower productivity that follows from the spread of economic activities in the region.

Figure 2.2 illustrates the development of the urban structure, with a focus on the distribution of employment. At point A is the classical model of complete concentration of employment in the centre and dispersion of the population around it. On the line BC we have a complete dispersion of employment. At C, employers find their workers at a local level, whereas at B there are many criss-cross connections, 'wasteful commuting' in the terminology of Hamilton (1982). The historical path that was outlined above started at O, given the high transport costs at the time. The railway-based structure led to growth and concentration of the city in the direction of A. The present development moves in the direction of the line BC, where both the direction of the development and the degree of dispersion from city to city may vary. The extent to which C will be the direction of the development depends among other things on the future level

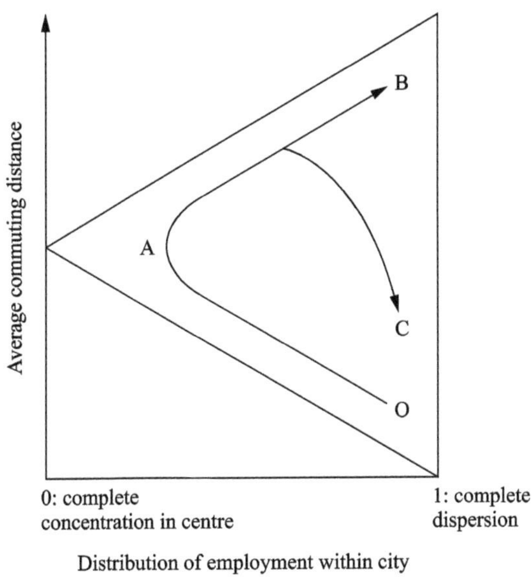


*Figure 2.2* Relationship between the distribution of employment in urban regions and mean commuting distances. Source: Brotchie *et al.* 1996.

of transport costs. It is clear that the distribution is not only influenced by the future development of transport costs and by spatial planning and zoning, but also by agglomeration advantages.

The literature on urban land use that developed after the seminal work of Alonso (1964), during the period of 1960–1990, concentrated on the urban housing market (Fujita 1989) and on location choice of households. Location choice of firms received much less attention. During the 1990s, a beginning was made on filling this lacuna, an example being the work of Fujita, Krugman and Venables (1999). In this approach, centrifugal and centripetal forces are distinguished. The factor land, which is essential for agriculture, is immobile and contributes to centrifugal forces. Labour is assumed to be completely mobile and provides opportunities for spatial concentration. A necessary condition for concentration in these models is the existence of scale economies within individual firms, otherwise firms could simply spread their production towards individual consumers. Marshall (1920) distinguished three main types of agglomeration economies: concentration of labour markets, face-to-face knowledge exchange and a large local market. The last of these has received most attention in the current line of models. When a certain location reaches a critical size because of a certain initial advantage, this leads to a lasting advantage because both consumers and delivering firms locate close by, saving transport costs. These advantages are not unlimited, however, because when the market grows, the centrifugal forces will, at some stage, induce urban developments to emerge at other places.

The above sketch of the forces of concentration and deconcentration is very global. In the tradition of 'new economic geography', this theory is made more precise with analytical tools where the theory of monopolistic competition appears helpful. It is important to note that this approach of agglomeration economies strongly concentrates on the manufacturing sector. However, the time when cities specialised in manufacturing lies far behind us. Therefore, there is reason in the present situation to focus on the two other agglomeration advantages mentioned by Marshall. The functioning of labour markets remains of undiminished importance in urban development: concentration of labour in certain areas has advantages for both workers and employers in matching processes. Also, the advantage of local knowledge spillovers is important. In the terminology of Glaeser (1999), this is an example of positive external effects or non-market interaction, where proximity and low transport costs are essential. The use of the analytical tools of new economic geography in these two directions is a promising area of research. From the perspective of the decreased transport costs it is important to note that where these costs have decreasing relevance for manufacturing, their roles in the functioning of labour markets, the service sector and the knowledge economy in particular will remain important. It is clear that a shift takes place from freight transport as the main driving force towards passenger transport, in the form of commuting and business traffic.

## SPATIAL ECONOMIC IMPACTS, ESTIMATION METHODS

To actually estimate the spatial economic impacts of changes in generalised transport cost, a large amount of literature is available (for overviews see Oosterhaven *et al.* 1998; Rietveld and Nijkamp 2000). An important distinction is that between *ex-post* analyses of historical changes and *ex-ante* analyses of expected future impacts. The latter is of special importance in evaluating proposals for transport infrastructure and price policies. Some methods are, of course, more suited to *ex-ante* analyses and others, to *ex-post* analyses. In this section, we briefly review the main methodologies by group.

### Microsurveys with firms

There is a rich, strongly normative theoretical literature on the influence of infrastructure and accessibility on the location decisions of individual firms. This literature started around 1900 with emphasis on the importance of minimising transport cost (Weber 1909). This is not surprising in view of the high absolute and relative costs of transport of that time, as discussed above. Current literature tends to de-emphasise the importance of transport cost as compared with other cost, such as labour cost (Dicken 1986). An interesting exception is McCann (1998), who replaces the concept of transport cost with that of logistic cost, which includes all costs related to moving goods in space and time through the whole of the supply chain. McCann argues that logistic costs play a central role in the locational decisions of most large multinational firms. The theoretical literature, however, does not serve to answer the empirical question about the impact of specific types of infrastructure in specific locations (Oosterhaven *et al.* 1998). For this purpose, microsurveys with firms provide better answers.

First, there are series of *general surveys*, with questions about the importance of all kinds of location factors, including accessibility. Naturally, the answers differ from country to country because firms are confronted with different locational bottlenecks in different countries and so tend to bias their answers in the direction of those location factors that they want to see improved. Also, the answers differ according to the type of firms and sectors that are interviewed as different sectors have different cost profiles and different market positions. The conclusion seems to be that centrality and the reliability of access are important, but not the actual transport cost. In fact, for most sectors, Europe presents a rather level playing field within which secondary and even subjective factors of location play an increasing role (Pellenbarg 1998).

The second strand of *surveys* tries to investigate the historical or future impacts of specific infrastructure. The outcome of this type of research is often rather dubious as the purpose of the surveys is seldom hidden; firms therefore tend to answer positively even if the project at hand is of little importance to their own firm. Such strategic and socially desirable answers are very difficult to avoid. Besides, when different variants of the same infrastructure are under investigation, under different scenarios for future economic development, such as in many social cost–benefit analyses (CBA), a questionnaire approach becomes unwieldy. Furthermore, it should be noted that both types of surveys do not indicate which firms (further away) are indirectly influenced by the actions of the directly affected firms (closer by).

## Quasi production functions, accessibility and potential models

In macroeconomics, the infrastructure debate started with the claim that the productivity decline in the USA was caused by a lack of investment in infrastructure (Aschauer 1989). Since then a whole series of articles has appeared that partly substantiate, but more often weaken, the original statement. The most common approach is the quasi production function approach:

$$Y_r^t = f(L_r^t, K_r^t, \text{infrastructure stock}_r^t) \tag{2.1}$$

where $Y$ is domestic output of region $r$, $L$ is labour, $K$ is capital and $t$ is time period. Besides labour and capital per region or nation and time period, several components – or the total stock – of infrastructure are included in a macro production function in order to explain the level of the change of domestic output. This approach has a number of difficulties.

1. There are complicated econometric issues relating to the one-sided nature of using only time series (data on different time periods, $t$) or only cross sections (data on different regions, $r$), which is done most often (see Sturm 1998).
2. The direction of causality is not easily detected statistically as infrastructure may both follow and lead economic growth. To sort this out, observations on many spatial units ($r$) over long periods of time ($t$) are needed, but these are seldom available.
3. Measurements of the infrastructure stock fail to take account of the actual use of infrastructure services, which determines its productivity contribution.
4. Historical macroelasticities are of no use when decisions about individual projects have to be taken because such projects are both type- and location-specific.

As a result of these difficulties, no clear conclusion about the effects of infrastructure investment has been reached. Production macroelasticities of infrastructure are found to vary considerably among the different studies. In many studies they are found to be insignificant, and in some studies even to be negative (see Sturm 1998). Comparable studies have been undertaken using macroregional data, but these suffer from the same problems and their conclusions are not any clearer (see Rietveld and Nijkamp 2000).

The last two problems may be solved by using a detailed spatial division of the study area, and by using for each region, $r$, a measure of economic accessibility rather than infrastructure stock (see: Jones 1981; Rietveld and Bruinsma 1998):

$$\text{Accessibility}_r = \Sigma_s Y_s f(c_{rs}) \qquad (2.2)$$

In (2.2), $f$ is a downward sloping (gravity or preferably entropy) distance decay of the transaction cost between region $r$ and region $s$ ($c_{rs}$). The inverse of (2.2) gives the economically weighted average transaction cost of location $r$ to the whole study area. Obviously, (2.2) allows approximation of the increase in economically useful infrastructure services available to a certain region that will result from investing in specific lines or nodes of the networks included. Moreover, (2.2) shows that it is not only the region within which the actual investment takes place that will profit from improved accessibility. In fact, a whole series of regions or nations will profit from any investment, as indicated by the summation and the distance decay.

The *economic potential*, which is directly derived from (2.2), provides an approximation of the significance of changes in accessibility for the regional economy at hand:

$$\text{Potential}_r = Y_r \Sigma_s Y_s f(c_{rs}) \qquad (2.3)$$

This almost directly follows from the fact that (2.3) is proportional to the total flow of traffic or trade from region $r$ to the whole of the study area (see: Jones 1981; Wilson 2000). This in turn is proportional to the total size of the economy of region $r$. Evers *et al.* (1987) and Evers and Oosterhaven (1988) were the first to use (2.3) to estimate the economic impacts of new infrastructure. They developed a variant of it, with border dummies and a modal split parameter, as a multi-sectoral potentials model, which they used to estimate the employment impacts of a proposed high-speed rail connection between Amsterdam and Hamburg. Their approach was shown to produce the 'right' spatial pattern of impacts, but not necessarily the right macro level of these impacts (Rietveld 1989). Later on, Bröcker (1995) showed that this gravity type of spatial impact pattern might also be produced by the even more satisfactory use of a spatial computable general equilibrium (SCGE) model.

The use of (2.2) in regression analyses, along with other independent variables, in fact comes down to estimating the reduced form of an unknown structural model. Cheshire, using such an approach, concludes that apart from transport cost, tariffs and non-tariff barriers also play significant roles in explaining inter-regional growth differences within the EU (Cheshire and Cabonaro 1996; Cheshire and Magrini 2002). The SASI model[2] even goes one step further and incorporates regional sectoral production functions with (2.2) into a recursive model with a labour supply module, intended to estimate the spatial impacts of large European transport infrastructure and pricing projects (Wegener and Bökeman 1998). Bröcker *et al.* (2002) presents the most recent version of the SASI model along with a description of CGEurope, an SCGE model for the extended EU.

## Regional and macroeconomic models

Using (2.2) in (2.1) provides a solution to the last two problems of the quasi production function approach. To solve the first two problems, a structural equation approach is needed. The conceptual basis of a more comprehensive approach is given in Figure 2.3 (adapted from: FNEI 1984; Rietveld and Nijkamp 2000). The dotted arrow represents the direct cross-effect of (generalised) transport time and cost savings on the demand for all non-transport products, whereas the other arrows represent the indirect economic effects of these savings. The latter can be positive as well as negative.

For sectors and products with a comparative advantage, increased accessibility may boost a region's exports, whereas for other sectors and products it may lead to increased competition on a region's home market and a contraction of local output, income and employment. Both positive and negative effects may be enhanced because of (firm internal) economies of scale. These effects will be further modified and complicated because of inter-industry, consumption and investment demand feedbacks, which may lead to further (external) cluster and agglomeration economies for other, not directly affected, firms. Finally, for the whole study area, besides obvious interregional redistributive impacts, there may be (national or EU-wide) net positive effects, or even negative effects. The larger the study area taken, the more likely a net positive effect becomes; positive comparative advantages and economies of scale will dominate at higher spatial levels of analysis.

As clarified by Figure 2.3, regional and national economic models need to be multisectoral in order to capture the sectoral different nature of the primary

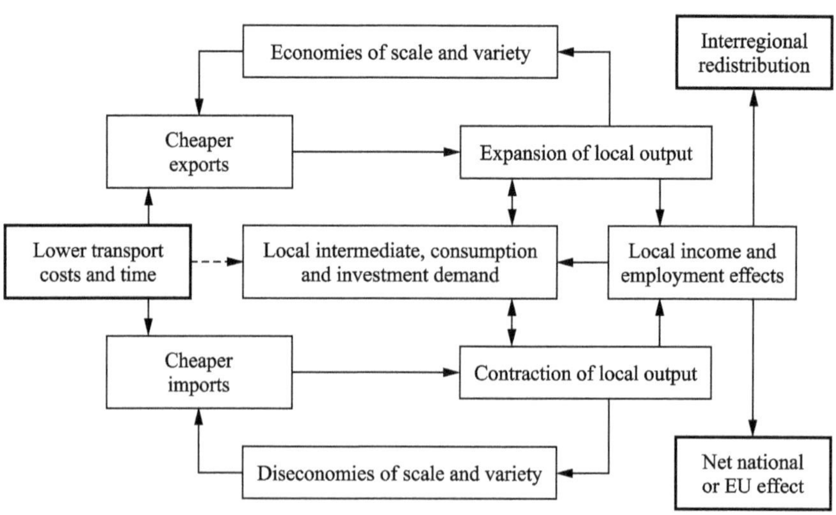


*Figure 2.3* Causal scheme for the spatial impacts of a transport improvement.

impacts of infrastructure. Also, the exogenous transaction cost reduction needs to be specified by sector such that the differentiated impacts on import, export and domestic prices will be captured. A detailed transport model is therefore needed to generate this information. But even then, regional and national economic models will suffer from a lack of spatial dimension, except for the presence of imports and exports to the rest of the world. Consequently, they will still have great difficulty in differentiating the impact of transport infrastructure investments between regions.

## LUTI and SCGE models

It has been shown that spatially detailed multisectoral models provide the only way to model the economic impact of new transport infrastructure adequately. Two broad classes of models satisfy this requirement, namely land-use/transportation interaction (LUTI) models and spatial computable general equilibrium (SCGE) models.

LUTI models consist of linked transport models and land-use (although location is a better term) models. They mostly employ a system dynamics type of modelling and are primarily developed to predict future growth and to analyse policy scenarios for large urban conglomerations (for example, Lee *et al.* 1995). There is a whole series of such models for different conglomerations. LUTI models have a decades-long history of gradual development and currently they are typically very disaggregated, with numerous spatial zones, sectors, household types, transport motives, modes of transport, etc. (see: DSC/ME&P 1998; Wilson 1998).

SCGE models typically are comparative static equilibrium models of interregional trade and location based on microeconomics, using utility and production functions with substitution between inputs (Bröcker 1998). Firms are either operating under constant economies of scale and perfect competition or under increasing economies of scale in markets with monopolistic competition. When operating under perfect competition, SCGE models lack the ability to model the cumulative causality of internal and external economies of scale emphasised in Figure 2.3. For social CBA they have little value added because the total benefits will equal the direct transport benefits, as long as the cross-border effects outside the study area are small (SACTRA 1999; CPB/NEI 2000). Their main benefit is their ability to show the interregional redistribution of the direct transport benefits across the study area.

The Dixit–Stiglitz (1977) type of monopolistic competition has become the workhorse of the ill-called 'new economic geography' (NEG) models (Krugman 1991; Fujita *et al.* 1999). As these models explicitly assume market imperfections (and sometimes also estimate their extents), they are very well equipped to measure additional welfare benefits in the rest of the economy as well as the direct transport benefits. Empirical applications are found in Venables and Gasiorek (1996) and Bröcker *et al.* (2002). Interesting theoretical simulations using an SCGE model with a land market are found in Fan *et al.* (1998), and simulations with congestion cost can be found in Brakman *et al.* (2001). A Dutch empirical application will be discussed in the next section.

The practical feasibility of LUTI models is large. The transport submodels are mostly based on discrete (multinomial) choice and are rather detailed. The location submodels are normally much cruder. As the relative cost of freight transport has decreased, and while locational decisions in the manufacturing sector are few, uncertainty about interregional manufacturing locational choice in particular is large. This is much less the case for service activities. Within large agglomerations they relocate quite often, while the relative time cost of passenger transport has been increasing or remained constant due to increased congestion and rising real incomes, as discussed earlier. Moreover, to a large extent the location of services follows that of people and industrial activities, which is easier to model. Consequently, the LUTI models are especially useful for estimating the impact on intra-urban location decisions, rather than for estimating the interregional location effects of transport measures.

Related to the difficulty of modelling location behaviour, the location modules tend to model production, price and non-transport consumption decisions by using fixed input–output ratios. As a consequence, most LUTI models provide reasonable estimates of direct transport user benefits, but they are ill-equipped to evaluate the additionality of the spatial impacts in the wider economy in terms of consumer welfare.

SCGE models are typically well suited for this evaluation task (see Venables and Gasiorek 1998). The SCGE modelling problem, at the moment, is not theoretical in nature, but empirical and computational. The consistent estimation of all the necessary consumers' and producers' substitution elasticities is problematic, if only because of the lack of adequate data. Moreover, the calibration of these models such that they reproduce recent history and provide plausible (that is, stable) projections into the future is problematic also, especially because of the highly non-linear character of the behavioural equations. The latter, however, is needed to model economies and diseconomies of scale, external economies of spatial clustering, continuous substitution between capital, labour, energy and material inputs in the case of firms, and between different consumption goods in the case of households.

For CBA, the most problematic aspect of SCGE is its comparative static nature. The best that can be done presently is to create a kind of pseudodynamics by comparing different equilibria in which increasing parts of the model are made endogenous. The standard distinction in NEG models is between the short term, in which labour is immobile, and the long term, in which it is not (Krugman 1991; Fujita *et al.* 1999). This distinction may usefully be extended into the following three types of equilibria:

1 Short-term, in which production, trade and consumption are variable, but not the number of firms (i.e. varieties) and workers per region.

2. Medium-term, in which the number of firms per region is variable until, through interregional firm migration, economic profit is zero everywhere.
3. Long-term, in which the number of workers per region is also variable until, through interregional labour migration, real wages are equal everywhere.

Others might consider the equilibrium character of SCGE its most problematic property, but this is more easily remedied. Introducing disequilibrium, for instance to explain persistent regional unemployment differentials, will mostly result in simpler models. On the labour market this could, for instance, be done by assuming that nominal wages are set at the national level and apply to all regions (van den Berg, 1999). In fact, LUTI models quite often use precisely this type of solution and then use a recursive structure to create a dynamic system, which moves to equilibrium in a step-wise fashion.

## AN APPLICATION OF AN SCGE MODEL

The use of SCGE to model the spatial economic impacts of transport infrastructure and price policies is well illustrated by means of the first Dutch SCGE model, called RAEM (an acronym of Ruimtelijk Algemeen Evenwichts Model).

### The RAEM-1 model

The first version of RAEM (Knaap and Oosterhaven 2001; Knaap 2004) has one type of household, 14 industries, 548 municipalities and nationally set wages, and only calculates changes in the short-term equilibrium, as defined above. It can be considered an extension of work by Venables (1996), who was first to incorporate inter-industry linkages into a theoretical NEG model. It also resembles the empirical CGEurope model by Bröcker *et al.* (2002), but RAEM is more detailed in that 14 different sectors have been specified and biregional input–output data (RUG/CBS 1999) are used to set the expenditure shares of its Cobb-Douglas upper-level production and utility functions. The 14 sector-specific elasticities of substitution at the lower CES (constant elasticity of substitution) levels of both functions are calibrated on the interregional trade flows from the same biregional input–output tables. This is done simultaneously with the calibration of the four parameters of the transport cost mark-up function.

The latter function deviates from the existing literature as RAEM-1 had to serve the evaluation of various railway infrastructure proposals. Theoretical NEG models only discuss manufacturing, but the real economy is dominated by services that depend far more on passenger travel than on freight transport. Therefore, RAEM assumes that sales at the firm level depend not only on freight transport, but also on personal business travel and shopping travel by the customers of the firm.

This is modelled by using a bimodal transport cost mark-up on f.o.b. prices ($p$):

$$p^* = \left[f_f\left(d_f\right)\right]^{\pi} \cdot \left[f_p\left(d_p\right)\right]^{1-\pi} \cdot p \tag{2.4}$$

where $\pi$ gives the share of freight transport ($f$) and $1-\pi$ the share of passenger travel ($p$) in the total transport cost per sector. The functional form of $f$ is taken from Bröcker *et al.* (2002):

$$f\left(d\right) = 1 + \upsilon \cdot d^{\omega} \tag{2.5}$$

where $\upsilon$ and $\omega$ are parameters to be estimated for freight and business/shopping travel and $d$ is distance cost. For freight, RAEM uses a $548 \times 548$ municipality-by-municipality distance matrix. For people, it uses separate travel time matrices by public transport and by car during non-peak hours, weighted by their modal shares in business/shopping travel (see: Elhorst *et al.* 2000; Knaap 2004).

## The empirical application of RAEM-1

We discuss the application of RAEM to two quite different magnetic levitation railway (maglev) proposals: namely, an urban conglomeration project and a core–periphery project, each with two variants (see Figure 2.4):

1. Inner urban ring: a maglev connecting the four largest cities (Amsterdam, The Hague, Rotterdam and Utrecht) in the urbanised Randstad region, running along the inner edges of these cities.
2. Outer urban ring: a competing maglev connecting the city centres of Amsterdam, The Hague, Rotterdam and Utrecht and a planned new town (Bollenstad) between The Hague and Amsterdam.
3. South-east route: a maglev between Schiphol Airport in the urbanised core and Groningen in the more peripheral, rural North, running along the south-east coast of the large lake in the middle of the country.
4. North-west route: a competing maglev running along the north-west dyke between the Dutch shallows and the North sea.

Each proposal has been evaluated in relation to different macroeconomic scenarios. Here we only compare with the European Coordination Scenario (CPB 1997). With the help of regional employment allocation and regional population projection models, the national total of people and jobs expected in 2020 has been divided over the 548 municipalities in the Netherlands (TNO *et al.* 2000). The EC Baseline Scenario consists of the projected railway and road networks for 2020, with travel times and volumes for 2020 (see Elhorst *et al.* 2000).

The maglev projects primarily lead to exogenous changes in the travel time matrix for public transport. Table 2.7 gives the representative travel times between

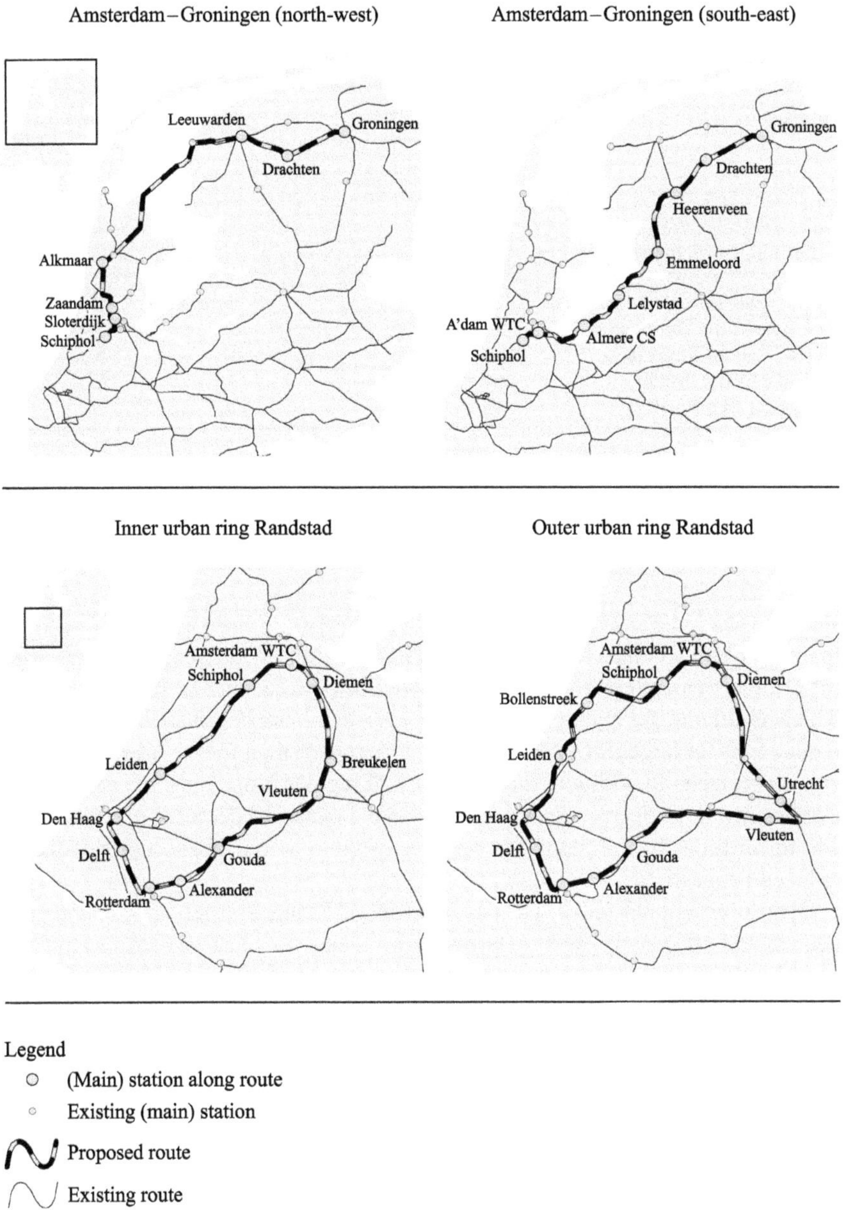


*Figure 2.4* Routes of the four maglev proposals.

*Table 2.7* Average travel times between main cities for proposed maglev routes

| Journey | *Average travel time[a] (minutes)* | | | |
|---|---|---|---|---|
| | *EC-baseline* | | *Proposed maglev route* | |
| | *Car* | *Public transport* | | |
| *Core–periphery projects* | | | *South-east* | *North-west* |
| Groningen–Schiphol | 135 | 173 | 100 | 96 |
| *Urban conglomeration projects* | | | *Inner ring* | *Outer ring* |
| Amsterdam–The Hague | 51 | 98 | 87 | 98 |
| The Hague–Rotterdam | 33 | 55 | 51 | 54 |
| Rotterdam–Utrecht | 64 | 75 | 74 | 61 |
| Utrecht–Amsterdam | 40 | 76 | 76 | 76 |

Source: Elhorst, Oosterhaven and Romp (2004).

Notes
a Including egress and digress time to stations of departure and arrival.

the major cities connected by each of the proposals. It demonstrates that total travel time by maglev falls below the travel time by car on several connections, which is unique for public transport. It also demonstrates that the travel time reduction is far larger for the core–periphery projects than for the urban conglomeration projects. In addition, the frequency of regular trains on some competing, existing rail links decreases, as a reaction to the expected decrease in passengers, and travel times by car along the corridor of the new rail links improve, due to reduced congestion.

Both interregional redistribution, in terms of changes in labour demand, and net national efficiency effect, in terms of the change in consumer surplus, played a role in the evaluation of these projects. Both types of effect could be estimated with RAEM by taking the difference between the EC-baseline equilibrium (with the old travel time matrices) and the project variant equilibria (with the new travel time matrices and modal shares for 2020).

Table 2.8 gives a summary of the expected interregional employment shifts. The subregions are grouped into five main regions, namely the northern Netherlands, the eastern Netherlands, the north wing of the Randstad, the south wing of the Randstad and the southern Netherlands.

The spatial employment shifts of the core–periphery projects are the most spectacular. The south-east route produces a gain in the two northernmost provinces of 4,500 jobs, and the north-west route surpasses this with 6,800 jobs. The difference is due to a difference in intervening opportunities. The intermediate region in the case of the south-east variant (Flevoland) is a much stronger competitor of the large Randstad market than the intermediate region in the case of the north-west route (northern North-Holland).

*Table 2.8* Employment effects of four proposed maglev routes

| | *Employment effects*[a] | | | |
|---|---|---|---|---|
| *Regions* | *South-east route* | *North-west route* | *Inner ring* | *Outer ring* |
| Northern Netherlands | | | | |
| Province of Groningen | 3638 | 4220 | −53 | −96 |
| Northern Friesland | 321 | 2185 | −24 | −55 |
| Southern Friesland | 668 | 420 | −28 | −50 |
| Province of Drenthe | −1176 | −626 | −84 | −126 |
| Eastern Netherlands | | | | |
| Province of Overijssel | −2066 | −1908 | −177 | −352 |
| Gelderland, except Tiel and surroundings | −3068 | −3393 | −701 | −252 |
| Northern Randstad | | | | |
| Northern North-Holland | −1038 | 1866 | 81 | −85 |
| Greater Amsterdam | 2374 | 2922 | 717 | 122 |
| Province of Flevoland | 2455 | −451 | 278 | 167 |
| Greater Utrecht (incl. Gooi + Tiel a.s.) | −932 | −2827 | 1032 | 1871 |
| Southern Randstad | | | | |
| Leiden and Bollenstreek | 265 | 112 | −5 | 158 |
| Greater The Hague | 116 | −107 | 358 | −135 |
| Greater Rotterdam | 531 | 174 | −170 | 372 |
| Remainder of South-Holland | 84 | −219 | 441 | 292 |
| Southern Netherlands | | | | |
| Zeeland and Western North-Brabant | 134 | −43 | −272 | −304 |
| Rest of Province of North-Brabant | −1385 | −1777 | −673 | −835 |
| Province of Limburg | −590 | −635 | −354 | −404 |

Sources: Elhorst *et al.* (2000); Romp and Oosterhaven (2001); Romp *et al.* (2001).

Notes

a Exclusive of the sizable employment impacts of total (housing and labour) migration, as these are not calculated by RAEM-1.

At the opposite end of the lines, the effects are also of interest. Many commentators expected these projects to only benefit the periphery, but that is clearly false. The absolute cost advantages at both ends of the line are the same. The number of firms that could profit in the core is even larger, but the peripheral market to which this profit applies is again smaller. The result of these three factors is an employment gain in greater Amsterdam of 2,400–2,900 and in the case of the south-east route a further gain in greater Rotterdam of 500 jobs, due to the ordinary high-speed rail line from Brussels through Rotterdam to Amsterdam, bypassing The Hague, which will be finished in the EC-baseline scenario in 2020. The rest of the Netherlands obviously lose out, which tends to be overlooked. They lose on both the large Randstad market (from northern firms) and on the smaller northern market (from Randstad firms).

The overall shift of employment due to the urban conglomeration projects is smaller, but it also has a clear spatial structure. Firms outside the Randstad region lose competitive position on the big Randstad market to Randstad firms, which get better access to each other's submarkets, leading to a loss of 2,400–2,600 jobs in regions in the northern, eastern and southern Netherlands. Between these regions, interesting differences may be noted, depending on the distance to the Randstad market. Regions closer by suffer more than those further out as the latter have smaller market shares to start with. Regions just outside the Randstad, such as Flevoland, again win a little as a result of two opposing forces. They lose in their direct neighbouring Randstad submarkets to firms from other parts of the Randstad, but they gain enough in the rest of the Randstad to compensate for that loss. Without the full data on the changes in the trade flows from a SCGE model, such shifts could not be observed or predicted.

Within the Randstad, interesting differences can be noted when the inner ring is compared with the outer ring. Both Greater Utrecht and Greater Rotterdam profit more from the outer ring, as their central stations get hooked on (see Figure 2.4). Greater Amsterdam and Greater The Hague, however, profit more from the inner ring, which gives them a fast bilateral connection, whereas the outer ring makes a detour through the Leiden region (see Figure 2.4). Finally, within the Randstad region, Greater Utrecht profits most for both options, for two reasons. First, it gets better access to the three economically largest regions: Amsterdam, Rotterdam and The Hague. Second, it lies between the rest of the Netherlands and the Randstad and is thus blocking off the competition from firms located there, which is again a kind of intervening-opportunities effect.

Table 2.9 gives the net national efficiency effect calculated by RAEM, which was incorporated into the social CBAs of these four projects. The south-east route produces a larger gain as it incorporates intermediate Flevoland much better in the Randstad economy and terminates in bigger municipalities. Given the comparable investment cost, the south-east route will most likely be the more socially profitable one.

The difference between the two Randstad projects is surprisingly small. The outer ring connects two big city centres and has one more station, but its detours reduce the time gains between the other stations, which compensates for

*Table 2.9* Net present values of consumers' surplus increase for four proposed maglev routes

| *NPV of consumer surplus increase*[a] *(€ million)* | | | |
|---|---|---|---|
| *South-east route* | *North-west route* | *Inner ring* | *Outer ring* |
| 1,421 | 862 | 724 | 803 |

Source: Elhorst, Oosterhaven and Romp (2004).

Notes

a NPV in 2010, at a discount rate of 4 per cent, in prices of 2000. The construction of the maglevs is planned for the period 2011–2015. The consumer surplus is assumed to reach the RAEM equilibrium value in five steps of 20 per cent over the period 2016–2020.

the gain. Given its higher investments cost, the outer ring alternative will most likely be the less socially profitable one.[3]

## SUMMARY AND CONCLUSION

The real transport costs of freight have decreased substantially over the past centuries. The decrease of passenger travel cost is somewhat less, especially in and around the large urban agglomerations. A closer investigation of the contribution of changes in transport networks to accessibility changes of European regions is that these effects are relatively small: the favourable position of the core regions remains unchallenged. However, persistent congestion in core regions may lead to an improvement of the relative positions of regions close to the core regions.

The overall reduction of transport cost has led to the relative increase in importance of other kinds of costs. This has made some economic activities footloose, but it has not lead to the 'death of distance'. The point is that transaction costs remain of great importance, and parts of these transaction costs are strongly distance-related. For example, transaction costs make frequent face-to face contacts necessary and this calls for clustering of the pertinent economic activities. This development also explains why the decrease of urban transport during the past 150 years has not led to the disappearance of employment centres in urban fields. Transport costs may be expected to remain important factors influencing passenger travel and locational patterns in the service sector.

There is a range of methods that can be used to estimate these impacts in a quantitative manner. From the overview it is concluded that land-use/transportation interaction (LUTI) models provide the best-tested approach at the level of large urban conglomerations. Spatial computable general equilibrium (SCGE) models provide a theoretically more-satisfying approach, which is especially suited for modelling interregional impacts for whole countries (or for parts of the EU). In the empirical application, the first Dutch SCGE model is shown to generate quite plausible results, both for two urban conglomeration magnetic levitation (maglev) projects and for two core–periphery maglev projects. Interregional redistribution effects in terms of increases in labour demand occur at both ends and along the length of the new maglev lines, whereas firms in other regions lose competitive position to the markets that get better connected. Additional national efficiency effects, in addition to the direct transport benefits, are also estimated, whereas a LUTI model with perfect competition and constant returns to scale would not have been able to estimate such effects.

## ACKNOWLEGDEMENTS

The authors thank J. Paul Elhorst, Thijs Knaap and Ward Romp for their contributions to the empirical application of the RAEM model.

## NOTES

1 McCallum (1995) and Helliwell (1996) find similar results for trade between the USA and Canada.
2 Developed by the Socio-Economic and Spatial Impacts of Transport Infrastructure Investments and Transport System Improvements (SASI) project.
3 This is confirmed in the full social CBA of these four projects (see Elhorst *et al.* 2004).

## REFERENCES

Alonso, W. (1964) *Location and Land Use*, Cambridge, MA: Harvard University Press.

Aschauer, D.A. (1989) 'Is public expenditure productive?', *Journal of Monetary Economics*, 23: 177–200.

Bairoch, P. (1990) 'The impact of crop yields, agricultural productivity and transport costs on urban growth between 1800 and 1910', in A. Hayami, J. de Vries and A.D. van der Woude (eds) *Urbanization in History*, Oxford: Oxford University Press.

Berg, M.M. van den (1999) 'Location and International Trade, in Theory and Practice', PhD thesis, Rijksuniversiteit Groningen.

Brakman, S., Garretsen, H. and Marrewijk, C. van (2001) *An Introduction to Geographical Economics*, Cambridge: Cambridge University Press.

Bröcker, J. (1995) 'Chamberlinian spatial computable general equilibrium modelling', *Economic Systems Research*, 7: 137–49.

Bröcker, J. (1998) 'Operational spatial computable general equilibrium modeling', *The Annals of Regional Science*, 32: 367–87.

Bröcker, J., Kancs, A., Schürmann, C. and Wegener, M. (2002) *Deliverable 2: Methodology of the Assessment of Spatial Economic Impacts of Transport Projects and Policies*, IASON Project, Delft: TNO Inro.

Brotchie, J.F., Anderson, M., Gipps, G.P. and McNamara, C. (1996) 'Urban productivity and sustainability', in Y. Hayashi and J. Roy (eds) *Transport, Land Use and the Environment*, Dordrecht: Kluwer.

Cairncross, F. (1997) *The Death of Distance*, Cambridge, MA: Harvard Business School Press.

Cheshire, P.C. and Cabonaro, G. (1996) 'Urban economic growth in Europe: testing theory and policy prescriptions', *Urban Studies*, 33/7: 1111–28.

Cheshire, P.C. and Magrini, S. (2002) 'The spatial economic impact of Euroland and the implications for policy', in J.R. Cuadrado-Roura and M. Parellada (eds) *Regional Convergence in the European Union, Facts, Prospects and Policies*, Berlin: Springer.

Clark, C. (1958) 'Transport – maker and breaker of cities', *Town Planning Review*, 28: 237–50.

CPB (1997) *Economie en Fysieke Omgeving, Beleidsopgaven en Oplossingsrichtingen 1995–2020*, The Hague: Central Planning Bureau.

CPB/NEI (2000) *Evaluatie van Infrastructuur Projecten. Leidraad voor Kosten-Batenanalyse*, The Hague: Central Planning Bureau.

Crafts, N. and Venables, A.J. (2001) 'Globalization in history: a geographical perspective', NBER conference on Globalization in Historical Perspective.

Dicken, P. (1986) *Global Shift: Industrial Change in a Turbulent World*, New York: Harper & Row.

Dixit, A.K. and Stiglitz, J.E. (1977) 'Monopolistic competition and optimum product diversity', *American Economic Review*, 67: 297–308.

Dollar, D. (2001) 'Globalization, Inequality and Poverty Since 1980', World Bank Working Paper, mimeo: World Bank.

DSC/ME&P (1998) *Review of Land Use/Transportation Interaction Models*, Report to SACTRA, London: Department of Transport, Environment and the Regions.

Elhorst, J.P., Knaap, T., Oosterhaven, J., Romp, W.E., Stelder, T.M. and Gerritsen, E. (2000) *Ruimtelijk Economische Effecten van Zes Zuiderzeelijn Varianten*, REG-Publicatie 22, Rijksuniversiteit Groningen.

Elhorst, J.P., Oosterhaven, J. and Romp, W.E. (2004) *Integral cost-benefit analysis of Maglev technology under market imperfections*, SOM Research Report 04C22, University of Groningen.

Evers, G.H.M., Meer, P.H. van der, Oosterhaven, J. and Polak, J.B. (1987) 'Regional impacts of new infrastructure: a multi-sectoral potentials approach', *Transportation*, 14: 113–26.

Evers, G.H.M. and Oosterhaven, J. (1988) 'Transportation, frontier effects and regional development in the Common Market', *Papers of the Regional Science Association*, 64: 37–51.

Fan, W., Treyz, F. and Treyz, G. (1998) 'Towards the development of a computable geographic equilibrium model', 45th North American RSAI Meetings, Santa Fe.

FNEI (1984) *Economische Betekenis van Transportinfrastructuur*, Groningen: Federatie van Noordelijke Economische Instituten.

Fujita, M. (1989) *Urban Economic Theory, Land-Use and City Size*, Cambridge: Cambridge University Press.

Fujita, M., Krugman, P. and Venables, A. (1999) *The Spatial Economy*, Cambridge, MA: MIT Press.

Garreau, D. (1988) *Edge City*, New York: Anchor books.

Glaeser, E. (1999) 'The Future of Urban Research: Non-market interactions', mimeo: Harvard University.

Glaeser, E. and Kahn, M.E. (2004) 'Sprawl and urban growth', in V. Henderson and J.-F. Thisse (eds) *Handbook of Regional and Urban Economics, volume 4*, Amsterdam: North Holland.

Hall, P. (1994) 'Squaring the circle: can we resolve the Clarkian paradox?, *Environment and Planning B*, 21: 579–94.

Hamilton, B.W. (1982) 'Wasteful commuting', *Journal of Political Economy*, 90: 1035–53.

Harley, C.K. (1988) 'Ocean freight rates and productivity 1740–1913: the primacy of mechanical invention reaffirmed', *Journal of Economic History*, 60: 819–41.

Helliwell, J.F. (1996) 'Do national borders matter for Quebec's trade?', *Canadian Journal of Economics*, 29: 509–22.

Henderson, V. and Mitra, A. (1996) 'The new urban landscape developers and edge cities', *Regional Science and Urban Economics*, 26: 613–43.

Hummels, D. (2001) 'Time as a Trade Barrier', mimeo: Purdue University.

Isserlis, L. (1938) 'Tramp shipping cargoes and freights', *Journal of the Royal Statistical Society*, 101: 53–146.

Jones, S.R. (1981) *Accessibility Measures, a Literature Review*, Crowthorne: Transport and Road Research Laboratory.

Knaap, T. and Oosterhaven, J. (2001) 'Het eerste ruimtelijke algemene evenwichtsmodel voor Nederland, met resultaten voor de magneetzweefbaan Schiphol-Groningen', *Maandschrift Economie*, 65/2: 89–107.

Knaap, T. (2004) 'Models of Economic Geography; Dynamics, Estimation and Policy Evaluation', PhD thesis, SOM Research School, University of Groningen.

Krugman, P. (1991) *Geography and Trade*, London: MIT Press and Leuven University Press.

Lee, S.Y., Haghani, A.E. and Byan, J.H. (1995) *Simultaneous Determination of Land Use and Travel Demand with Congestion: A system dynamics modeling approach*, TRB paper No. 950716, Washington DC.

Lösch, A. (1940) *Die Räumliche Ordnung der Wirtschaft*, Jena.

Maddison, A. (2001) *The World Economy: A millennial perspective*, Paris: OECD.

Marshall, A. (1920) *Principles of Economics*, London: Macmillan.

McCallum, J.C.P. (1995) 'National borders matter', *American Economic Review*, 85: 615–23.

McCann, P. (1998) *The Economics of Industrial Location: A logistics-costs approach*, Heidelberg: Springer-Verlag.

MuConsult (2001) 'De remmen los. Historisch analyse van de prijs/prestatieverhouding in het vervoer', Amersfoort.

Oosterhaven, J., Sturm, J.E. and Zwaneveld, P. (1998) *Naar een Theoretische Onderbouwde Aanpak van Voorwaartse Economische Effecten: Modelmatige Definitie*, Delft: TNO Inro/RUG.

Pellenbarg, P.H. (1998) 'Het huidige belang van infrastructuur en vervoer voor regionale en nationale vestigingsbeslissingen', in J.P. Elhorst and D. Strijker (eds) *Het Economisch Belang van het Vervoer, Verleden, Heden en Toekomst*, REG Publicatie 18, Rijksuniversiteit Groningen.

Perrels, A. and Hilbers, H. (2000) *Internationale Benchmarks voor prestatievergelijking infrastructuur*, Delft: TNO Inro.

Rietveld, P. (1989) 'Employment effects of changes in transportation infrastructure: methological aspects of the gravity model', *Papers of the Regional Science Association*, 66: 19–30.

Rietveld, P. (2001) 'Obstacles to openness of border regions in Europe', in M. van Geenhuizen and R. Ratti (eds) *Gaining Advantage from Open Borders. An active space approach to regional development*, Aldershot: Ashgate Publishing.

Rietveld, P. and Bruinsma, F. (1998) *Is Transport Infrastructure Effective? Transport Infrastructure and Accessibility: Impacts on the space economy*, Berlin: Springer-Verlag.

Rietveld, P. and Nijkamp, P. (2000) 'Transport infrastructure and regional development', in J.B. Polak and A. Heertje (eds) *Analytical Transport Economics*, Cheltenham: Edward Elgar.

Rietveld, P., Zwart, B., Wee, B. van and Hoorn, T. van den (1999) 'On the relationship between travel time and travel distance of commuters', *Annals of Regional Science*, 33/3: 269–88.

Romp, W.E. and Oosterhaven, J. (2001) *Indirect economics effects of a rail link along the Afsluitdijk*, Vakgroep Algemene Economie, Rijksuniversiteit Groningen.

Romp, W.E., Thissen, M.J.P.M., Oosterhaven, J. and Elhorst, J.P. (2001) *Indirecte Effecten Rondje Randstad: Migratie en Banen*, REG Publicatie 25, Rijksuniversiteit Groningen.

RUG/CBS (1999) *Regionale Samenhang in Nederland, Bi-regionale Input-output Tabellen en Aanbod- en Gebruiktabellen voor de 12 Provincies en de Twee Mainport Regio's*, REG Publicatie 20, Rijksuniversiteit Groningen/CBS, Groningen.

SACTRA (1999) *Transport and the Economy*, Standing Advisory Committee on Trunk Road Assessment, London: TSO.

Storper, M. and Venables, A.J. (2004) 'Buzz, face-to-face contact and the urban economy', *Journal of Economic Geography*, 4: 351–70.

Sturm, J.E. (1998) *Public Capital Expenditure in OECD Countries: The Causes and Impact of the Decline in Public Capital Spending*, Cheltenham: Edward Elgar.

TNO/RUG/VU/TUD (2000) *Indirecte Effecten Zuiderzeelijn, Hoofdrapport*. TNO Inro, Rijksuniversiteit Groningen, Vrije Universiteit Amsterdam, Technical University Dresden, Delft.

Thünen, J.H. von (1826) *Der Isolierte Staat in Beziehung auf Landwirtschaft and Nationalekonomie*, Hamburg.

Venables, A.J. (1996) 'Equilibrium locations of vertically linked industries', *International Economic Review*, 37: 341–59.

Venables, A.J. and Gasiorek, M. (1996) *Evaluating Regional Infrastructure: A Computable Equilibrium Approach*, Report to the European Union.

Venables, A.J. and Gasiorek, M. (1998) *The Welfare Implications of Transport Improvements in the Presence of Market Failure*, Report to SACTRA.

Weber, A. (1909) *Über den Standort der Industrien*, Mohr, Tübingen.

Wegener, M. and Bökeman, D. (1998) *The SASI Model: Model Structure*, Berichte aus dem Institüt für Raumplanung 40, Üniversität Dortmund.

Wilson, A.G. (1998) 'Land-use/transport interaction models, past and future', *Journal of Transport Economics and Policy*, 32: 3–26.

Wilson, A.G. (2000) *Complex Spatial Systems: The modelling foundations of urban and regional analysis*, Harlow: Pearson Education.

# 3 Agglomerations in equilibrium?

*Jan G. Lambooy and Frank G. van Oort*

## INTRODUCTION

In this chapter we will provide insights of the simultaneous usefulness of two scientific approaches that both focus on the relation between geography and economics: 'old' economic geography and 'new' geographical economics (GE, in the literature often called the 'new economic geography'). Depending on the research goals and the particular circumstances, the two approaches appear complementary to each other. Both approaches stress the importance of spatially determined externalities for explaining regional growth differences. As an example with universal implications, we analyse the development of the spatial pattern of the relatively new information and communications technology (ICT) sector in the Netherlands by using the theory of agglomeration advantages. Starting from regional economics and economic geography paradigms, we compare the research outcomes with those stemming from the GE framework of analysis.

The relatively new GE approach is accepted as a valuable one, providing new insights on fields traditionally studied by economic geography and regional economics. We argue, however, that the economic geographical approach can contribute through theoretical and empirical studies on more specific issues, where GE cannot shed light (as yet) due to its self-imposed theoretical constraints and assumptions. Also, economic geography is inherently more open to heterodox economic theories, such as evolutionary and institutional economics. Four examples of this kind of heterodox approach, which we will illustrate and discuss in this chapter, are:

- the importance of *life-stages* of firms, technologies and sectors, or development paths of firms, sectors, cities and systems of cities,
- specific *spatial structures* not showing (clear) relations with the (in GE assumed) forces of economic agglomeration,
- specific urban and regional factors *explaining* why agglomeration forces influence sectors and firms differently, depending on the period of economic development and the various technological trajectories, and,
- factors related to *forces* that cannot, at least not yet, be explained with equilibrium approaches, such as the relation to institutional structures,

path-dependent development, the way selection works out for new technologies and firms, innovation, the rise of new technologies and new regional concentrations of firms, spillover mechanisms and (co-)evolution.

Although our illustration is based on Dutch data for new firm formation and economic growth, we argue that these four heterodox aspects of economic theory and empirics are attached to economic development trajectories in a wide range of regions and countries in the same manner.

In this chapter we will start by showing how different theories deal with the choice of location in different stages of the life cycles of firms and sectors. Although there are common elements in economic geography and GE as to the analysis of the concept of externalities, the relation with various levels of geographical scale and the inclusion of development paths is not considered in GE. In economic geography and evolutionary economics, a more dynamic approach focused on technologies, firms and regions influenced by time- and region-specific contingencies and technological knowledge can be used in empirical research to explain the significance of agglomerations and external effects. In the following sections the region-specific focus, and not the 'representative firm, region or city', will be used to explain agglomeration. Different spatial levels of scale in the Dutch urban context and measurable agglomeration indicators are introduced. We then focus on an empirical application (taken from Van Oort and Atzema 2004), which concludes upon the various assumptions on heterogeneity, scale, sector and development paths in the case of the location of new ICT firms in the Netherlands in the period 1996–2000. The heterodox aspects, the determinants and spatial scales, are found to be simultaneously relevant for firm dynamics and economic growth. The final section summarises our main findings and concludes that this kind of research shows the differences, but also the relations, between geographical economics and economic geography in explaining location and competition.

## CONCEPTUAL FRAMEWORKS ON AGGLOMERATION EXTERNALITIES IN GE, ECONOMIC GEOGRAPHY AND EVOLUTIONARY ECONOMICS

Theories on agglomeration advantages have been widely used in economic geography and regional economics since Von Thünen's famous book on the spatial structure of the economy (1842), Marshall's approach of 'industrial districts' and his introduction of the concept of 'externalities' (1890) and Weber's (1909) book on industrial location. More particularly, Hoover laid the foundations of a renewed theory (Hoover 1937; 1948) when he made the distinction between 'localisation economies' and 'urbanisation economies'. For the development of more general location theories, Isard's contribution in developing 'regional science' has to be mentioned, especially because he was also using advanced mathematical modelling in his approach to spatial problems (Isard 1960). In traditional economic geography the focus was on explaining the choice of location of firms and the 'hierarchy of cities' (Christaller 1933). Its theoretical basis was strongly oriented on microeconomics, with an accent on decision-making of firms when determining their optimal location in a world with transport costs and spatial differences in wages and opportunities to be profitable, and on the theory of monopolistic markets (Lambooy 1980). Krugman (1991) revived the discussion on agglomeration advantages once again; his theory was based on a more generalised framework, an approach using advanced mathematical models. His ideas on agglomeration and the economic mechanism behind that phenomenon were more or less similar to those used in economic geography, but he used more advanced methods to enable the theory to be more general. He also paid attention to locational questions (interregional and international trade included) and the structure of the system of cities (Krugman 1998). Krugman called his approach 'new economic geography', acknowledging the scientific value for economic theory of looking at spatial patterns and the spatial element in the economy and in economic theory. Brakman *et al.* (2001) call this approach 'geographical economics' (GE), a better name than 'new economic geography', because it includes space but is primarily based on economics. We will use this term as well. It is in many respects different from 'old' economic geography; specifically, by accepting general equilibrium models and disregarding specific attributes of cities, regions and international relations. However, it has to be emphasised that there are many overlapping fields of interest and methods, and one of the goals of this chapter is to make that clear.

The observation that economic activities are not spread homogeneously in space, but clustered in concentrations of different sizes, is an important common element in economic geography and regional economics on the one hand and GE on the other. However, differences between both approaches cannot be denied. Martin and Sunley (1996) mention, for instance, the differences in the weights of the factor levels of spatial scale and the acceptance of heterogeneous actors and non-economic (e.g. psychological and socio-political) factors. Another important difference is the acceptance of general and specific spatial behaviour and structures. The GE models are based on the idea that it is possible to construct and use spatial general equilibrium models. 'Old' economic geography emphasises the existence of specific situations where it is not always useful to work with that kind of model. The reasons for this are that economic geography has a preference for the assumption of heterogeneousness, for the strong relation with empirical studies and for the applicability of the results in policy-oriented studies for specific cities, regions or international relations. In the GE approach, one of the main issues is the thesis that the forces converging in, or leading towards, an equilibrium state as a standard, influencing economic behaviour and structure, are independent of scale ('scale-free processes'): increasing returns, economies of scale, monopolistic competition and the relation of transport costs and wages to spatial behaviour (Fujita *et al.* 1999). In the words of Brakman *et al.* (2001: 323), 'By using highly stylised models, which no doubt neglect a lot of specifics about urban, regional and international phenomena, geographical economics is able to show that the same mechanisms are at work at different levels of spatial agglomeration'. In this sense both approaches are complementary. The GE tradition, however, distinguishes (simultaneously) little to no variation in types of firms (sectors), life cycles of firms (firm formation or incumbent firm growth) and scales within regional and urban space. This is what we call the 'representative firm, region or city' in GE analyses. Geographical and evolutionary economic theories explicitly depart from this.

Both the GE and economic geography conceptualisations build on location theory, especially on the concept of externalities or spillovers.[1] Externalities or spillovers occur if an innovation or growth improvement implemented by a certain enterprise increases the performance of other enterprises without the benefiting enterprise having to pay (full) compensation (Van Stel and Nieuwenhuijsen 2004: 394). Spatially bounded externalities are related to an enterprise's geographical or network contexts and are not related to internal firm performance. All discussions of spatial externalities link to a threefold classification, as made by Hoover (1948) and Isard (1960) in which the sources of agglomeration advantages are grouped together as:

- *Internal increasing* returns to scale. These may occur to a single firm due to production-cost efficiencies realised by serving large markets. There is nothing inherently spatial in this concept other than that the existence of a single large firm in space implies a large local concentration of factor employment.
- *Localisation economies.* Whether due to firm size or a large initial number of local firms, a high level of factor employment (labour demand) may allow the development of external economies within the group of local firms in a sector.
- *Urbanisation economies.* A high level of factor employment (labour demand) may also allow the development of external economies available to all local firms irrespective of sector.

Localisation economies usually take the form of Marshallian (technical) externalities whereby the productivity of labour in a given sector in a given city is assumed to increase with total employment in that sector. In short, they arise from labour market pooling, creation of specialised suppliers and the emergence of technological knowledge spillovers. The strength of local externalities is assumed to vary, so that these are stronger in some sectors and weaker in others. The associated economies of scale comprise factors that reduce the average cost of producing commodities. External scale economies apply when the industry in which the firm belongs (rather than the firm itself) is large. Under further assumptions on crowding (congestion costs that increase with population triggers dispersion), perfect product and labour mobility within and between locations and the influence of large agents, an urban system is composed of (fully) specialised cities, provided that the initial number of cities is large enough. Once cities exist, urbanisation economies also become important. The concept of agglomeration externalities in this framework is used by both regional economists and geographical economists (Meardon 2001; Brakman *et al.* 2001).

Relatively higher wages, along with congestion and higher land prices, together make up centrifugal and centripetal forces that shape agglomeration and city development in the GE models. Within the 'old' geography, 'untraded interdependencies' that function as externalities and spillovers are a particular focus of recent geographical research (Fingleton 2001; Sjöberg and Sjöholm 2002). Historically, in geography there has always been a much larger emphasis on spatial differentiation and on the interaction of the relevant urban or regional environment with locational choices made by individual firms and investors than in the GE models (Lambooy 1988). More generally, the main differences between the GE context of analysis and the geographical one is the role that the treatment of individual choice by entrepreneurs and behaviour play in them. The influential behavioural geographical literature, which started with Pred (1966) and Webber (1972), focuses on rational choice, incomplete information, limited cognitive capacities of entrepreneurs and differences in information absorption in life stages of firms. In particular, newly founded firms (starting entrepreneurs) have limited experience in their business, and locational choices (concerning first location, in-situ growth or movement) will be limited to certain information-dense regions or cities where (transaction) cost minimisation and profit optimising opportunities are thought to be optimal. Regionally, the living and working location of newborn entrepreneurs will not diverge much. Large urban agglomerations are often better 'incubator' places than other locations in this respect. Relatively large product markets, a diverse supply of input factors and common infrastructures are important factors for urban location. The stylised fact that the life phase of (especially new and young) firms in different industries is highly influential on agglomeration is largely ignored in GE models – the 'representative firm' is common in this theory (Dumais *et al.* 2002). We plead for differentiation on this, also policy-sensitive, dimension.

The locational choices of firms do not tell the whole story of agglomeration processes, however. Theories focusing on choice and behaviour can be extended to meso- and macroeconomic growth theories, as in evolutionary economics. This theory can bridge behavioural and more-structural approaches of agglomeration. Structures are more than the aggregation of individual choices, they are the results of many interactive processes (Lambooy 2002; Boschma and Frenken 2003). Evolutionary economic theory focuses more on the creation of new spatial structures and less on explaining equilibrium states. Within the same spatial and institutional context, firms and entrepreneurs come to different locational behaviour. In evolutionary economic theory, 'new' industrial locations might occur by means of chance or by 'catastrophes' (usually led by the introduction of new technologies). Neo-Schumpeterian, endogenous growth (caused particularly by innovation) can cause a process of creative destruction in the 'old' agglomerations of economic activity (such as the Ruhr region in Germany) and can develop relative new concentrations elsewhere (such as Silicon Valley). Still, after a certain period, agglomerated location occurs on the macro level again: externalities and spillovers become localised and regional clustering and co-location is profitable (again) for firms. From then on, path dependency becomes important in explaining persisting agglomeration of economic activity. Neither 'old' geographical theories nor the GE models can deal with these phenomena in one single conceptualisation, like evolutionary economics can.

When behavioural and evolutionary explanations for interregional economic development are to be taken seriously, attention should also be paid to the behavioural causes of agglomeration by *entrepreneurs*. The concept of externalities then also has to be related to research on information transmission between (actors in) firms and the cognitive and interactive character of the construction of locational preferences. Although we thus plead to start by accepting spatial and firm-level heterogeneity much more than is done in the present GE models, research results relating to agglomeration, path dependency and heterogeneous sectoral development trajectories do not contradict those of the theory of GE. The theoretical base of general equilibrium research should thus not be refuted as useless; on the contrary, we think that it can contribute to our understanding of general tendencies.

However, contrary to the detailed and everyday-life applications of geographical and evolutionary concepts, it is not always entirely clear what is meant with the approach since there are many possible definitions and uses of general equilibrium theory. One of these is the 'pure' Walrasian–Arrow–Debreu approach, which, as mathematical economists have stated (Hommes, *et al.* 2002; Walker 1997), is more a mathematical theory than an economic one. This theory can be strongly criticised on mathematical grounds as an unsatisfactory basis for further economic theory building. In our empirical analyses in this chapter it will be made clear that there are almost always many solutions possible (multiple and indeterminate optima), and certainly quite often not just one optimal solution. The new non-linear dynamic theories shed some doubt on the stability of the calculated equilibria, although it can be combined with a focus on converging developments towards equilibrium states. Walker (1997: 35, 106) is even more negative, and states that the 'Arrow–Debreu–Hahn constructions are not supported by the features of a reasonably functioning model and have no relation to the real economy'.

A second way to approach this theory is by accepting the general equilibrium approach just as a general theory of the interrelation of markets; it can become a powerful tool to show the interdependencies and the clearing mechanisms, particularly if it shows a process of Pareto-improvements. With such an approach the interregional interdependencies of markets can be fruitfully analysed.

A third way to use this theory is to apply it with a change in the basic assumptions. Peneder's more-dynamic approach (Peneder 2001) shows the shortcomings in Krugman's analysis as soon as the assumption of two sectors and two regions are changed into the acceptance of more regions and more sectors. Some conclusions made by Krugman collapse when complexity is increased. In our opinion, urban and regional economic phenomena can be explained by referring to non-linear dynamics, which Krugman does not combine satisfactorily with his general equilibrium approach, but which Peneder does. One of the improvements made by the Peneder is that external shocks (structural technological changes) are allowed, unlike in the original general equilibrium models which only allowed endogenous shocks (endogenous technological change). As Frank Hahn says, 'what is needed is more theory and more applied and empirical foundations of how agents and the economy react to mistakes' (Hahn 2002: 229). In line with this, we suggest that important explanations for urban and regional phenomena are in the build-up of micro-level and meso-level behavioural and locational elements of firms and industries. In the following sections we will focus on this empirically.

## DETERMINANTS OF AGGLOMERATED ECONOMIC DEVELOPMENT

The role accorded to agglomeration economies (spatially determined externalities) in determining growth has long been a central theme in urban and regional economics as well as in the GE approach. In theoretical terms, the topic has acquired greater importance in the years following seminal contributions by Romer (1986) and Lucas (1993), when economic growth was modelled in an endogenous framework. In these types of models, knowledge spillovers between economic agents, an important source of agglomeration economies, play a crucial role in the growth and innovation process leading to external economies of scale in production. At the core of the new economic growth theory lies the concept of technological change as a non-rival and partially excludable good (as opposed to the neoclassical view of knowledge as an entirely public good). On this basis, new technological knowledge (as applied in the ICT sector) is usually tacit, meaning that its accessibility, as well as its growth spillovers, are bounded by geographic proximity of high-technology firms or knowledge institutions, and by the nature and extent of the interactions among these actors in an innovation system (Acs 2002). A large and growing empirical literature has developed around testing this idea using data from cities (Glaeser *et al.* 1992; Henderson *et al.* 1995; Dumais *et al.* 2002; Van Oort 2004). The assumption here is that if knowledge spillovers are important to growth and firm dynamics they should be more easily identified in cities, where many people are concentrated into a relatively small and confined space and where knowledge is transmitted more easily. In our empirical application in this chapter we examine how agglomeration economies, actually indicators of knowledge spillovers, affect the creation of new establishments, and draw upon a unique data set for the Netherlands. The analysis focuses on the ICT sector, an important growth industry, where business start-up and innovation are pronounced (Beardsell and Henderson 1999). As we have argued, our empirical focus is on the identification of a measurable, explanatory framework, the influence of life stages of firms and sectors in the externalities debate and the identification of spatial (urban) structures suitable for testing agglomeration hypotheses that both GE and economic geography frameworks find important. The spatial, longitudinal and sectoral detail of the data used allows for more-sophisticated testing of these questions than within previous studies (Van Oort and Atzema 2004). The data provide counts (relative to the population) of newly established and existing businesses and their employment levels by industry for 580 municipalities (cities) over a five-year period extending from 1996 to 2000. The approach taken is quite similar to that by Rosenthal and Strange (2001), who analysed determinants of establishment births in US ZIP codes using Dun & Bradstreet MarketPlace data.

In this section we suggest a set of agglomeration indicators that can be used to test for the relation between agglomeration and new firm formation in the ICT industry (the analysis is shown in a later section). In line with the international literature, indicators are chosen for economic diversity, specialisation and local competition. These statistical indicators are broader than commonly used 'pure' innovation indicators, such as patent citations (Van Oort 2004). For example, knowledge spills over between firms via informal contacts between employees or when employees switch jobs and take their knowledge with them. Indeed, the most important type of knowledge that plays a role in growth and innovation processes is not necessarily ground-breaking innovations, but may be learning opportunities for everyday people. Empirical tests of this theory have often looked at cities to identify settings in which these external factors most effectively foster (endogenous) economic firm dynamics. Previous results, however, have been sharply divided (Van Oort and Atzema 2004). On the one hand, a group of researchers – most clearly represented by Glaeser *et al.* (1992) – find that employment growth and firm dynamics are enhanced by diversity of activity across a broad range of sectors. These externalities are often called 'urbanisation economies'. Research lead by Henderson *et al.* (1995), on the other hand, finds faster growth when more activity is concentrated in a single sector (specialisation). Externalities attached to this type of spatial dependence are often labelled 'localisation economies' (see p. 63). The lack of agreement on the relative importance of industrial concentration, diversity and their spatial composition sends an ambiguous message regarding policy choices for promoting or managing growth, firm formation and innovation in urban areas (Rosenthal and Strange 2001).

In this chapter, knowledge-based theories of endogenous development are tested at the city (municipal) level. The density of economic activity in cities facilitates face-to-face contact as well as other forms of communication. Several hypotheses have been proposed concerning conditions under which knowledge spillovers affect growth. One hypothesis, originally developed by Marshall (1890) and later formalised by Arrow (1962) and Romer (1986) (collectively referred to as 'MAR'), contends that knowledge is predominantly sector-specific and hence that local or regional specialisation will foster growth and new firm formation. The theory of Marshallian externalities states that intraregional spillover effects occur alongside agglomeration effects due to labour market pooling and input sharing –for recent elaborations see Feser (2002) and Rosenthal and Strange (2001). Furthermore, (local) market power is also thought to stimulate firm dynamics as it allows the innovating firm to internalise a substantial part of the rents. A possible conjecture in this regard is that a local competition variable (at the municipal level) is an indicator of both product market and labour market competition for non-manufacturing establishments (e.g. ICT services) that sell goods and services only locally, but for manufacturing establishments (e.g. ICT manufacturers) that are more likely to sell in national markets is an indicator of labour market competition only. This spatial embedding should ideally be incorporated in empirical analysis.

A second hypothesis, proposed by Porter (1990), also states that knowledge is predominantly sector-specific, but argues that its effect on growth and firm dynamics is enhanced by local competition rather than market power because firms need to be innovative in order to survive. A third hypothesis, proposed by Jacobs (1969) and Quigley (1998), agrees with Porter that competition fosters growth, but contends that regional diversity in economic activity will result in higher growth rates because many ideas developed by one sector can also be applied fruitfully in other sectors. A fourth hypothesis, of course, could be developed by combining aspects of the other three to emphasise the role of industrial diversity in a non-competitive environment. Table 3.1 summarises the spatial externality circumstances distinguished in these respective hypotheses.

Our analysis will empirically relate these hypotheses (controlling for sectoral and spatial heterogeneity) to spatial patterns of new ICT firm formation in the Netherlands. Note that while case study research is able to obtain many specific organisational details but is poor on the question of applicability of high-technology spatial regularities to situations elsewhere, the measurable set of indicators in our analysis allows for interregional comparison of locations at the loss of organisational detail.

## DEFINITIONS OF URBAN STRUCTURE IN THE NETHERLANDS

Spatial proximity (clustering) is considered by many observers to be important for 'explaining' localised growth and new firm formation in high-technology sectors, the ICT industry in particular. The marginal cost of transmitting tacit knowledge rises with distance. As tacit knowledge and human interaction become more valuable in the innovation process, geographical proximity becomes crucial to the innovation and growth processes. The exchange of tacit knowledge may require a high degree of mutual trust and understanding. It is especially in the

*Table 3.1* Stylised and hypothesised relations of agglomeration circumstances with innovation and economic growth

| | *MAR* | *Porter* | *Jacobs* | *Fourth hypothesis* |
|---|---|---|---|---|
| Concentration | + | + | – | – |
| Diversity | – | – | + | + |
| Competition | – | + | + | – |

contiguous proximity way of thinking about space (cities) that the two noted contradicting outcomes concerning agglomeration economies (urbanisation versus localisation) discussed above come to the fore.

The geographic literature also provides clues for non-contiguous (regime) types of spatial dependence. Quality of life aspects, regional labour markets, specialised networks and city size appear as significant locational considerations, both to professional workers and to growing ICT firms (Van Oort and Atzema 2004). The spatial structures of proximity (contiguous nearness at the municipal level) and heterogeneity (urban hierarchical and regional, not necessarily contiguous, spatial dependence) have been captured in our analyses in spatial lag (or spatial error) estimates and spatial regimes, respectively. The spatial coefficient in spatial lag estimation shows whether the dependent variable in a model (in our case localised new firm formation) is dependent on neighbouring values of this dependent variable. If so, conclusions can be reached on the significance and magnitude of this spatial dependence (Anselin 1988). Spatial heterogeneity, conversely, is modelled by spatial regimes, involving change-of-slope regression estimation over various types of locations that theoretically 'perform' differently. Four sets of spatial regimes are distinguished, each indicating aspects of urban structures at different spatial scales. At the meso level we distinguish a labour market induced connectedness regime from a non-connectedness regime (Figure 3.1). This spatial regime concerns commuting-based labour market relations. In Figure 3.1, core and suburban municipalities together comprise the connected regime, as opposed to the other types of locations, which are characterised as non-connected. The four types of locations have been distinguished, initially based on municipal data for 1990–99. The classification is based on the dependency of a municipality's population upon employment and services proximity and accessibility. Urban core areas have an important employment function. More than 15,000 persons commute into these municipalities (while living somewhere else) on a daily basis. Municipalities where more than 20 per cent of residents commute to central core locations are labelled suburban. The literature finds in general that urban areas in the connected regime show higher economic growth and innovation rates than areas in the non-connected regime. As becomes clear from Figure 3.1, locations in the connected regime are not necessarily adjacent to each other.

At the macro level, three national zoning regimes have been distinguished: the Randstad core region, the so-called 'intermediate' zone and the national periphery (Figure 3.2). Distinguishing between macroeconomic zones in the Netherlands is based on a gravity model of total employment derived from 1997 data. The Randstad region in the Netherlands historically comprises the economic core provinces of Noord-Holland, Zuid-Holland and Utrecht, the intermediate zone mainly comprises the growth regions of Gelderland and Noord-Brabant, while the national periphery is built up by the northern and southern regions of the country. This zoning distinction is hypothesised as important in many studies on endogenous growth (e.g. Van Oort 2004) in the Netherlands, in the sense that the Randstad region traditionally is thought to have better economic potential for development.

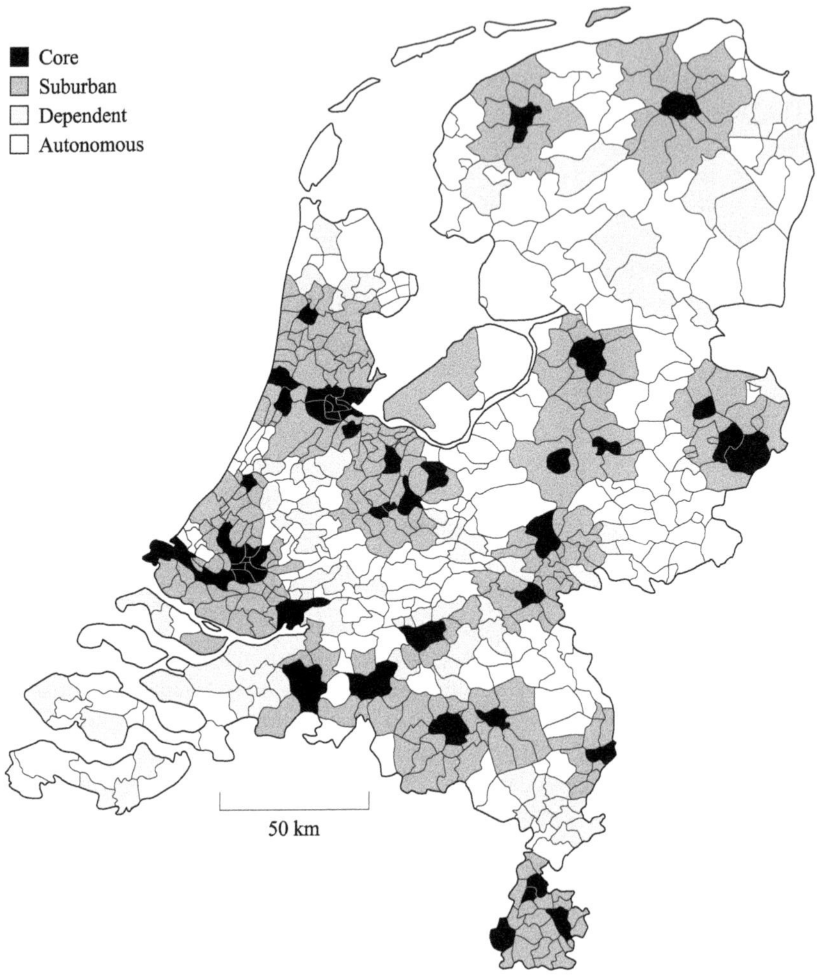


*Figure 3.1* Connectedness spatial regime: labour market.

The third set of spatial regimes is constructed using the degree of urbanisation of municipalities (Figure 3.3). A population threshold of 45,000 inhabitants, standard for distinguishing medium-sized cities in the Netherlands, is used for the distinction in urban and non-urban regimes respectively. The municipalities identified in Figure 3.3 as large and medium-sized together make up the urban regime, the other municipalities make up the non-urban regime.

These forms of spatial heterogeneity constitute three spatial levels of urban constellation: the urban level (urban size) itself, the meso-level functional (commuting) region and the national core–periphery (Randstad, intermediate zone, national periphery) distinction.

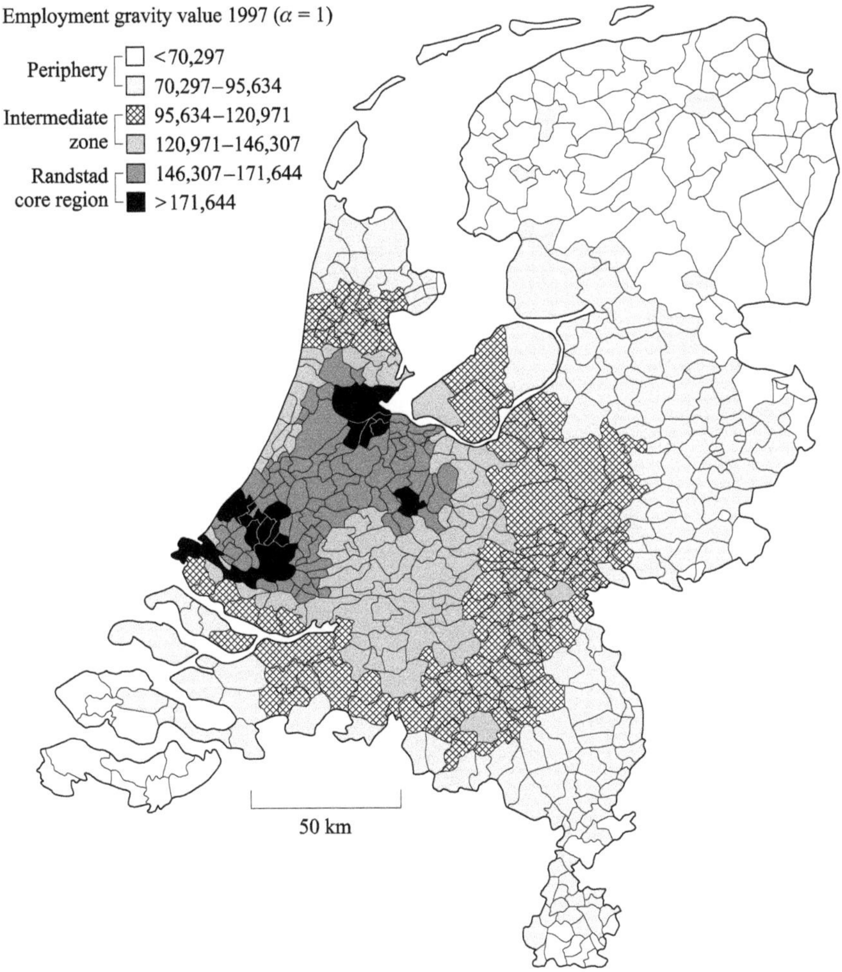


*Figure 3.2* National zoning spatial regimes.

## NEW FIRM FORMATION IN THE DUTCH ICT SECTOR

In this section, we present the spatial pattern of new firm formation rates in 580 municipalities in the Netherlands and econometrical analyses of these patterns related to the agglomeration indicators (page 63) and measures of spatial clustering and spatial heterogeneity (page 69).

The technique most conveniently used for spatial statistical descriptions of data is exploratory spatial data analysis (ESDA). ESDA is aimed at describing and visualising spatial distributions, identifying atypical localisations or spatial outliers, detecting patterns of spatial association, clusters or hot spots,

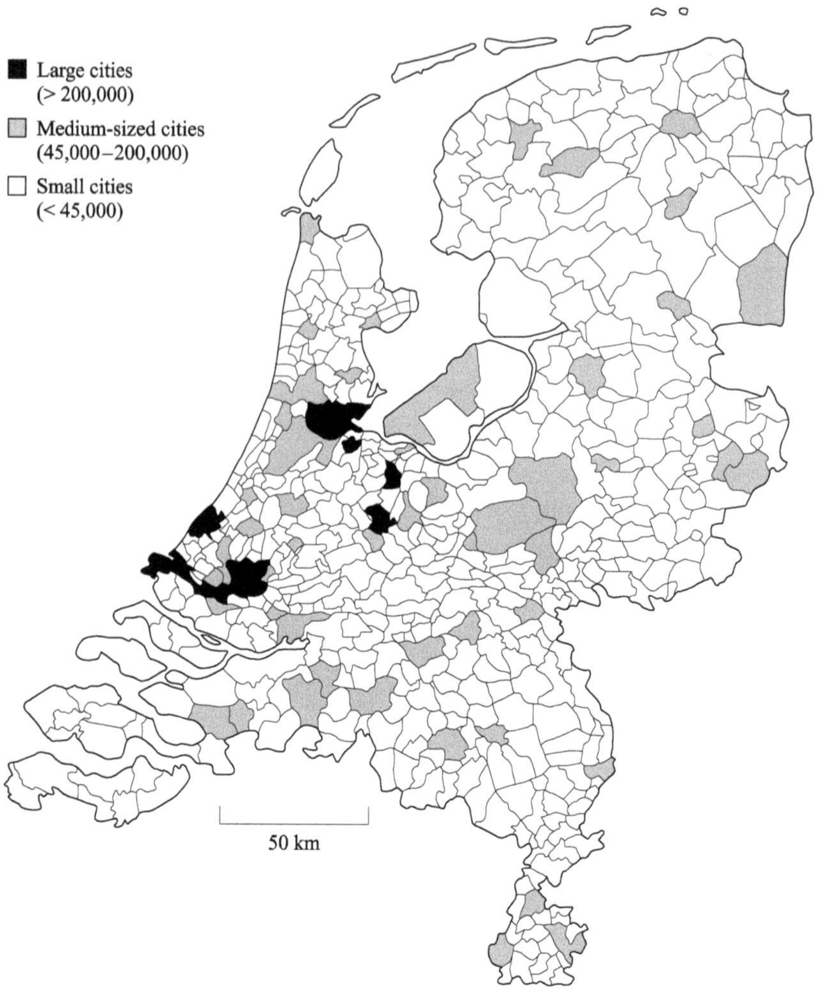


*Figure 3.3* Urban size spatial regimes.

and suggesting spatial regimes or other forms of spatial heterogeneity (Anselin 1988).

Spatial autocorrelation can be defined as the coincidence of value similarity with locational similarity. Positive spatial autocorrelation occurs when high or low values of a random variable tend to cluster (agglomerate) in space; negative spatial autocorrelation occurs when geographical areas tend to be surrounded by neighbours with very dissimilar values. Our measurement of spatial autocorrelation is based on Moran's *I* statistic, which is the most widely known measure of spatial clustering (for technical details, see Van Oort 2004). A positive and significant

$z$-value for Moran's $I$ (as can be judged from accompanying low probability values) indicates positive spatial autocorrelation. Similar values of the variable, either high or low, indicate more spatial clustering than might result from pure chance. In contrast, a negative and significant $z$-value for Moran's $I$ indicates negative spatial autocorrelation, the opposite of spatial clustering.[2]

Analysis of *local* spatial autocorrelation can be carried out using the tool of the Moran scatter plot, which can be used to visualise local spatial instability. Four different quadrants of the scatter plot, which correspond to four types of local spatial association between a location and its neighbours, can be distinguished:

- HH comprises locations with a high value surrounded by locations with high values.
- LH indicates locations with a low value surrounded by locations with high values.
- LL denotes locations with a low value surrounded by locations with low values.
- HL locations with a high value surrounded by locations with low values.

HH and LL refer to positive spatial autocorrelation, indicating spatial clustering of similar values, whereas LH and HL represent negative spatial autocorrelation, indicating spatial clustering of dissimilar values. The locations in each quadrant of the new firm formation rates are mapped in Figure 3.4. It is clear from Figure 3.4 that new ICT firms have little presence in the south wing of the Randstad region (The Hague and Rotterdam). Instead, the north wing of the Randstad region and the municipalities more remote from the Randstad core region (along the A-2 highway axis, Amsterdam–Eindhoven) show high concentration values.

In Table 3.2, econometric models on the new firm formation rates are summarised. These analyses are taken and adjusted from Van Oort and Atzema (2004). The models in Table 3.2 are numbered (1) to (5) (technical explanation on the models is provided in the footnote to the table). The degrees of localised concentration, diversity and competition are introduced according to the definitions given in Van Oort (2004). Besides concentration indices (location quotients) of ICT firms, concentration indices for industrial, distribution, business service and consumer service activities are introduced in the model (see Van Oort 2004 for an exact definition of these activities). Sectoral diversity is measured as a Gini coefficient over big industries per municipality. Gini measures *lack* of diversity. Likewise, localised competition, in line with the Glaeser *et al.* (1992) approach, is measured by relative firm size both for ICT firms and for all firms in the localised economy in an aggregated sense.

The ordinary least squares (OLS) model for the percentage of new firm formation (model (1)) shows the significance of both concentration indicators (of the 'own' ICT sector, as well as in general for business services in a positive sense, and for consumer services in a negative sense) and the diversity indicator. The third agglomeration indicator, measuring localised (labour market or service market) competition circumstances, shows a positive relationship with new firm

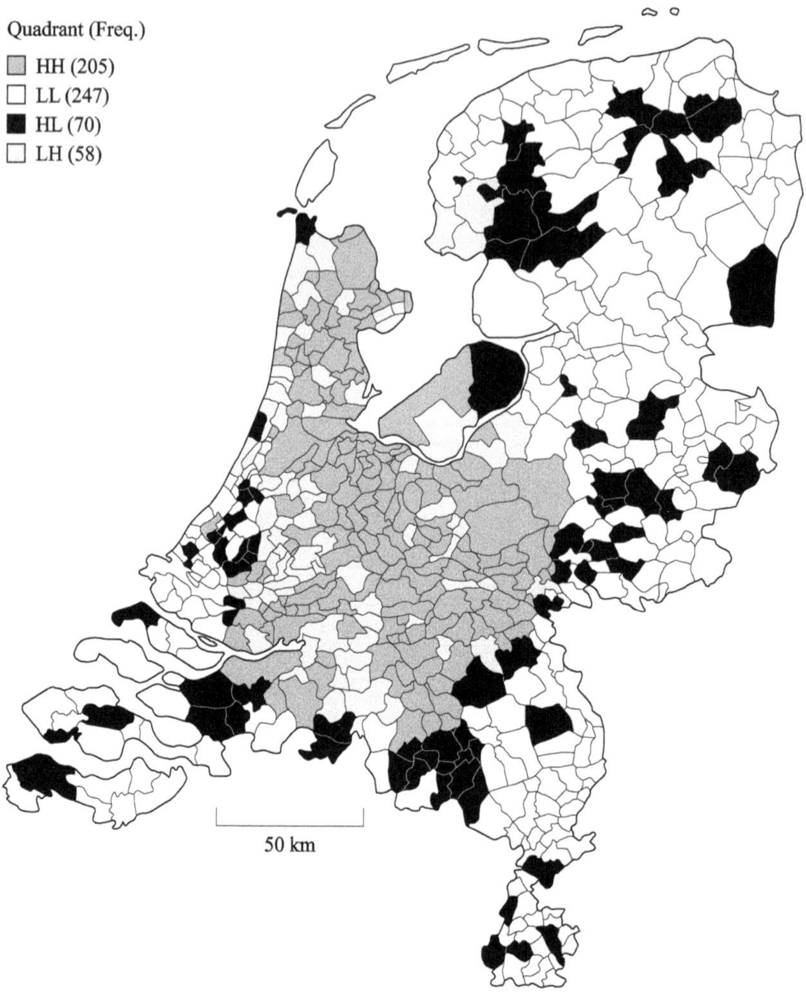


*Figure 3.4* Moran scatter plot map (log) of new firm formation rates in ICT industries in the Netherlands (average 1996–2000).

formation rates when measured for the 'own' ICT sector. But this indicator shows a strong negative relationship when measured in general terms, taking all firms within a municipality into account and independent of sectoral composition. Interestingly, these results do not provide unambiguous support for any of the three endogenous development theories discussed above. Results for (own, ICT) sectoral specialisation support the MAR and Porter hypotheses, but results for industrial diversity do not.

Results for industrial diversity support the Jacobs hypothesis. Results for (own, ICT) levels of localised competition support the Porter and Jacobs hypotheses of growth, but not the MAR hypothesis. The general indicators of concentration stress the importance of business service specialisation as an important correlate to new firm formation, and the negative influence of consumer service specialisation in general. The general competition indicator is clearly negatively related to firm formation rates, concluding on the MAR hypothesis of economic dynamics – a very confusing picture indeed.

However, the results presented are still very much of interest from the broader perspective of those concerned with the location tendencies of start-up establishments in the ICT sector. These firms tend to cluster in municipalities that already are employment centres, and rich in industrial diversity. The test statistics for model (1) in Table 3.2 reveal the presence of spatial autocorrelation dependency of the model. Model (2), therefore, is estimated using a spatial lag specification. Spatial lag models make use of maximum likelihood estimation techniques, in which the explained variance is no longer an adequate measure for model fitting. The spatial coefficient indeed turns out to be highly significant. Introducing spatial dependency in the model alters the coefficients slightly when compared to the OLS base model. Relative specialisation of distribution activities in particular hampers firm dynamics, while industrial diversity is no longer unambiguously connected to new firm formation rates. The likelihood-based measure (*ML* in the summary statistics of the tables) can be used to compare the model fit with that of the basic OLS model. It turns out that for the new firm formation model, the fit considerably improves when the spatial lag is added to the model, as indicated by an increase in the log-likelihood. The interpretation of the model outcomes change when the spatial lag specification is applied: the significance of specialisation and competition indicators, together with the insignificance of the diversity indicator, favours the MAR hypothesis.

Models (3) and (4) give spatial lag estimations, but with the allowance of structural change of coefficient estimates between spatial regimes. Model (3) shows that the concentration indicators work out more favourably in connection with new firm formation in urban municipalities, as opposed to non-urban ones. The significance of industrial diversity makes the result, again, theoretically more ambiguous. The spatial Chow-Wald test confirms the significance of the spatial regime. The model fit again improves considerably when compared with the OLS and spatial lag model without the urbanisation regimes. The relations found thus work out most profoundly in urban environments. This conclusion confirms the urban setting of the endogenous development theories, as outlined above. But other definitions of urbanisation also appear to be significant for ICT business development. Model (4) shows that the Randstad region most notably 'exhibits' the significant set of agglomeration economies, as opposed to the national periphery and (to a lesser extent) the intermediate zone. The model fit is slightly less than in the urban regimes model, but still considerably better than the OLS and spatial lag (sec) model. Model (5) shows the significance of the connected spatial regime, as opposed to the unconnected regime. The analyses show that urbanisation matters for new ICT firm formation on all different scales of urban analyses in the Netherlands, defined both by contiguous proximity (as envisaged by the spatial

*Table 3.2* OLS and combined spatial-lag and spatial-regime models for new firm formation in ICT activities in the Netherlands

| *Explanatory variables* | *(1) OLS* | *(2) Spatial lag* | *(3) Spatial lag Urban regimes* | | *(4) Spatial lag Macro zoning regimes* | | | *(5) Spatial lag Connectedness regimes* | |
|---|---|---|---|---|---|---|---|---|---|
| | | | *Urban* | *Non-urban* | *Randstad* | *Intermediate zone* | *Periphery* | *Connected* | *Non-connected* |
| Constant | 0.536 | −0.375 | −0.120 | −0.092 | −0.377 | 0.231 | −0.195 | −0.357 | 0.198 |
| | (0.933) | (−0.726) | (−0.208) | (−1.455) | (−0.484) | (0.092) | (−0.700) | (−0.419) | (0.254) |
| Concentration ICT | 0.789 | 0.687 | 0.654 | 0.056 | 0.616 | −0.062 | 0.056 | 0.683 | 0.626 |
| firms | **(7.867)** | **(7.614)** | **(7.361)** | (0.601) | **(6.384)*** | (−0.086)* | (0.707)* | **(3.629)** | **(5.968)** |
| Concentration | −0.029 | −0.022 | −0.008 | −0.092 | −0.041 | 0.016 | −0.062 | −0.004 | −0.056 |
| industry | (−1.239) | (−1.008) | (−0.347) | (−1.455) | (−1.199) | (0.403) | (−1.158) | (−0.014) | (−1.765) |
| Concentration | −0.119 | −0.199 | −0.142 | −0.660 | −0.189 | −0.030 | −0.133 | −0.280 | −0.119 |
| distribution | (−1.144) | **(−2.665)** | (−1.771) | **(−3.544)** | (−1.585) | (−0.204) | (−0.952) | **(−2.848)** | **(−1.068)** |
| Concentration | 0.292 | 0.188 | 0.239 | −0.314 | 0.257 | 0.392 | 0.062 | 0.237 | −0.038 |
| business services | **(4.394)** | **(3.153)** | **(3.854)*** | (−1.640)* | **(2.796)*** | **(3.382)*** | (0.485)* | **(2.821)*** | **(−0.433)*** |
| Concentration | −0.234 | −0.238 | −0.059 | −1.106 | −0.072 | 0.182 | −0.418 | −0.383 | −0.127 |
| consumer services | **(−2.244)** | **(−2.539)** | (−0.590)* | **(−4.887)*** | (−0.505)* | (0.089)* | **(−2.575)*** | **(−3.086)** | **(−0.864)** |
| Lack of diversity | −1.114 | −0.559 | −0.820 | −0.575 | −1.133 | −1.503 | −0.684 | −1.005 | −0.132 |
| | **(−2.934)** | (−1.639) | **(−2.167)** | (−0.676) | **(−2.011)** | **(−1.940)** | (−1.116) | **(−2.253)*** | **(−0.241)*** |
| Size ICT firms | 1.029 | 0.815 | 0.793 | 0.091 | 0.731 | 0.744 | 1.106 | 0.909 | 0.757 |
| (competition) | **(19.820)** | **(17.429)** | **(15.985)** | **(7.133)** | **(10.192)** | **(7.268)** | **(11.967)** | **(13.637)** | **(11.893)** |
| Size all firms | −0.465 | −0.352 | 0.011 | −0.357 | −0.404 | −0.280 | −0.406 | −0.215 | −0.509 |
| (competition) | **(−6.353)** | **(−5.338)** | (0.052)* | **(−5.108)*** | **(−3.907)** | **(−1.943)** | **(−3.358)** | **(−2.487)** | **(−5.035)** |
| Employment 1996 | 0.148 | 0.073 | 0.084 | −0.052 | 0.084 | 0.068 | −0.055 | 0.209 | 0.035 |
| ICT firms | (1.534) | (0.847) | (1.002) | (−0.590) | (0.917) | (0.096) | (−0.694) | (1.081) | (−0.368) |
| Employment 1996 | −0.073 | 0.007 | −0.038 | 0.056 | −0.016 | −0.068 | 0.556 | −0.097 | −0.026 |
| all firms | (−0.678) | (0.008) | (−0.383) | (0.595) | (−0.130) | (−0.094) | (0.595) | (−0.488) | (−0.214) |
| Spatial | – | 0.969 | 0.973 | | | 0.974 | | | 0.964 |
| coefficient, $\rho$ | | **(26.843)** | **(22.948)** | | | **(23.241)** | | | **(20.125)** |

| | | | | | |
|---|---|---|---|---|---|
| *Summary statistics* | | | | | |
| $n$ | 580 | 580 | 580 | 580 | 580 |
| $R^2/ML$ | *0.657/ −474.63* | *−421.386* | *−400.74* | *−404.96* | *−405.126* |
| LM (*BP*) | 4.095 (0.393) | 6.840 (0.077) | 1.527 (0.216) | 2.981 (0.170) | 2.092 (0.148) |
| LM ($\rho$) | 324.78 (0.000) | – | – | – | |
| LM ($\lambda$) | 56.61 (0.000) | – | – | – | |
| LR ($\rho$) | – | 106.49 (0.000) | 114.54 (0.000) | 106.86 (0.000) | 97.302 (0.000) |
| Chow-Wald | – | – | 42.822 (0.000) | 33.810 (0.051) | 50.057 (0.000) |

Source: Van Oort and Atzema (2004), tables 6 and 7, pp. 284, 285.

Notes
OLS = ordinary least squares, $n$ = 580, period 1996–2000, $t$-values in parentheses. Values of log-likelihood are not comparable over populations of all and old establishments. Following Anselin (1988), LM ($\rho$) and LM ($\lambda$) are statistics for the presence of a spatial lag in the dependent variable and in the residual, respectively, with a critical value of 3.84 at the 5 per cent level of significance (marked +). LR ($\rho$) tests for the significance of the spatial dependence coefficient. LM (*BP*) tests for homoscedasticity of regression errors using the Breusch-Pagan Lagrange multiplier test for normal-distributed errors. The spatial weight matrix used is w_1 (row standardised), probability levels ($p$ values) are presented in the tables. Significant $p$ levels are printed in bold. The spatial Chow-Wald test is distributed as an $F$ variate and tests for structural instability of the regression coefficients over regimes (Anselin 1988). Significant results (95 per cent confidence interval) of the spatial Chow-Wald in general and on individual coefficients (rejection of $H_0$ of joint equality of coefficients over regimes) are marked (*). All variables are log transformed and corrected for extreme values (found in ESDA analyses discussed).

lag significance) and by the spatial heterogeneous regimes. This extends considerably the current debate on urbanisation and localisation externalities, which focuses mainly on proximity-based spillovers and knowledge transfer.

## CONCLUSIONS

In this chapter, we have provided insights into the simultaneous usefulness of two scientific approaches that focus on the relation between geography and economics: 'old' economic geography and 'new' geographical economics (GE). We suggested four heterodox aspects attached to urban and regional economic growth that are currently relatively unwarranted for in the GE-models. These are:

- the importance of *life stages* of firms, technologies and sectors, or development paths of firms, sectors, cities and systems of cities,
- specific *spatial structures* not showing (clear) relations with the, in GE assumed, forces of economic agglomeration,
- specific urban and regional factors *explaining* why agglomeration forces influence sectors and firms differently, depending on the period of economic development and the various technological trajectories, and
- factors related to *forces* that cannot, or not yet, be explained with equilibrium approaches, e.g. the relation with institutional structures, path-dependent development, the way selection works out for new technologies and firms, innovation, the rise of new technologies and new regional concentrations of firms, spill-over mechanisms and (co-)evolution.

Although our illustration is based on Dutch data of new firm formation and economic growth, we argue that these four heterodox aspects of economic theory and empirics apply to economic development trajectories in a wide range of regions and countries in the same manner. The empirical analyses made clear that there are almost always many solutions possible (multiple and indeterminate optima), and certainly quite often more than one optimal solution. New non-linear dynamic theories shed some doubt on the stability of the calculated equilibria, although they can be combined with converging developments towards equilibrium states. In the evolutionary economic and geographical research traditions, much more emphasis exists on the interaction of the relevant urban or regional environment with the locational choices made by individual firms and investors. In these traditions, a strong preference exists to allow for differentiation of firms and types of behaviour and locations. The assumptions of the 'representative firm' and the 'representative space', as have been accepted in GE, are not considered as being useful for reaching relevant conclusions about all empirically observable spatial dynamics and structures on all spatial scales imaginable.

Although we start by accepting spatial and firm-level heterogeneity, the results are not contradicting to the theory of GE. However, we met with certain phenomena that could not be satisfactorily explained with that approach. In particular, there is a need for the inclusion of the existence of multiple equilibria for regions and sectors, evolutionary patterns and spatially heterogeneous attributes. However, many phenomena, such as external effects, need a more empirical analysis to understand the mechanisms of agglomeration forces. We do not to say that the GE-approach is not useful for explaining empirical observations, but for the application in policy-oriented research it might be too abstract. In particular, we see room for both kinds of approaches in explaining and using the economic effects of agglomeration advantages.

## NOTES

1 In general, firm-internal increasing returns to scale are fostered by firm-external (agglomerated) scale economies, which are called 'externalities'. Pecuniary externalities are those that somehow are being paid for by market transactions; spillovers are unpaid externalities (Van Oort 2004: Ch. 2). In this chapter we do not distinguish the concepts so explicitly.

2 The concept of negative spatial autocorrelation is harder to grasp; it reflects a lack of clustering, more so than would be the case in a random pattern. Perfect negative spatial autocorrelation is represented by a checkerboard pattern.

## REFERENCES

Acs, Z.J. (2002) *Innovation and the Growth of Cities*, Cheltenham: Edward Elgar.

Anselin, L. (1988) *Spatial Econometrics: Methods and models*, Dordrecht: Kluwer.

Arrow, K.J. (1962) 'The economic implications of learning by doing', *Review of Economic Studies*, 29: 155–73.

Beardsell, M. and Henderson, V. (1999) 'Spatial evolution of the computer industry in the USA', *European Economic Review*, 43: 431–56.

Boschma, R.A. and Frenken, K. (2003) 'Evolutionary economics and industry location', *Review for Regional Research*, 23: 183–200.

Brakman, S., Garretsen, H. and Marrewijk, C. van (2001) *An Introduction to Geographical Economics*, Cambridge: Cambridge University Press.

Christaller, W. (1933) *Central Places in Southern Germany*, Englewood Cliffs, NJ: Prentice Hall.

Dumais, G., Ellison, G. and Glaeser, E.L. (2002) 'Geographic concentration as a dynamic process', *The Review of Economics and Statistics*, 84: 193–204.

Feser, E.J. (2002) 'Tracing the sources of local external economies', *Urban Studies*, 39: 2485–506.

Fingleton, B. (2001) 'Theoretical economic geography and spatial econometrics: dynamic perspectives', *Journal of Economic Geography*, 1: 201–25.

Fujita, M., Krugman, P. and Venables, A. (1999) *The Spatial Economy: Cities, regions and international trade*, Cambridge, MA: MIT Press.

Glaeser, E.L., Kallal, H.D., Scheinkman, J.A. and Schleifer, A. (1992) 'Growth in cities', *Journal of Political Economy*, 100: 1126–52.

Hahn, F. (2002) 'On the Possibility of Economic Dynamics', in C.H. Hommes, R. Ramer and C.A. Withagen (eds) *Equilibrium, Markets and Dynamics: Essays in honour of Claus Weddepohl*, Berlin: Springer.

Henderson, V., Kuncoro, A. and Turner, M. (1995) 'Industrial development in cities', *Journal of Political Economy*, 103: 1067–85.

Hommes, C.H., Ramer, R. and Withagen, C.A. (2002) *Equilibrium, Markets and Dynamics; Essays in honour of Claus Weddepohl*, Berlin: Springer.

Hoover, E.M. (1937) *Location Theory and the Shoe and Leather Industries*, Cambridge, MA: Harvard University Press.
Hoover, E.M. (1948) *The Location of Economic Activity*, New York: McGraw-Hill.
Isard, W. (1960) *Methods of Regional Science*, Cambridge, MA: MIT Press.
Jacobs, J. (1969) *The Economy of Cities*, New York: Vintage.
Krugman, P. (1991) *Geography and Trade*, Cambridge, MA: MIT Press.
Krugman, P. (1998) 'What's new about the new economic geography?', *Oxford Review of Economic Policy*, 14: 7–17.
Lambooy, J.G. (1980) *Economie en Ruimte*, Assen: Van Gorcum.
Lambooy, J.G. (1988) *Ruimtelijk-economische Dynamiek*, Bussum: Coutinho.
Lambooy, J.G. (2002) 'Knowledge and urban economic development: an evolutionary perspective', *Urban Studies*, 39: 1019–35.
Lucas, R.E. (1993) 'Making a miracle', *Econometrica*, 61: 251–72.
Marshall, A. (1890) *Principles of Economics*, New York: Prometheus Books.
Martin, R. and Sunley, P. (1996) 'Paul Krugman's geographical economics and its implications for regional development theory: a critical assessment', *Economic Geography*, 72: 259–92.
Meardon, S.J. (2001) 'Modeling agglomeration and dispersion in city and country: Gunner Myrdal, Francois Perroux, and the New Economic Geography', *American Journal of Economics and Sociology*, 60: 25–57.
Peneder, M. (2001) *Entrepreneurial Competition and Industrial Location: Investigating the structural patterns and intangible sources of competitive performance*, Cheltenham: Edward Elgar.
Porter, M. (1990) *The Competitive Advantage of Nations*, New York: Free Press.
Pred, A.R. (1966) *The Spatial Dynamics of US Urban-industrial Growth 1800–1914: Interspective and theoretical essays*, Cambridge, MA: MIT Press.
Quigley, J.M. (1998) 'Urban diversity and economic growth', *Journal of Economic Perspectives*, 12: 127–38.
Romer, P.M. (1986) 'Increasing returns and long-run growth', *Journal of Political Economy*, 94: 1002–37.
Rosenthal, S.S. and Strange, W.C. (2001) 'The determinants of agglomeration', *Journal of Urban Economics*, 50: 191–229.
Sjöberg, O. and Sjöholm, F. (2002) 'Common ground? Prospects for integrating the economic geography of geographers and economists', *Environment and Planning A*, 34: 467–86.
Van Oort, F.G. (2004) *Urban Growth and Innovation: Analysis of spatially bounded externalities in the Netherlands*, Aldershot: Ashgate.
Van Oort, F.G. and Atzema, O. (2004) 'On the conceptualization of agglomeration economies: the case of new firm formation in the Dutch ICT-sector', *Annals of Regional Science*, 38: 263–90.
Van Stel, A.J. and Nieuwenhuijsen, H.R. van (2004) 'Knowledge spillovers and economic growth: an analysis using data of Dutch regions in the period 1987–1995', *Regional Studies*, 38: 393–407.
Von Thünen, J.H. (1842) 'Der Isolierte Staat', in P. Hall (ed.) (1966) *Von Thünen's Isolated State*, London: Pergamon.
Walker, D.A. (1997) *Advances in General Equilibrium Theory; The Hennipman Lectures*, Cheltenham: Edward Elgar.
Webber, M.J. (1972) *Impact of Uncertainty on Location*, Cambridge, MA: MIT Press.
Weber, A. (1909) *Theory of the Location of Industries*, Chicago, IL: Chicago University Press.

# 4 Policy competition in theory and practice

*Ruud A. de Mooij, Joeri Gorter and Richard Nahuis*

## INTRODUCTION

There are widely diverging views on policy competition. Politicians of left-wing parties usually believe that policy competition erodes useful public tasks, thereby reducing welfare. Capital flight, for instance, induces a 'race the bottom' in taxes on capital, social provisions and environmental legislation, while public expenditures are increasingly geared towards infrastructure. This erodes expenditures on healthcare or social protection. In this spirit, the Dutch social democrats state on their website that 'it is important in Europe to prevent sharp tax competition (which leads to poor governments)'.[1] The socialist party maintains that 'the harbour which imposes the toughest regulations in terms of safety, environmental protection and labour conditions will lose competitiveness and eventually disappear'.[2]

Right-wing parties have a very different perspective. They argue that policy competition is attractive because it disciplines inefficient governments that would otherwise spend too much. The threat of losing competitiveness or capital forces bureaucrats to perform more efficiently. The Dutch employers' organisation, for instance, says that 'many European countries reduce their corporate tax rates to attract firms. This is not a wrong thing. It reflects the prosperous implications of healthy policy competition in Europe' (Schraven 2000).

This chapter explores these opposing views on policy competition from an economic perspective. In particular, it focuses on three questions:

- What are the fundamentals behind the different views on policy competition?
- What does the empirical evidence suggest about the claims from the alternative views?
- How do the insights from the new economic geography literature modify these results?

## POLICY COMPETITION IN THEORY

### Theory of policy competition

An inflow of foreign direct investment is usually thought to be attractive for the welfare of citizens. Indeed, employees may benefit from extra capital as labour productivity tends to rise, and so do gross wages. This is especially so if foreign capital brings along spillovers in the form of new technologies and knowledge. Furthermore, the inflow of foreign capital can reduce unemployment in the short term and broaden the corporate tax base. This would improve the fiscal position of governments. For these reasons, governments adopt explicit policies to attract foreign companies. In the Netherlands, for instance, the Commissioner for Foreign Direct Investment aims to promote the country to multinational companies. Similarly, the fiscal authority regularly negotiates with new foreign investors about their tax treatment after settling in the Netherlands. More generally, governments try to design their policy frameworks so as to create an attractive place for foreign investors.

If governments thus compete with each other to attract the same capital, they engage in a process of policy competition. This not only applies to national governments, but can also occur among local governments. Moreover, policy competition not only refers to attracting physical capital, but also human capital. Indeed, attracting highly talented people is accompanied by similar benefits such as attracting new firms.

The key issue is whether policy competition is good for social welfare. This section elaborates on this question. Our starting point is the traditional literature on policy competition in which trade costs or agglomeration economies do not play a role (see the section on policy competition and location). The traditional literature primarily deals with corporate taxation. It yields two opposing views:

- Competition between governments is an efficient mechanism.
- Policy competition yields a suboptimal outcome.

### Policy competition as an efficient mechanism

The starting points of the first view are the two welfare theorems from economics. These teach us that markets lead to an efficient outcome as long as some basic conditions are met, such as an appropriate definition of property rights and no externalities. This suggests that, in principle, society is best off when transactions are traded in private markets. One way of seeing this is that the market mechanism is extremely powerful in revealing information about preferences. Indeed, the confrontation between demand and supply yields prices that adequately reflect relative scarcities. At these price signals, consumers set their marginal rates of substitution between different goods equal to the marginal rate of transformation that producers face in production. This ensures allocative efficiency. Whereas the market mechanism thus produces the necessary information about relative scarcities, it would be virtually impossible for a government to do so. Indeed, a government would face substantial transaction costs associated with information gathering and difficulty in determining the efficient allocation. Although market failures may justify some form of government intervention, the burden of proof is usually put at the government. Hence, the market is believed to be efficient, and only when there are clear signs of market failures can there be a case for government intervention.

For similar reasons, policy competition may be preferred in principle over centralisation of policies. Tiebout (1956) developed a theorem which is similar to the welfare theorems. It states that, under particular conditions, competition between governments will lead to an efficient policy mix. In the Tiebout world, this happens because mobile households will move to the jurisdiction where they find a combination of taxes and public expenditure that best fits with their own needs and preferences. By 'voting by their feet', households reveal information about their preferences. This is exactly the information a central government does not have in developing an optimal policy. Competing governments are thus able to take account of the true preferences of individual households regarding public goods. Moreover, they face appropriate incentives to supply these public goods efficiently (i.e. at low tax rates) and not to waste any tax money. Indeed, in case of inefficient combinations of taxes and public goods, households may decide to move to other locations so that land and housing prices will fall and the welfare level of the remaining households declines. Eventually, the selection mechanism would cause a migration of households, and the inefficient jurisdiction would be left without people.

Critics of Tiebout argue that the main assumption of the model, namely labour mobility, does not hold true in practice. Therefore, voting by feet will not play a major role in the European Union (EU). However, the proponents of policy competition have further arguments to strengthen their case. They argue that even without mobility of households, decentralised governments are in a better position to gather the right information about local preferences as compared with a centralised government. Policy can thus take better account of local preferences. Moreover, the public choice literature maintains that central policies yield more government failures than do decentralised policies (Buchanan and Tullock 1962; Brennan and Buchanan 1980). This is because of less accountability in the case of centralisation, which means that governments can grow to become leviathans. Lobby groups affect the behaviour of bureaucrats, who no longer take into account the interests of the average tax payer but rather those of the most influential pressure groups.[3] Policy competition between decentralised governments makes it more difficult to pursue such policies and thus adds to the disciplining impact of elections. The tendency to become a leviathan is thus reduced and governments become smaller, more reliable and more efficient.[4]

## Failures of policy competition

The second view on whether policy competition is good for social welfare considers that it is a threat. The failure of policy competition can be formally illustrated with a model developed by Zodrow and Mieszkowski (1986). This model contains two countries that supply public goods, financed by a corporate income tax. Capital is mobile internationally, while labour is immobile. If public goods benefit households (in terms of utility) but not firms (in terms of productivity), then Zodrow and Mieskowski's model shows that policy competition leads to too low a level of supply of public goods. The reason is that public goods are costly for governments because financing them via the corporate tax yields capital flight, thereby reducing the income of immobile residents. Individual governments therefore find it attractive to supply fewer public goods and reduce the corporate tax to maximise the welfare of their residents. If both governments act in this way, then we end up with too low tax and an underprovision of public goods in both countries. There is a so-called 'fiscal externality' because individual governments do not take account of the impact of their lower tax on the tax base of their neighbouring country. With coordinated action, governments would be able to raise their tax and supply more public goods without changing the allocation of capital across the two countries. Analogous to market failures, one may speak about a coordination failure of policy competition as an allocative mechanism to determine policies. Indeed, without coordination, governments find themselves in a prisoner's dilemma.

Critics of this second view emphasise that the externality does not materialise in the case of productive public expenditures. These can be broadly interpreted, including all expenditures that benefit productivity, such as justice (to ensure property rights), education, healthcare and infrastructure. With these forms of public expenditures, the corporate tax more or less acts as a benefit tax because mobile capital benefits from the public investments paid out of the tax on this capital income. As is know from economic theory, the application of the benefit principle is not distortionary, even in the case of policy competition (Oates and Schwab 1988). If government would be able to tax immobile households to finance these productive expenditures, governments could even spend too much on public capital as the benefit principle no longer applies (Keen and Marchand 1997).

Another point of criticism is that there exist other fiscal externalities that work in opposite directions (see Gorter and De Mooij 2001; for more about tax exportation, see Huizinga and Nicodeme 2003). For instance, tax exportation means that national governments can face incentives to raise taxes on immobile capital in order to shift the incidence of the tax onto foreign owners of this capital. Capital can be immobile due to location-specific rents. Indeed, the corporate tax is usually a tax on both the normal return on capital and economic rents. If all governments thus try to shift their tax incidence to foreign capital owners, the tax rates on capital could even become too high due to externalities.

The qualifications to the Zodrow-Mieszkowski result emphasise that only when government expenditures feature a consumptive character will policy competition erode public intervention. It is important to understand what drives this result. In our view, it is the restriction on the instrument choice of the government. Indeed, there is no redistribution in the Zodrow-Mieszkowski model as it assumes a representative agent. Yet, it assumes that the government only has access to a highly distortionary tax on mobile capital, and public goods only benefit immobile households. There is no reason why the government cannot adopt more-efficient taxes in the model, such as a tax on labour or consumption. Thus, the Zodrow-Mieszkowski result is driven by a poorly-motivated restriction on the instrument set of the government. They thus do not explain why a government would normally adopt a corporate income tax to raise revenue, which is essentially redistribution. If one takes account of redistribution, it then becomes clear where tax competition imposes a threat, namely the socially desirable distribution of income can become unsustainable. (For papers on tax competition and income redistribution, see Fuest and Huber 2001a; 2001b; Kessler *et al.* 2002.)

Sinn (2003) adds that policy competition (or 'systems competition' as he calls it) erodes the opportunities for not only income redistribution, but also public insurance. Indeed, the welfare state provides insurance against various (labour-market) risks. Government intervention is justified since asymmetric information causes adverse selection so that private markets fail. The government can enforce the insurance contract by means of compulsory insurance without exit options. Yet, if labour is mobile internationally, then policy competition introduces an alternative exit route, thereby causing adverse selection of public insurance. Indeed, people with low risk will move to countries with little insurance while people with high risks will move to countries with higher insurance. Even in the Tiebout model, adverse selection will thus cause underprovision of (public) insurance.

To sum up, policy competition is a possible threat to redistribution when capital is mobile. If labour is also mobile, it then causes a threat to (social) insurance as well. Hence, policy competition provides a potential threat to the welfare state.

## Policy competition: harmful or healthy?

What can we conclude from the previous discussion? In policy debates, people tend to add terms like 'harmful' or 'healthy' to policy competition. Economic theory provides a case for both of them. Indeed, policy competition can be healthy because it disciplines bureaucrats who may otherwise act in their self-interest, or it can reduce informational problems that governments face regarding social preferences for public goods. Policy competition is therefore healthy from an efficiency point of view.

Policy competition is harmful in terms of its impact on the possibilities for governments to redistribute income. It is therefore harmful when considered from an equity point of view. Although economic theory cannot assess the relative weights of equity and efficiency arguments, it reveals that the terms 'harmful' and 'healthy' policy competition largely reflect people's different views on the well-known trade-off between equity and efficiency.

With respect to this trade-off, high-skilled people will usually prefer efficiency and thus favour policy competition as they have higher incomes, are more mobile, face lower labour market risks and have more property. For low-skilled people, the opposite holds true (Huber 1999; Sørensen 2000). With policy competition, the high-skilled will therefore gain at the expense of the low-skilled, e.g. from lower corporate tax, higher public investments in infrastructure, less progressive income taxation and a smaller welfare state. In fact, in every market it is the one that is competed for that will gain from more intense competition. In private markets, it is the consumer who will benefit from lower prices. With policy competition, it is the mobile factor that gains because there is less redistribution from mobile to immobile factors.

How should one deal with the pros and cons of policy competition? The opponents of policy competition sometimes argue that governments should put limitations on the mobility of capital or reverse the process of economic integration. This option, put forward by some antiglobalisation movements, is extremely costly in terms of efficiency because all the gains from regional economic integration will be reduced. An alternative option is centralisation of policies. This, however, has a number of other drawbacks, as the discussion above reveals. The coordination failures associated with policy competition therefore do not provide a sufficient condition for international centralisation of policy, but a necessary condition. In dealing with the drawbacks of policy competition, one can also think of laxer forms of policy coordination. Setting rules and regulations within which the process of policy competition can materialise, e.g. through common standards, minimum tax rates or a ban on certain forms of policy competition, may be a more attractive option. Like any market, the market for policy also needs rules for it to be an appropriate allocation mechanism.

## POLICY COMPETITION IN PRACTICE

What will policy competition imply for various institutions? How intensely will governments compete? Which deviations can countries afford compared with their neighbours? Are there indications that globalisation and European integration make policy competition more intense? It is difficult to answer these questions, especially since empirical indicators for measuring the intensity of policy competition are lacking. Indicators used to measure the intensity of competition in private markets, such as the number of competitors, entry barriers, profit margins and the like, are not relevant for policy competition among governments. Yet, the theory of tax competition reveals a number of hypotheses that can be empirically explored. This section elaborates on this. It not only explores competition with respect to corporate taxes, but also analyses competition in social policy and environmental policy.

## Is there a race to the bottom?

### *Tax competition*

The theory of tax competition predicts that corporate taxes will fall if capital becomes more mobile internationally under the influence of economic integration. Razin and Sadka (1991) even find that the optimal corporate tax will move to zero. This could lead to a reduction in public goods supply, as the Zodrow-Mieszkowski model predicts. Alternatively, it could lead to a shift in the tax burden to taxes on labour (Bucovetsky and Wilson 1991). Do trends in taxes support this claim?

Table 4.1 shows the changes in effective tax rates on capital and labour in the EU since the 1970s. They are derived from the OECD revenue statistics and refer to the EU-15. The table reveals that the average tax burden on labour in the 1970s increased by 6.4 per cent while the average tax on capital dropped by 0.3 per cent. This seems consistent with a process of tax competition. Yet, in the 1980s and 1990s, the tax burden on both labour and capital increased. Recent developments even suggest that the tax burden on capital increases relative to that on labour (European Commission 2003).

These findings are not undisputed, however. Indeed, the *ex-post* measure based on revenue statistics may not provide adequately control for business cycle developments and may thus hide a reduction of taxes during an economic boom or an increase during a recession. Indeed, Devereux, Griffith and Klemm (2002) show that the mean statutory corporate tax rate in 13 EU countries (excluding Denmark and Luxemburg) has dropped from 48 per cent in 1982 to 33 per cent in 2001. The late 1980s and the years around the new century in particular show declines in tax rates. In many countries, however, this reduction in rates was accompanied by a broadening of the tax base. For instance, Devereux, Griffith and Klemm (2002) show that the net present value of fiscal depreciation allowances fell from 83 per cent of the price of the capital good in 1982 to 74 per cent in 2001. Nevertheless, the average effective tax rates also fell during the past two decades, especially in recent years. This provides an indication that tax competition might be more important than suggested by the development in revenues. There is consensus, though, that the reduction in statutory tax rates is more pronounced than the reduction in effective tax rates on capital. This can be explained by increasing

*Table 4.1* Development of the average tax in the EU, 1970–1998

| | *Change (%)* | | |
|---|---|---|---|
| | *1970–1979* | *1980–1989* | *1990–1998* |
| Effective tax on capital in the EU | −0.3 | 2.6 | 1.7 |
| Effective tax on labour in the EU | 6.4 | 3.3 | 1.6 |

Source: Martinez-Mongay (2000).

opportunities for profit shifting by multinational companies, the incentives for which are determined by statutory tax rates rather than by effective tax rates.

### *Social dumping*

Non-wage labour costs associated with social security premiums, sickness payments and other costs of labour market regulations comprise around 40 per cent of the total labour costs in Europe on average (Chen and Funke 2003). Differences in these costs can affect the locational decisions of firms. Moreover, talented workers who represent low risks for the labour market may be encouraged to look for jurisdictions with small non-wage labour costs as these allow for higher after-tax wages. Governments thus face an incentive to cut back social policies. Accordingly, they could reduce the non-wage labour costs, thereby attracting mobile production factors and increase production and welfare. When governments thus start competing intensively with each other, they may end up in a process of social dumping. If social dumping has been important in the recent past, we should observe a gradual decline in social spending in the EU.

Figure 4.1 illustrates the development of social spending as a percentage of GDP in Europe between 1980 and 1998. We observe that social spending has gradually increased from 20.1 per cent of GDP in 1980 to 23.8 per cent in 1998 on average. The Mediterranean countries in particular have seen their social expenditures increase from 13.8 to 21.4 per cent of GDP. Only in the late 1990s is there a modest decline in social expenditure in the Anglo-Saxon and Scandinavian countries. This is primarily due to the economic boom during that period, which reduced unemployment levels.[5] Figure 4.1 thus does not provide support for a process of social dumping. Indeed, it suggests that externalities in

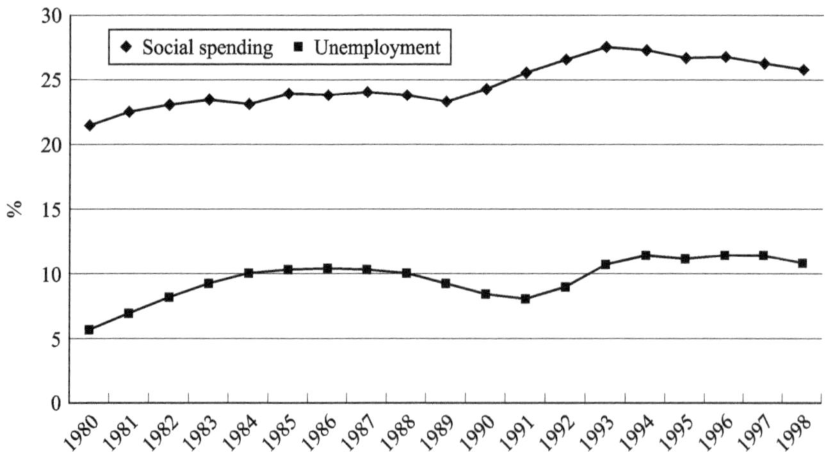


*Figure 4.1* Social expenditures 1980–1998 in relation to GDP and unemployment in relation to the total labour force. Source: OECD Social Expenditure Database.

social policies are likely to be small. The reasons can be twofold. First, social policies not only involve a cost for mobile factors, but also a benefit. For instance, De Grauwe and Polan (2003) empirically explore the impact of social expenditures in OECD countries on indicators for competitiveness. They find no significant effect, suggesting that social expenditure can well be reconciled with a good competitive position for countries. A second reason for small externalities is that production factors are less mobile than is often believed. European labour mobility is rather low across borders. Also, firms may be less mobile than is often thought because agglomeration benefits and other location-specific rents lock firms in at particular locations.

To sum up, there is no reason to believe that the process of social dumping has reduced social expenditures. This opinion is shared among many economists (see for example Bean *et al.* 1998).

### *Ecological dumping*

Environmental regulation may raise production costs for firms. Governments competing for international capital may therefore be tempted to reduce their environmental standards so as to reduce production costs and attract foreign capital. In this way, policy competition may lead to a process of ecological dumping.

A number of EU countries that have raised taxes on pollution, however, largely applied exemptions for industries. This can be seen as a form of policy competition as governments fear the loss of capital once they impose taxes on polluting industries. Figure 4.2 illustrates this by showing the development in the EU of the tax burdens (measured as the excise as a percentage of the user price) on four types of energy used by industry, namely fuel oil, diesel, gas and electricity.[6] We find that only a small number of countries tax fuel oil (eight), gas (four) and electricity (seven). For countries that do tax these fossil fuels, the average tax rate has increased since 1978. This also applies to diesel excises, which more than doubled between 1978 and 2001, largely due to the minimum excise that was imposed in the early 1990s. These trends suggest that policy competition is especially important for countries to exempt industries from any tax, rather than imposing only low tax rates.

## Do governments respond to each other?

It can be suggested that the absence of dumping or a race to the bottom means that there is no policy competition. However, this is not necessarily the case. Governments may compete, but without reducing tax, social expenditures or environmental controls.

Recently, a number of studies have tried to assess empirically the importance of tax competition between countries in an alternative way. In particular, they estimate so-called 'fiscal reaction functions'. These measure the responsiveness of a country's tax rate to the rates of neighbouring countries. These studies typically show that countries in the OECD and Europe do indeed systematically respond to

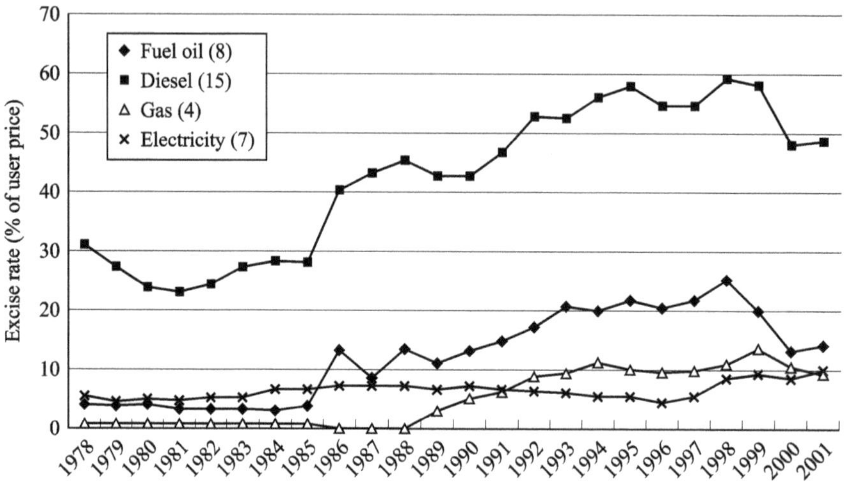


*Figure 4.2* Excises on energy sources for industrial users 1978–2001. Source: IEA database.

each other's corporate tax rates. For instance, Devereux, Lockwood and Redoano (2002) find that strategic tax responses are strong and highly robust for both statutory tax rates and (marginal and average) effective tax rates in 16 OECD countries. For the EU, Altshuler and Goodspeed (2002) find similar results for alternative specifications for the tax game. Their results suggest that a 10 per cent higher tax rate in neighbouring countries implies an 8 per cent higher rate in a particular European country. These findings provide evidence for the claim that governments aggressively compete with their corporate tax systems for foreign direct investment. Altshuler and Goodspeed find, however, that the responsiveness of European tax rates has not increased between 1980 and 1996. This suggests that tax competition has not intensified, even though this might have been expected under a process of European economic integration.

Strategic policy responses have also been explored in the area of environmental policy, however these results are inconclusive. Levinson (2003) for instance shows that decentralisation of environmental policy in the USA in the early 1980s has not significantly reduced the stringency of environmental rules. It therefore seems that US states are not engaged in a competition for firms via their environmental regulations. Yet, the estimated reaction functions by Fredriksson and Millimet (2002) suggest that environmental regulations in the US states are affected by the policies in neighbouring states.

## Do policies converge?

Policies may also converge under the influence of policy competition. This is especially true in the EU, where countries today assess each other's policies under the open method of coordination. Governments may therefore believe that they cannot differ too much from their neighbours as this may come at the expense of foreign investment.

Do we indeed observe a process of convergence? Table 4.2 provides an indication of the variance between EU countries with respect to three policy variables across time: the effective tax rate on companies, social expenditures as a percentage of GDP and the diesel excise as a percentage of the user price. The figures show the coefficient of variation, i.e. the standard deviation divided by the mean. The developments suggest that there is a clear convergence in the average tax on companies and in social expenditure. The coefficient of variation for the effective tax rate decreased from 0.369 in 1990 to 0.218 in 1999. This is particularly due to a reduction in the tax rate in high-tax countries, such as Germany and Finland, and a rise in low-tax countries, such as Portugal and Greece. The variance in the diesel excise declined from 0.598 in 1981 to 0.117 in 1999. This is particularly because of an increase in southern EU countries and in Scandinavia. For social expenditures, we observe a decline from 0.258 in 1981 to 0.177 in 1999, due particularly to a rise in southern EU countries.

We also explored beta convergence, i.e. we regressed the average relative change in different institutional variables of Table 4.2 on the initial value. A negative beta implies convergence because a high initial value causes a relative decline in its value. The parameter beta also measures the speed of convergence. Table 4.3 gives the results. We find convergence in all three policy parameters. The speed of convergence is highest in the tax rate on companies (25.3 per cent) and lowest for social expenditures (4.1 per cent). A beta coefficient of –0.253 means that the difference from the EU-mean will decline annually by 25.3 per cent. This can be translated into the so-called half-time value, i.e. the number of years that a country needs to make up half of the difference from the EU mean. Table 4.3 reveals that it takes a country slightly more than 3 years to make up half the difference from the EU mean in the average tax on companies. For social expenditures it takes more than 17 years, and for diesel excises it takes almost 11 years.

*Table 4.2* Development of coefficient of variance for EU policy areas, 1981–1999

| *Policy variable* | *Coefficient of variation* | | | | | | |
|---|---|---|---|---|---|---|---|
| | *1981* | *1984* | *1987* | *1990* | *1993* | *1996* | *1999* |
| Effective tax on companies[a] | – | – | – | 0.369 | 0.325 | 0.227 | 0.218 |
| Social expenditures, in % GDP | 0.258 | 0.234 | 0.205 | 0.206 | 0.218 | 0.175 | 0.177 |
| Diesel excise, in % user price | 0.598 | 0.442 | 0.342 | 0.359 | 0.161 | 0.137 | 0.117 |

Notes

a Own calculations, on the basis of figures from Gorter and De Mooij (2001).

*Table 4.3* Beta convergence and half-time value for EU policy areas

| *Policy variable* | *Beta (t-value)* | *Half-time value* |
|---|---|---|
| Effective tax on companies 1990–1999 | −0.253 (−4.02) | 3.1 |
| Social expenditure in % GDP 1980–1999 | −0.041 (−3.84) | 17.3 |
| Diesel excise in % user price 1978–2001 | −0.066 (−7.42) | 10.9 |

### Do countries differ from each other?

Although institutions have converged, there remain important differences among countries. This is not surprising in light of the different circumstances, historical developments and preferences among countries. The literature of tax competition has explored whether differences can be explained by certain characteristics of countries, especially size.

Bucovetski (1991) has shown that large countries, measured in terms of population, will set higher taxes on capital than will small countries. The reason is that tax differences cause changes in the before-tax return to capital as the after-tax returns should be equal in a world with freely moving capital across borders. The adjustment of the before-tax return for a small country is larger than for a large country because a given capital flow between two countries is relatively small for the large country and relatively large for the small country. Therefore, employees in the small country will benefit relatively much more from a reduction in the corporate tax as it substantially raises their wage. In the large country, employees hardly suffer from a relatively high corporate tax because only a small fraction of its capital flows to the small country. As a result, large countries will, all other things being equal, set higher taxes than will small countries.[7]

To test this hypothesis, we have simply regressed the tax burden on capital on the size of the population in the EU-15; Table 4.4 shows the result. It reveals that size indeed exerts a positive impact on the tax burden, both for corporate taxes and for diesel excises. In particular, an extra 10 million inhabitants in a country raises, on average, the effective corporate tax by 2.1 per cent and the diesel excise by 1.9 per cent (both statistically significant).[8]

## POLICY COMPETITION AND LOCATION

In the previous sections the spatial dimension was rather implicit. In this – what we will denote in the remainder as – neoclassical world, countries are locations

*Table 4.4* Impact of population size on tax rates

| | *Population* | t-*value* |
|---|---|---|
| Effective tax on companies, average 1990–1999 | 0.21 | 4.03 |
| Diesel excise in % user price, average 1992–2001 | 0.19 | 4.53 |

with a distance between them that is indeterminate. The geographical dimension in the neoclassical world is limited to an assumption about which production factors or goods can cross national borders (costless) and which cannot. One drawback of the models in this class is that they cannot account for the lack of policy competition. Despite the leaps forward in the process of European economic integration, there is not much evidence for a race to the bottom. Introducing explicitly the spatial or geographic dimension to the analysis, as does the so-called 'new economic geography', helps to overcome this limitation. At the heart of the new economic geography are agglomeration externalities. These are advantages (or disadvantages) of spatial clustering. In these theoretical explorations, further economic integration possibly leads to *less* intense policy competition.

The relevance of the spatial dimension is illustrated by the list of most important considerations for firms' choice of location. Table 4.5 shows results of interviews by Ernst & Young with managers of international firms (within services as well as manufacturing). The table reports the percentage of managers that answered 'very important' or 'crucial' to the question of how much importance a certain factor had for their decision where to locate.

The most important factors according to Table 4.5 are not directly related to policy. For example, the size of the (local) market is by far the most important decision variable for most companies. For manufacturing firms, locating near to a harbour or river and the presence of raw materials are often important. After these factors, some policy variables play a role. Infrastructure is the most prominent one. High-quality infrastructure (more specifically, railways and roads), an airport in the vicinity and well-developed communications facilities are important for services as well as for manufacturing firms. The wage costs (including social security contributions) and the price of land are also mentioned by managers.

*Table 4.5* The most important factors for the location of multinational firms (manufacturing and services), according to managers' questionnaire responses

| *Location factor* | *% of managers that replied 'very important' or 'crucial'* | |
|---|---|---|
| | *Manufacturing* | *Services* |
| Size of nearby market | 76 | 60 |
| Quality of infrastructure | 44 | 61 |
| Quality of the labour force | 32 | 26 |
| Presence of raw materials | 31 | – |
| Wage level | 31 | 35 |
| Location of a nearby airport | 27 | 27 |
| Price of land | 24 | 23 |
| Language | 23 | 30 |
| Location of nearby harbour | 20 | – |
| Corporate tax | 17 | 15 |
| Quality of telecom | 16 | 34 |

Source: Ernst & Young (1993).

Remarkably, the corporate tax rate appears rather low on the list. However, there are competing studies where the corporate tax rate is argued to be an important factor.[9]

## What does location imply?

By explicitly introducing location, one also introduces distance. Distance implies that there are costs of transporting goods and production factors. The new economic geography emphasises transport cost for intermediate and final goods. This focus on goods rather than factors is because the latter are 'transported' or replaced only once, while goods are to be transported more than once. In such a setting, clustering of activities can be beneficial for all firms. Indeed, because individual firms ignore the (positive) impact of their presence in a specific location on other firms, there is an externality. It is referred to as the 'agglomeration-externality'. This need not be due only to transport costs, but also to learning externalities. That is, by producing, firms add to the local knowledge stock to the benefit of other firms in the location. Other examples of agglomeration-externalities include reduced search cost in a pooled labour market (think of positive and negative fluctuations in the demand for labour that cancel out) or the development of specialised intermediate goods producers that is only possible if there is enough demand for their products.

The agglomeration externalities have the character of a flywheel: once they are set in motion they keep on going for a long time. This is because individual decisions of producers and consumers reinforce each other. (The opposite effect is also possible; congestion effects can dominate. Think of someone entering a traffic jam; in this case it is less attractive for the next person to use their car as the traffic jam is more severe. In the remainder of our discussion we assume that agglomeration externalities dominate the congestion externalities.)

This type of externality implies that the economy is characterised by increasing returns to scale: adding firms to the economy implies that the productivity of existing firms goes up.[10] This contrasts with the neoclassical world, where declining marginal productivity is a crucial assumption. In particular, decreasing returns implies that an increasing supply of a production factor decreases the return, thereby inherently stabilising the equilibrium. Increasing returns implies that an equal distribution of economic activity across space is not the only plausible outcome. On the contrary, in a hypothetical world where all activity is initially equally distributed, the new economic geography models predict a highly uneven outcome.

Using a standard new economic geography model, Figure 4.3 illustrates the essence of agglomeration externalities.[11] The horizontal axis shows the distribution of economic activity between country 1 and country 2 (the further to the right-hand side of the figure, the larger the share of country 2). The vertical axis indicates the ratio of the returns to mobile production factors in the two countries. Suppose that the initial distribution of activity is equal (point C in the figure). If country 2 increases the cost of production (for example by imposing a tax) relative

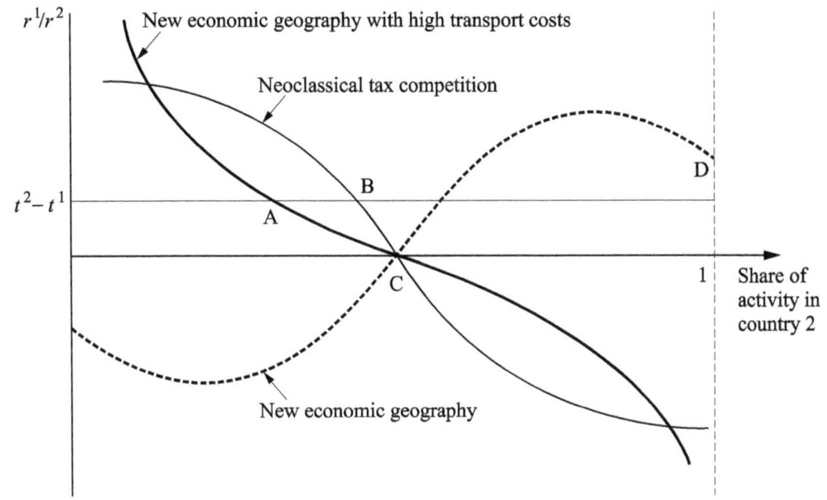


*Figure 4.3* Allocation of economic activity in a neoclassical world and in the 'new economic geography' world.

to country 1, the gross return to the mobile factor will increase in country 2. In the neoclassical tax-competition literature, this happens due to a reallocation of the mobile factor from country 2 to country 1 (which affects the marginal productivity in both countries). The new equilibrium is in point B. With agglomeration externalities – the new economic geography models – two possibilities arise. On the one hand, the mobile factor reacts more strongly to differences in returns; more capital will flow from country 2 to country 1 as compared with the neoclassical model. We then end up at point A, a 'separating equilibrium'. On the other hand, the agglomeration-externalities can also imply that a situation as point C is unsustainable. Hence the equilibrium situation from which to start our experiment is one where all mobile factors are allocated in one point, say D. In such a core–periphery pattern, nothing happens if country 2 raises its tax somewhat because the agglomeration externalities will – up to a very high tax level – lock in the firms in country 2.[12]

Agglomeration effects are determined by the size and wealth (and possibly the quality) of a location (or market).[13] These in turn are determined by the size of the local population, their wealth and income (after taxes) and the size of market in the neighbourhood of the location (see also Table 4.5). Moreover, the presence of intermediate goods producers plays an important role. The size of the market is an endogenous outcome determined by the decisions of consumers and firms where to locate. The key variables for policy competition in such an environment are those variables that affect the decisions of firms and consumers.

Possible instruments are the production of public capital, such as high-quality legal institutions, research and other knowledge institutes, a good infrastructure and the creation of a pleasant place to live for consumers and managers. Furthermore the government can invest in infrastructure that reduces transport costs to other (national or international) locations. Such infrastructure could be highways, railways or airports.

In addition, of course, taxes affect the decision of where to locate. In the remainder we will focus on taxes and on infrastructure.

## Tax competition and agglomeration

Despite the integration of European capital markets, we do not observe a clear race to the bottom in European capital income taxes. This is somewhat surprising in light of the theoretical predictions of the traditional literature on tax competition. Does the new economic geography perhaps provide an explanation here?

The combination of increasing returns to scale and transport costs implies that profits in agglomerations are higher than elsewhere. Increasing returns force firms to determine their location, while transport costs make it attractive to locate in agglomerations (see point D in Figure 4.3). In this location, firms are close to the market. The reduced transport costs in the agglomeration drive a wedge between the rates of return in the core and in the periphery. This reflects agglomeration rents. It implies that, although capital is mobile *ex ante*, it is immobile ex post when agglomeration tendencies have created rents. Kind *et al.* (2000) refer to this as a 'lumpy world', while Baldwin *et al.* (2003) talk about 'quasi fixed factors'. This allows governments to tax capital efficiently, i.e. taxing location-specific rents is efficient and does not imply capital flight. It gives rise to a so-called 'sustain point tax gap,' i.e. a maximal sustainable tax differential between the core and the periphery at which the core can keep its locational advantage compared with the periphery.

Agglomeration economies imply that economic integration does not necessarily reduce the optimal tax on capital, but may also increase it. Ludema and Wooton (2000) and Baldwin *et al.* (2003) show that in the early phase of economic integration, the sustain point gap tends to rise due to increasing agglomeration rents. During this phase, economic integration may well lead to a 'race to the top'. This conclusion deviates from the findings in the traditional literature on tax competition and may explain why a tax race to the bottom has not materialised.

The new economic geography literature usually divides Europe into a core and a periphery. The core consists of regions with important agglomerations, while agglomeration rents in the periphery are generally low. Baldwin and Krugman (2000) thus argue that countries in the core of Europe should impose higher taxes than countries in the periphery. We tested this hypothesis by exploring whether the average effective tax rate on companies (derived from European Commission 2001) in the core of Europe is systematically higher than in the periphery. In particular, we regressed the tax rate on a measure for agglomeration, namely GNP per $km^2$, of an EU member state. The regression suggests a correlation of 0.39, which is statistically significant. This is consistent with the positive impact of agglomeration on tax rates.

The core–periphery result provides little reason for tax coordination. Indeed, countries can tax capital up to the sustain point gap. Moreover, public expenditures may further strengthen the attractiveness of the core as a location (Brakman *et al.* 2002). Baldwin and Krugman (2000) therefore conclude that tax harmonisation either hurts the core, or the periphery, or both, as compared to the non-cooperative equilibrium.[14] However, tax competition may still be unattractive in a world with agglomeration, for two reasons. First, capital is only quasi fixed. As soon as tax differences exceed the sustain point gap, some investors will move towards the periphery. This erodes the agglomeration benefits and so other investors will follow. Ultimately, a large number of firms will leave the region. Second, if the initial equilibrium is not characterised by a core–periphery but by a separating equilibrium (i.e. point A in Figure 4.3), the result becomes opposite to tax competition. Indeed, the forces that provide a stable core–periphery equilibrium, make the separating equilibrium unstable. This makes it difficult for fiscal authorities to raise taxes since a slightly higher tax induces a strong adverse impact on locational choices. Kind *et al.* (2000) show that the optimal tax on capital in a non-cooperative setting is even negative. Tax competition is so intense that governments provide subsidies to prevent investors from leaving for other locations. Tax coordination could then be attractive for reducing the intensity of tax competition. Baldwin *et al.* (2003) therefore conclude that the non-cooperative tax rates are generally too low and so an increase in all rates will benefit all jurisdictions.[15] The desirability of tax coordination or tax competition is thus highly dependent on the initial equilibrium, i.e. a core–periphery pattern or a separating equilibrium.

## Competition in infrastructure and agglomeration

Governments can also compete through the provision of high-quality infrastructure. We can distinguish two types of public infrastructure investments, namely intraregional and interregional connections. Intraregional (or local) infrastructure positively affects the productivity of a region. As mobile factors (firms or capital owners) benefit most from this type of investment, governments might have an incentive to invest excessively in this infrastructure, and to finance these by taxing immobile factors. The excessive investment is analogous to the too-low tax on mobile capital in the case of tax competition (as described above).

Policy competition with respect to interregional infrastructure works differently. The crucial difference to intraregional infrastructure is that interregional connections ‘go two ways’. For example, a road from Brussels to Paris, connects Brussels better to Paris but also Paris better to Brussels. You often hear pleas to improve the transport possibilities of peripheral regions to the core region in order to enhance the development of the periphery. In the Netherlands, a discussion is going on to connect the rural north with the Randstad (the busy west) by means of a high-speed rail connection in order to make the north more attractive as a location for firms. Similar considerations played a role when the Dutch government had to decide on a high-speed rail connection between Amsterdam and Paris. That line ought to connect the Netherlands with the core of Europe. Insights derived from the new economic geography literature suggest that investments like these might backfire on the peripheral regions (Martin and Rogers 1995). Improving the connection between a peripheral region and the wealthy core might possibly benefit the core region at the expense of the backward peripheral region. The reason for this is that a high-speed connection will also better connect the core to the backward region. This implies that firms can even more easily combine the benefits of being located in the core with supplying their goods to the backward region. Ultimately, the backward region is a *less* attractive location for firms.

If different governments compete for economic activity by investing in the improvement of their connections between each other, the question arises of whether they tend to overinvest, as was the case with intracountry or intraregional infrastructure. Theory alone does not provide the answer. If one country improves a connection with another country, the investing country does not take into account that their investment is also beneficial for the other country. This tends to lead to underinvestment. However, the investing country also improves its attractiveness as a location, as it might become relatively better connected to other countries as well. This form of policy competition leads possibly to overinvestment. Only if policy competition is fierce, the latter effect dominates and there is overinvestment.

As has already been hinted at, for interregional infrastructure, more dimensions play a role because new or better infrastructure is usually integrated within an existing network. Let us return to the example of the Netherlands, where the peripheral north is going to be better connected to the Randstad in the west. If the north would also be better connected with the north of Germany (to Hamburg, for example), the north could become the heart of an entire network, a so-called 'hub'. Firms in the north could then serve cheaply customers both in the Randstad and in Hamburg (Krugman 1993). Is creating a hub the thing to do? Nahuis and Tang (2002) analysed whether a hub strategy is indeed good for peripheral regions. Their analysis revealed several caveats. First, the backward region should be comparatively much better connected to other regions in order to compensate for their disadvantage of having a small home market. Second, if a backward region follows such a strategy, other regions or countries are likely to respond to the deterioration of their own competitive positions. These regions are likely to follow similar infrastructure investment plans and thereby they will undo the efforts of the backward region to become a hub. The analysis reveals that the incentive for rich regions to invest is indeed increasing in the quality of the infrastructure of the backward region. The authors show that attaining a hub position by improving connections with other regions one by one is not a viable strategy.

However, in real life, hubs do exist – think of Frankfurt, Chicago or Rotterdam. We take the example of a hub that is based on a harbour, Rotterdam, for reasons that will become clear in a moment. Why is it that this place became a hub, while the theory discussed above suggests that such a position will be undone by other countries' or regions' investments? There are three characteristics that make Rotterdam different from, for example, the north of the Netherlands. First, Rotterdam has the natural advantage of a deep-water harbour. Second, Rotterdam is part of an agglomeration – the Randstad, discussed above. The final, and most important, difference is that a harbour differs fundamentally from a road. A harbour is a so-called 'point infrastructure' whereas highways and railways are 'line infrastructure'. Point infrastructure connects one place with the complete existing network. An improvement in the harbour of Rotterdam connects it better with all harbours in the world. Think similarly of an airport, such as Frankfurt. An improvement in your point infrastructure therefore immediately improves your attractiveness as a location relative to all similar point infrastructures. So, once a country has a lead – due to a natural advantage or early investment – this is not easily undone by investments of others.[16]

## CONCLUSIONS

Traditional economic theory can be used to support both healthy and harmful policy competition. To illustrate this, the literature on tax competition, staring with Zodrow and Mieszkowski (1986), suggests that policy competition will cause an underprovision of public goods; the Tiebout (1956) hypothesis, in contrast, suggests that policy competition will lead to an efficient policy.

More-modern theories of tax competition put fewer restrictions on the instrument sets of governments. This yields more useful insights in the desirability of policy competition: it suggests a trade-off between the efficiency gains from policy competition and the adverse implications for equity. Hence, the distinction between healthy and harmful tax competition boils down to different perspectives on the classical trade-off between efficiency and equity.

Most views on policy competition assume that economic integration goes along with more intense policy competition. However, the average tax burden on capital income has not declined to very low levels, while social expenditures have been maintained and environmental policies have not become less stringent. The insights from the 'new economic geography' offer an explanation for this. It stresses agglomeration economies, i.e. the gains from spatial concentration of economic activities. It allows for a relatively high tax burden on capital due to location-specific rents. Economic integration may imply that agglomeration economies become more important and so taxes on capital and social expenditures may rise, rather than fall. This result does not imply, however, that governments can substantially raise their tax rates on capital. Indeed, the new economic geography also stresses potentially disastrous implications if capital taxes become too high.

Policy competition in infrastructure in the presence of agglomeration economies is also important. Strategic behaviour of governments can be attractive to internalise external effects of infrastructure. However, policy competition can also cause an oversupply of infrastructure. The literature also suggests that it seems unlikely that interregional infrastructure is a good instrument for reducing regional income differentials.

## NOTES

1 www.pvda.nl
2 www.sp.nl
3 Not everyone shares this view. Some theories, for instance, find that local politicians are more vulnerable to lobby groups than central politicians, see for example Bahrdan and Mookherjee (1999).
4 The empirical support for leviathan, measured by a positive relationship between the size of government and the degree of centralisation, is weak, see for example Oates (1985) and Anderson and Van den Berg (1998).
5 The correlation coefficient between social expenditures and unemployment is 0.7.
6 As either not all EU countries tax these sources of energy, or because data for some countries are lacking, we present the development for those countries that do feature positive excises. The number of countries considered in the figure is between brackets for each energy source.
7 Large countries can also yield larger agglomeration rents, thereby raising higher taxes (Haufler and Wooton 1999).
8 Kanbur and Keen (1993) show that large countries will find it optimal to set higher indirect taxes in the presence of cross-border shopping. For small countries, the loss in tax revenue from the lower tax rate is relatively small while there is a relatively large inflow of cross-border shoppers from the large country. For large countries, the opposite holds true.
9 Brunetti *et al.* (1997) explored the impediments to entrepreneurship and find that the corporate tax rate is the most important factor whereas infrastructure is only sixth on the list. De Mooij and Ederveen (2003) collected 25 studies on the effect of corporate taxes on foreign investments. A meta-analysis of these studies reveals that a 1 percentage point higher effective corporate tax rate leads to a reduction of 3 per cent in foreign investments.
10 In this type of model, for individual firms an increasing returns production function is the standard specification, however the increasing returns are countered by a downward-sloping demand curve.
11 For such a model, see for example Fujita *et al.* 1999.
12 Figure 4.3 also implies that a temporary policy shock can have permanent effects. If a government temporarily provides favourable conditions for firms (for example by giving a subsidy), firms will all locate in that country. Afterwards, higher tax can be introduced without causing the firms to leave.
13 This is a slightly broader definition than what is commonly referred to as 'the size of the market' in economic geography models. We include in the discussion the quality of publicly provided facilities as well as the attractiveness of a location to live in (for managers and workers).
14 A milder form of tax coordination, e.g. through a minimum rate, can increase welfare.
15 Baldwin and Forslid (2002) argue, however, that tax competition will lead to the optimal mix of public and private goods. The reason is that Baldwin and Forslid (in contrast to Baldwin *et al.* 2003) do not allow for capital and the owner to reside in different locations. High taxes and a large supply of public goods can then compensate as public goods are also important for location decisions, see Brakman *et al.* (2002).
16 Welfare analysis in a network setting, as provided in Nahuis and Tang (2002) yields similar results to the two-country case. Depending on the existing quality of the infrastructure, infrastructure-based policy competition can lead to both over- and underinvestment.

## REFERENCES

Altshuler, R. and Goodspeed, T.J. (2002) 'Follow the Leader? Evidence on European and U.S. tax competition', mimeo: Hunter College.

Anderson, J.E. and Van den Berg, H. (1998) 'Fiscal decentralization and government size: An international test for leviathan accounting for unmeasured economic activity', *International Tax and Public Finance*, 5/2: 171–86.

Bahrdan, P. and Mookherjee, D. (1999) 'Relative Capture of Local and Central Governments: An essay in the political economy of decentralization', University of California, Berkeley, Center for International and Development Economics Research (CIDER) Working Paper: C99/109.

Baldwin, R. and Forslid, R. (2002) 'Tax Competition and the Nature of Capital', CEPR Discussion Paper 3960.

Baldwin, R. and Krugman, P. (2000) 'Agglomeration, Integration and Tax Harmonization', CEPR Discussion Paper 2360.

Baldwin, R., Forslid, M., Ottaviano, M. and Nicoud, R. (2003) *Economic Geography and Public Policy*, Princeton, NJ: Princeton University Press.

Bean, C., Bentolila, S., Bertola, G. and Dolado, J. (1998) *Social Europe: One for all?*, Monitoring European Integration, CEPR.

Becker, R. and Henderson, V. (2000) 'Effects of air quality regulations on polluting industries', *Journal of Political Economy*, 108: 379–421.

Besley, T., Griffith, R. and Klemm, A. (2001) *Fiscal Reaction Functions*, London: Institute for Fiscal Studies.

Brakman, S., Garretsen, H. and Van Marrewijk, C. (2002) 'Locational Competition and Agglomeration: The role of government spending', mimeo: University of Groningen.

Brennan, G. and Buchanan, J. (1980) *The Power to Tax: Analytical foundations of a fiscal constitution*, Cambridge: Cambridge University Press.

Brunetti, A., Kisunko, G. and Weder, B. (1997) *Institutional Obstacles for Doing Business: Data description and methodology of a worldwide private sector survey*, survey conducted for the World Development Report.

Buchanan, J.M. and Tullock, G. (1962) *The Calculus of Consent: Logical foundations of constitutional democracy*, Ann Arbor, MI: University of Michigan Press.

Bucovetsky, S. (1991) 'Asymmetric tax competition', *Journal of Urban Economics*, 30: 167–81.

Bucovetsky, S. and Wilson, J.D. (1991) 'Tax competition with two tax instruments', *Regional Science and Urban Economics*, 21: 333–50.

Chen, Y-F. and Funke, M. (2003) 'Labour Demand in Germany: An assessment of non-wage labour costs', CESifo Working Paper no. 952.

CPB (2003) *Klimaatbeleid en Europese concurrentieposities*, CPB Document no. 24.

Devereux, M.P., Griffith, R. and Klemm, A. (2002) 'Corporate income tax: reforms and tax competition', *Economic Policy*, October 2002: 451–95.

Devereux, M.P., Lockwood, B. and Redoano, M. (2002) 'Do Countries Compete Over Corporate Tax Rates?', CEPR Discussion Paper no. 3400.

European Commission (2001) *Company Taxation in the Internal Market*, Com (2001) 582 final, Brussels.

European Commission (2003) *Structures of the Taxation Systems in the European Union*, data 1995–2001.

Fredriksson, P.G. and Millimet, D.L. (2002) 'Strategic interaction and the determination of environmental policy across US States', *Journal of Urban Economics*, 51: 101–22.

Fuest, C. and Huber, B. (2001a) 'Tax competition and tax coordination in a median voter model', *Public Choice*, 107/1–2: 97–113.

Fuest, C. and Huber, B. (2001b) 'Labour and capital income taxation, fiscal competition, and the distribution of wealth', *Journal of Public Economics*, 79/1, 71–91.

Fujita, M., Krugman, P. and Venables, A.J. (1999) *The Spatial Economy: Cities, regions, and international trade*, Cambridge, MA: MIT Press.

Gorter J. and De Mooij, R.A. (2001) *Capital Income Taxation in Europe: Trends and trade offs*. The Hague: Sdu Publisher.

Grauwe, P. de and Polan, M. (2003) 'Globalisation and Social Spending', CESifo Working Paper 885.

Haufler, A. and Wooton, I. (1999) 'Country Size and Tax Competition for Foreign Direct Investment', *Journal of Public Economics*, 71: 121–39.

Huber, B. (1999) 'Tax competition and tax coordination in an optimum income tax model', *Journal of Public Economics*, 71: 441–58.

Huizinga, H. and Nicodeme, G. (2003) 'Foreign Ownership and Corporate Income Taxation: An empirical evaluation', CEPR Discussion Paper no. 3952.

Jaffe, A., Peterson, S., Portney, P. and Stavins, R. (1995) 'Environmental regulations and the competitiveness of U.S. manufacturing: what does the evidence tell us?', *Journal of Economic Literature*, 33: 132–63.

Kanbur, R. and Keen, M. (1993) 'Jeux sans frontieres: tax competition and tax coordination when countries differ in size', *American Economic Review*, 83/4, 877–92.

Keen, M. and Marchand, M. (1997) 'Fiscal competition and the pattern of public spending', *Journal of Public Economics*, 66: 33–53.

Keller, W. and Levinson, A. (2002) 'Environmental regulations and foreign direct investment to U.S. states', *Review of Economics and Statistics*, 84/4: 691–703.

Kessler, A., Lülfesmann, C. and Myers, G. (2002) 'Fiscal Competition, redistribution, and the politics of economic integration', *Review of Economic Studies*, 69/241: 899–924.

Kind, H.J., Midelfart, K.H.M. and Schjelderup, G. (2000) 'Competing for capital in a 'lumpy' world', *Journal of Public Economics*, 78: 253–74.

Krugman, P.R. (1993) 'The hub effect: or, threeness in interregional trade', in W.J. Ethier, E. Helpman and J.P. Neary (eds) *Theory, Policy and Dynamics in International Trade: Essays in honour of Ronald W. Jones*. Cambridge: Cambridge University Press.

Levinson, A. (2003) 'Environmental regulatory competition: a status report and some new evidence', *National Tax Journal*, 56/1: 91–106.

Ludema, R.D. and Wooton, I. (2000) 'Economic geography and the fiscal effects of regional integration', *Journal of International Economics*, 52/2: 331–57.

Martin, P. and Rogers, C.-A. (1995) 'Industrial location and public infrastructure', *Journal of International Economics*, 39/3–4: 335–51.

Martinez-Mongay, C. (2000) *ECFIN's Effective Tax Rates: Properties and Comparisons With Other Tax Indicators*, Economic Papers of DG ECFIN 146.

Mooij, R.A. de and Ederveen, S. (2003) 'Taxation and foreign direct investment: a synthesis of empirical research', *International Tax and Public Finance*, 10: 673–93.

Nahuis, R. and Tang, P.J.G. (2003) 'Strategic Competition with Public Infrastructure: Ineffective and Unwelcome?', CPB Discussion Paper No. 008.

Oates, W.E. (1985) 'Searching for Leviathan: an empirical study', *American Economic Review*, 75: 748–57.

Oates, W.E. and Schwab, R.M. (1988) 'Economic competition among jurisdictions: efficiency enhancing or distortion inducing?', *Journal of Public Economics*, 35: 333–54.

Razin, A. and Sadka, E. (1991) 'Vanishing Tax on Capital Income in the Open Economy', NBER Working Paper no. 3796.

Schraven, J. (2000) *Versterking Fiscale Concurrentiepositie Nodig*, ESB 4272, 728–31.

Sinn, H.-W. (2003) *The New Systems Competition*, Oxford: Blackwell Publishing.

Sørensen, P.B. (2000) 'The case for international tax coordination reconsidered', *Economic Policy*, 31: 431–72.

Tiebout, C.M. (1956) 'A pure theory of local expenditures', *Journal of Political Economy*, 64: 416–24.

Zodrow, G.R. and Mieszkowski, P. (1986) 'Pigou, Tiebout, property taxation and the underprovision of local public goods', *Journal of Urban Economics*, 19: 336–70.

# 5 Clustering, optimum currency areas and macroeconomic policy

*Roel Beetsma and Koen Vermeylen*

## INTRODUCTION

European economic integration is making steady progress. Since 1993, most goods and services are traded freely in a common market. Markets that are not free yet, such as the energy market, will be liberalised soon. Since 1999, there is also a monetary union in Europe, in which currently 12 countries participate, with a common currency and a common central bank. The success of the euro will to a large extent depend on whether the participating countries constitute a so-called 'optimal currency area'.[1] This, in turn, largely depends on the extent to which the euro countries are hit by asymmetric shocks and how efficiently these shocks can be absorbed.

Not every economic sector reacts in the same way to economic shocks. Energy-intensive industries, for instance, are much more sensitive to oil price shocks than the service sector, and the export industry reacts differently to exchange rate fluctuations than a sector that imports its inputs from abroad. The fact that different economic sectors react differently to specific economic shocks does not necessarily pose a problem for macroeconomic policy. If all these sectors are spread geographically in a more or less homogeneous way, policymakers can focus on how the different sectors react *on average* to these shocks. Things are more complicated, however, if certain sectors are concentrated in a few specific regions, i.e. if the economy is characterised by geographical clustering of economic activities. In this case, not only the different sectors, but also different regions will react differently to economic shocks. The economy is then subject to *asymmetric* shocks.

A common market also implies, however, that (the asymmetry of) these shocks may well change over time. Steadily advancing economic integration in Europe may lead to regional clustering of specialised activities and therefore increase the asymmetry of economic shocks. The implications for macroeconomic policy at the national level become more important when the effect of asymmetric regional shocks on the national economy is strong. This is especially the case if the geographic displacement of certain economic activities moves across borders (which becomes easier in a more integrated Europe), and/or if the regional clustering of specific activities leads to a relatively strong growth in these activities,[2] such that their weight in the total economy increases. It is also possible that after economic and monetary union (EMU), business cycles of countries will become more correlated with each other (for instance, because of higher intra-industry trade), such that the prevalence of asymmetric shocks decreases. The consequences of EMU for national macroeconomic policy will then decrease.

Differences in economic or industrial activity as a result of clustering are not the only source of asymmetric shocks. Shocks can also be caused by macroeconomic policy itself or by unexplained changes in consumer or producer confidence. An important source of asymmetric shocks, which has disappeared with EMU, is fluctuation in exchange rates between member countries that do not reflect changes in so-called 'fundamentals', such as differences in inflation or economic growth rates. Asymmetric shocks that are the consequence of imperfect control or errors in national monetary policy have also disappeared.[3] Therefore, the extent to which macroeconomic policy needs to be adjusted because of EMU depends crucially on the relative importance of different sources of macroeconomic shocks.

The remainder of this chapter is structured as follows. First, we discuss the theoretical literature on the effect of economic and monetary integration on clustering. Then we discuss the empirical evidence of asymmetric shocks in the euro area. With this theoretical and empirical background, we investigate to what extent the euro area is an optimum currency area and what this implies for policy. Following that we discuss the criteria for an optimal currency area, and then explain the role of factor mobility in eliminating disequilibria between countries in a monetary union. Monetary and fiscal policy in a monetary union are then analysed, and the role of fiscal transfer mechanisms to absorb asymmetric shocks discussed. The final section presents a short summary and looks ahead to future developments.

## THE EFFECT OF ECONOMIC AND MONETARY INTEGRATION ON CLUSTERING

Economic and monetary integration probably has important consequences for the location strategy of firms and sectors, and therefore for the extent of clustering and the risk of asymmetric shocks.

The far-reaching integration in the euro area undoubtedly has led to lower transport and transaction costs and has intensified international trade. The classical international trade theory, and especially the Heckscher-Ohlin theorem, predicts that this will encourage labour-intensive sectors to move to regions where labour is relatively abundantly available and capital is relatively scarce, while capital-intensive firms will want to establish themselves in regions where labour is relatively scarce and capital is relatively abundant.

However, the major part of international trade in the euro area is intra-industry trade, rather than inter-industry trade. Or in other words: for most industrial sectors it is the case that countries in the euro area tend to import as well as export goods within the same sector. So if most trade is intra-industry trade, what determines whether a firm establishes itself in one country rather than in another?

According to Krugman (1991), firms often tend to locate themselves in the vicinity of other firms in order to take advantage of scale effects on input markets or spillover effects between firms (such as informal contacts with employees from other firms, so that firms can keep themselves informed about developments in firms in their immediate vicinity). Consequently, Krugman predicts in another paper (Krugman 1993) that EMU will lead to more clustering of firms in certain regions.

It should be pointed out, however, that lower transport and transaction costs do not necessarily lead to more clustering. If there is not sufficient migration of labour from regions with low labour demand to regions with high labour demand, more clustering will lead to larger wage differentials between regions. It is conceivable that at a certain point these wage differentials become so substantial that a further decrease of transport costs will stimulate firms to move to regions where the labour market is less under pressure. Ever lower transport costs, combined with little labour migration, may therefore lead to less clustering, rather than more clustering. This possibility was studied by Puga (1999).

Increased clustering affects both demand and supply shocks. To the extent that increased clustering leads to a more uniform supply of goods from a region or country, the variance of both demand and supply shocks will increase. This is simply due to the effect of less diversification, under the assumptions that the demand for each product is stochastic and demand shocks are not perfectly correlated across products. A similar argument holds for supply shocks. Industries differ in the extent to which they are sensitive for shocks in oil prices or other inputs, technological shocks, etc. More clustering therefore increases the risk of asymmetric shocks.

However, it is also possible that economic and monetary integration decreases the importance of asymmetric shocks. Thanks to intensified trade within EMU counties, demand shocks in one country have a stronger spillover effect on aggregate demand in the other countries, and the effect of productivity shocks in one country will be felt quicker in the rest. Furthermore, there are reasons to believe that intensified trade also leads to better fiscal policy coordination within EMU counties. The result of all this is that business cycles in the different EMU countries will become more synchronised.

This last hypothesis has been investigated by, among others, Frankel and Rose (1997; 1998). An econometric analysis of a dataset of bilateral trade and aggregate production for 20 industrialised countries over 30 years indeed shows that closer trade relations lead to more-correlated business cycles. A similar study by Artis and Zhang (1997) shows that in most European countries aggregate production has become increasingly correlated with aggregate production in Germany since the introduction of the European Monetary System – the predecessor of EMU – where exchange rates were stabilised within narrow bands (see also Artis 1999).

## ASYMMETRIC SHOCKS IN THE EUROPEAN UNION

Even though the results by Frankel and Rose (1998) and Artis and Zhang (1997) suggest that the economic and monetary integration in Europe has diminished the relative importance of asymmetric shocks, a lot of research has attempted to identify these shocks. In this section, we investigate to what extent different areas (countries and regions) in the European Union (EU) are subject to asymmetric shocks.[4] This gives an indication of the extent to which the common monetary policy in Europe can be successful, as well as the risks of policy conflicts.

A first wave of empirical studies tried to measure asymmetric shocks by looking at the correlations between the real exchange rates or the output fluctuations of the different countries. Neumann and Von Hagen (1994), for instance, showed that the variability of the real exchange rates in a core group of EMU member countries (France, Germany, Austria and the Benelux) has decreased substantially in the 1980s, and were comparable with the variability of the real exchange rates between the German Länder at the end of the 1980s.[5] Cohen and Wyplosz (1989) and Weber (1990) carried out similar studies, but for the variability of output fluctuations. De Grauwe and Vanhaverbeke (1993) studied correlations between real exchange rates as well as between output and employment fluctuations, both with national data and regional data within several EU countries.

A problem with all these studies, however, is that they do not make a distinction between the shocks and the consequences of these shocks: it is very possible that two countries are subject to the same shocks, but that the economy in one country adjusts faster than in the other. This would lead to a low correlation of output fluctuations, even though the underlying shocks are the same.

A second wave of empirical studies therefore tried to distinguish both the shocks and their consequences. The most commonly used method to achieve this is a vector autoregression analysis. In such an analysis, production and price data are regressed on their values in the (near) past, while unexplained production and price shocks are interpreted as supply and demand shocks. In order to be able to identify which part of the unexplained production and price fluctuations is the result of supply shocks and which part is due to demand shocks, it is assumed that supply shocks have a permanent effect on both the price level and the production, while demand shocks also have a permanent effect on the price level but only a temporary effect on production (this method is known as the Blanchard–Quah decomposition method; see Blanchard and Quah 1989).

In this way, Bayoumi and Eichengreen (1993) distilled time series for the demand and supply shocks to which several EMU countries were subjected between 1968 and 1988. In a core group consisting of France, Germany, Austria, Denmark and the Benelux, the demand and supply shocks appear to be strongly correlated with each other. The periphery, where the correlations are less clear, consisted of the UK, Ireland, Finland, Italy, Spain, Portugal and Greece. Sweden was somewhere between the core and the periphery.

The study by Bayoumi and Eichengreen stimulated a lot of follow-up research (for instance Erkel-Rousse and Mélitz 1995; Helg *et al.* 1995), and their results seem to be quite robust. Funke (1997) found lower correlations in a study based on time series up to 1992, but this can be fully ascribed to the German reunification (Bayoumi and Eichengreen 1997).

Instead of trying to derive time series for demand and supply shocks from production and price data, and consequently studying the correlations of these shocks between different EU countries, there is another, more direct way to investigate to what extent regions within the EU are subject to asymmetric shocks. This method is based on a dynamic factor model and was introduced into the literature by Forni and Reichlin (2001).

Forni and Reichlin (2001) assumed that every country in the EU consists of several regions, and that the growth rate of the production in every region is subject to a European-wide shock, a shock at the national level and a regional shock. The regional shock has no effect on other regions and the national shock has no effect on other countries. The estimation method of Forni and Reichlin is flexible enough to allow for every region to react differently to the shocks to which it is subjected. As Forni and Reichlin assume that all shocks are independent of each other, they can analyse for each region to what extent the variability of production was due to shocks at the European, the national and the regional levels.

In Germany, France, Italy, Belgium, the Netherlands and Spain, about half of regional output fluctuations can be explained by shocks at the European level, about 20 to 30 per cent by shocks at the national level and the rest by shocks at the regional level. For Greece and the UK, shocks at the European level are much less important: for Greece and the UK shocks at the European level only explain about 15 per cent of the regional output fluctuations, while national shocks account for 60 per cent and 75 per cent, respectively. Portugal lies between these two groups: the relative importance of national shocks compared with European shocks is bigger than in Germany, France, Italy, Belgium, the Netherlands and Spain, but smaller than in Greece and the UK.

One can also clearly identify clusters of regions where the output variability is strongly affected by shocks at the European level. In the regions along the Rhine, for instance, from south Holland in the Netherlands via the Ruhr area to Rheinland-Pfalz in Germany, European shocks explain more than 70 per cent of total output variability. The same holds for a cluster of regions around the southwest of the Alps, from Geneva, via Lyon and the Rhône delta, to Turin and Milan.

It is striking that these clusters are not located within one country, but rather they cross borders. Furthermore, all countries seem to have regions where shocks at the European level dominate, but hardly any regions where shocks at the national level dominate. The only exceptions are Greece and the UK, where in almost every region the output variability is mainly determined by shocks at the national level. This confirms previous results by, among others, De Grauwe and Vanhaverbeke (1993) and De Nardis *et al.* (1996): asymmetric shocks seem to matter especially at the regional level, but not really at the national level.

Finally, there is also empirical evidence on the degree of industrial specialisation in the different regions in the EMU area (which may be an indication of the extent to which they are vulnerable to asymmetric shocks). Midelfart-Knarvik and Overman (2002) computed for each EU country the Krugman index, which measures to what extent the industrial structure of the country deviates from the industrial structure in the EU. It turns out that for most countries this index has slightly increased between 1970 and 1997, which suggests that the industrial structure in most countries has become more specialised. At the regional level, however, no trend can be detected: about half of the regions were more specialised in 1997 than in 1970, while the other half were less specialised. Midelfart-Knarvik and Overman also observed that during the past few decades, labour-intensive industries, such as textiles, have moved more and more to labour-abundant regions in southern Europe, consistent with the Heckscher–Ohlin theorem.

## WHEN DO COUNTRIES FORM AN OPTIMUM CURRENCY AREA?

Almost as per the definition, countries form an optimum currency area if the advantages of a monetary union are greater than its disadvantages. Seminal work by Mundell (1961) argues that the main advantage of a monetary union is the disappearance of transaction costs related to currency exchange, while its main disadvantage is that macroeconomic disequilibria can no longer be eliminated by adjusting exchange rates.

These 'classical criteria' for the existence of an optimum currency area depend therefore on the trade-off between, on the one hand, lower transaction costs and, on the other hand, welfare losses due to the loss of a mechanism for absorbing asymmetric shocks. Since Mundell's analysis, other factors have been suggested which should be taken into account in deciding whether or not to form a monetary union. In particular, the EMU in Europe has spurred research on optimum currency areas. To put the discussion of the optimum currency area into a broad perspective, this chapter will examine not only the classical criteria for an optimum currency area, but also more-recent criteria. The focus on our discussion in the next paragraphs, however, will be on the question of how policymakers should deal with asymmetric shocks, resulting from geographical concentration of (specific) economic activities. More efficient absorption of these shocks will make it easier to comply with the classical criteria for an optimum currency area.

### The role of labour mobility

According to Mundell (1961), whether a set of countries form an optimum currency area depends to a large extent on how strongly the business cycles in the different countries are correlated with each other and how fast asymmetric shocks can be eliminated. Economic shocks that affect all countries in the area in the same manner can in principle be absorbed by a common monetary policy. There is also no problem if shocks are asymmetric but markets work perfectly and all prices are flexible. In that case, prices adjust such that disequilibria promptly disappear.

Consider, for instance, a monetary union with two countries, country A and country B. Suppose now that world demands change, such that the demand for products from country A decreases and the demand for products from country B increases. This leads to unemployment in country A, while the economy in country B starts to overheat. With perfect markets, however, the relative prices of the products of country A decrease until the demand for products from country A is restored and the unemployment has disappeared, while the demand for products from country B is curbed and its economy is stabilised.[6]

In practice, however, many markets are characterised by imperfections, such that prices (of products or labour) only slowly adjust. This is the reason why the classical work by Mundell (1961) stresses the importance of labour mobility for the existence of an optimal currency area. Suppose that in the example above relative prices cannot adjust. Unemployment in country A and overheating in country B can then be avoided by migration of sufficient labour from country A to country B.

## Avoiding competitive devaluations

An argument that has been put forward in favour of monetary unification in Europe is the problem of 'competitive devaluations' (see, for instance, Eichengreen, 1993). In the European Monetary System (EMS), exchange rates of the participating countries moved within narrow bands around a central parity, but this central parity was revised from time to time. Especially in the first half of the 1980s, a few countries (notably France and Italy) used this possibility rather freely. Their monetary policies were more expansive than in West Germany – the anchor country in the EMS – such that their currencies had to be devalued from time to time compared with the German mark. In the short run, such devaluations implied a competitive advantage as prices of tradable goods only adjust slowly after a devaluation. A devaluation can therefore be a handy instrument (politically) for stimulating the economy in the short run. However, as all participating countries in this exchange rate system have the same incentive to devalue, this may quickly lead to a situation where one country after the another devalues, resulting in higher overall inflation while nothing changes in real terms. In a monetary union, the possibility of such competitive devaluations is eliminated because monetary policy is determined centrally.

Furthermore, many economists doubt that flexible exchange rates are important for adjusting relative prices. Nominal exchange rates (and, because of price rigidities, real exchange rates also) exhibit strong fluctuations, especially in the short run that are often difficult to explain by relying on 'fundamentals'. Important examples are the fluctuations of the US dollar in the 1980s and the exchange rate between the US dollar and the euro since 1999. Therefore, it is doubtful that exchange rates between member countries in the euro area could play an important role in cushioning the effects of diverging business cycles.

One can, therefore, fix these exchange rates or introduce one currency, thereby avoiding the adverse effects of exchange rate movements that are not warranted by developments in the fundamentals.

## Changes in the strategic interactions between the most important players

Recent research has drawn attention to the fact that monetary unification not only affects the absorption of asymmetric shocks, but also has other effects that should be taken into account when evaluating whether an optimal currency area exists. More specifically, the literature points out that a monetary union changes the strategic interactions between the different agents who influence macroeconomic policy, such as the strategic interactions between monetary and fiscal policymakers, the interactions between the fiscal policymakers in different member countries, and the interactions among trade unions and between them and the other policymakers.

Beetsma and Bovenberg (1998) studied the altered strategic relation between fiscal and monetary policymakers. They built a model of a monetary union, which included a common central bank and national fiscal authorities that have strategic leadership compared to the central bank (known as 'Stackelberg' leaders). This seems a reasonable assumption as fiscal policy cannot be adjusted as easily as monetary policy. As monetary policy can always be loosened up somewhat afterwards in order to ease the potential negative employment effects of fiscal policy, the fiscal authorities have an incentive to set the tax rate and the government expenditures too high from a social point of view.[7] However, as the private sector anticipates this loose monetary policy when setting up its wage contracts, the resulting equilibrium is one with – from a social point of view – too-high inflation, taxes and government expenditures, and too-low employment. Monetary unification weakens the strategic position of each individual fiscal authority towards the central bank. The monetary policy response to a tax increase becomes smaller and therefore diminishes the incentive to set tax rates and government expenditures that are too high. The resulting equilibrium in a monetary union is, therefore, better than the one with national monetary policy.

Cukierman and Lippi (2001) analysed the effects of changes in the strategic position of trade unions. They assume that trade unions do not only care about traditional concerns, such as the real wage and/or the employment level, but also value an environment with low and stable inflation. High wage claims negatively affect aggregate employment and may therefore force the monetary authority to loosen up their policy, which leads to inflation. Trade unions may therefore want to mitigate their wage claims. With national monetary authorities, the claims of an individual trade union have a stronger effect on monetary policy than in a monetary union, as in the first situation the trade union is a relatively bigger player. Consequently, in a monetary union each individual trade union experiences a smaller negative effect from increasing its wage claims. In equilibrium, this will lead to higher unemployment and inflation. This strategic effect is analogous to the one in Beetsma and Bovenberg (1998), be it that there the weakened strategic position of the fiscal authority is beneficial in the monetary union, while in Cukierman and Lippi (2001), the weaker influence of each individual trade union has a negative effect on the desirability of a monetary union.

The European Central Bank (ECB) and the European Commission, but also other international organisations, often stress the necessity of structural reforms within Europe. Structural reforms concern, for instance, the flexibility of the labour market, pension reform to deal with the ageing problem and reform of social safety nets to eliminate poverty traps. Monetary unification increases the need for flexible labour markets. The economic trade-off to form a monetary union therefore also depends on the incentives that a union provides to engage in structural reforms. This is the basis for the analyses by Calmfors (2001), Sibert (1999) and Sibert and Sutherland (2000). The models in these articles start from the so-called 'inflation bias' (a suboptimally high inflation rate). Structural reform improves the functioning of the labour market and leads to a higher level of natural employment and production. In principle, this diminishes the incentive to loosen monetary policy and, therefore, leads to a lower inflation rate. In a monetary union, however, this hardly plays a role because the national authorities realise that structural reforms in one country have little effect on the common monetary policy. It is, therefore, important to coordinate (or impose) structural reforms at the level of the Union, for example by the European Commission.

## The role of factor mobility in absorbing asymmetric shocks

Even though labour mobility is hard to measure, there exists a consensus among economists that labour mobility is low in the euro area. Bayoumi and Eichengreen (1993) compared labour mobility in Europe with labour mobility in the USA and conclude that labour mobility in the USA is substantially higher. This should not surprise us. Even though formal barriers for free movement of labour within the EU have disappeared, there are several informal barriers that hamper labour mobility. Important barriers are due to differences in culture, language and institutions. These differences can also have direct financial consequences, such as non-transferable pension rights or double income taxation. Even labour mobility within countries, such as in the Netherlands, is low. The extent to which labour mobility can absorb diverging business-cycle developments within the euro area is therefore limited (at least for the near future).

Not only labour mobility, but also capital mobility may contribute to cushioning diverging business-cycle developments between countries. A recent branch in the literature investigates the empirical importance of capital mobility in cushioning national or local consumption risks. Ideally, private agents should spread their assets across countries or regions in such a way that the return on these assets largely eliminates country-specific fluctuations in disposable income. Consider individuals who receive all their labour income in a procyclical sector in

France (i.e. in a sector that on average does well when the economy is booming). To minimise their disposable income and consumption risk, they should invest their savings in countries where the business cycle has a low or negative correlation with the business cycle in France. The difference between aggregate production in a country (i.e. gross domestic product, GDP) and aggregate income of a country (i.e. gross national income, GNP) is factor income received from or paid to the rest of the world. As GNP determines the consumption possibilities of the average consumer in a country, an international portfolio policy to diminish consumption risks should lead to a GNP that is more stable than GDP.

This idea is behind the research carried out by Asdrubali *et al.* (1996). These authors investigated to what extent consumption risks in the USA are diversified by holding assets outside the state of residence. They found that almost 40 per cent of shocks in GDP at the state level are eliminated through the capital market (i.e. through portfolio investment in shares), while another 25 per cent is eliminated through credit markets (the debt market). These markets therefore play an important role in the USA in cushioning consumption risks. Follow-up research on risk diversification between countries in the EU and the OECD shows a much more limited role for these markets. Arreaza *et al.* (1997) found that government consumption and government transfers are important channels for smoothing consumption over time. Sørensen and Yosha (1998) make a distinction according to the time span across which consumption is smoothed. At an annual basis, about 40 per cent of fluctuations in GDP are eliminated, half of which is achieved through government savings (or dissavings), while the other half is accounted for by savings (or dissavings) at the firm level. Over a time span of three years, only 25 per cent of the shocks are eliminated, almost exclusively through borrowing and lending by the government.

The limited role that capital markets play confirms the 'home bias puzzle', the well-documented observation that by far the largest part of savings is held in the home country. This is a puzzle because from a theoretical point it is hard to explain why individuals take so little advantage of the possibility of spreading their risks by holding an internationally diversified portfolio. The advantages of such a portfolio seem to substantially outweigh its costs (such as transaction costs). As in the title to their paper, Gordon and Bovenberg (1996) therefore posed the question 'why is capital so immobile?' Notwithstanding increasing international capital flows, to which the media give ample attention, capital markets fulfil their role as insurance markets only to a limited extent.

## ASYMMETRIC SHOCKS AND MONETARY POLICY IN THE EURO AREA

The objective of business-cycle policy is to stabilise economic growth and inflation. This is important to ensure that economic growth is accompanied by full employment and is sustainable in the long run. Business-cycle policy, therefore, needs to react in an appropriate way to shocks that hit the economy.

As we have seen above, labour and capital mobility play only limited roles in absorbing asymmetric shocks, which should be taken into account by macroeconomic policymakers. Asymmetric shocks complicate macroeconomic policy substantially because central policymakers have to delineate a policy that holds for several countries simultaneously. In the euro area, for instance, the ECB has to design a monetary policy that holds for the Ruhr area as well as for the manufacturing towns in Galicia. A direct consequence of this is that asymmetric shocks also increase the risk of policy conflicts. It is therefore crucially important to make sure that the decision process within the ECB happens in such a way that the decision process is not paralysed whenever asymmetric shocks lead to conflicting policy preferences in the different member states.

## The effect of asymmetric shocks on common monetary policy in Europe

In the euro area, the common monetary policy should only pursue objectives at the level of the aggregate economy in the euro area. The formal objective of the ECB, as spelled out in the Treaty on the European Union (the 'Maastricht Treaty'), is to maintain price stability, which the ECB defines as an increase in the harmonised index of consumer prices (HICP) of between 0 and 2 per cent at an annual rate. Even though stabilising economic activity in the euro area is not a formal objective of the ECB, it is reasonable to assume that the ECB pays attention to this. The policy of the ECB can therefore to a certain extent be characterised as *flexible inflation targeting* (see, for instance, Svensson 2000).

Geographical concentration of economic activity and the related asymmetric shocks – to the extent that they affect the economies of the participating countries as a whole – may hamper monetary policy substantially because the ECB can never design a policy that is optimal for all countries. Asymmetric shocks are, therefore, a potential source of disagreement about which monetary policy to follow. Hence it is crucial that the decision-making process in the ECB deals with these disagreements in a clever way, such that they do not continually escalate into policy conflicts which mortgage monetary policy in the euro area.

The decision-making body in the ECB, where decisions about monetary policy are taken, is the Executive Committee. The Executive Committee is composed of the 12 presidents of the national central banks of the countries in the euro area, and the president, vice-president and the four directors of the ECB. How the Executive Committee takes its decisions is not determined by the Maastricht Treaty or by other European legislation, therefore it has to be determined by the Committee itself.

This leads to a number of important questions. First, will the members of the committee defend a monetary policy that is in the interest of their own country, or one that is in the interest of the euro area as a whole? And second, to what extent can member states influence the decision-making process indirectly, for instance by blocking appointments or by thwarting the ECB's monetary policy through other channels?

The first question has been analysed extensively by Aksoy, De Grauwe and Dewachter (2002). These authors investigated the extent to which the objectives of the members of the committee and the voting procedure affect the ECB's monetary policy and the consequences of this policy for social welfare in the euro countries.

Aksoy *et al.* studied three scenarios. In the first scenario, a 'nationalistic' scenario, all 18 members of the Executive Committee vote for the interest rate that is optimal for their own country. In the second scenario, a 'consensus' scenario, all 18 members vote for an interest rate that is a weighted average of the optimal interest rates for the different countries. In the third scenario, the 12 presidents of the central banks of the euro countries vote for the interest rate that is optimal for their own country, while the president, the vice-president and the four ECB directors vote for a weighted average of these interest rates. All scenarios assumed that the Executive Committee decides by simple majority.

The optimal interest rate for each euro country was estimated as follows. First, the authors estimated for each euro country how inflation and aggregate production react to shocks in the nominal interest rate. They then proposed an objective function for the central bank, where the central bank tries to stabilise inflation and aggregate production while at the same time wanting to avoid large swings in the interest rate. Using this objective function and the estimated response of inflation and aggregate production to shocks in the nominal interest rate, they could derive for each country the optimal interest rate as a function of the current economic situation in the country and the shocks it faced.

The authors then investigated, through numerical simulations, the extent to which the decisions of the ECB differ in the three scenarios. This yielded two important conclusions. First, in the first scenario (the nationalistic scenario), social welfare is lower than in the two other scenarios. This is because the volatility of the interest rate is higher. Second, if the president, the vice-president and the four ECB directors vote for a weighted average of the optimal interest rates for the different euro countries, it hardly matters anymore whether the 12 presidents of the central banks vote nationalistically or take into account the situation in the other countries. In other words, the ECB's monetary policy hardly differs between the second and the third scenarios. We can thus conclude that the asymmetries between the different euro countries probably do not lead to a suboptimal monetary policy, as long as the president, the vice-president and the four ECB directors base their voting behaviour on the aggregate euro economy.

There is a second important problem, however. Assume that a member country is hit by a large asymmetric shock and prefers a monetary policy that deviates substantially from the ECB's monetary policy. Is it then possible to avoid this country trying to influence indirectly the decision-making process, for instance by blocking appointments or by putting pressure on the Council of Economics and

Finance Ministers, to thwart the ECB's policy? This was the question studied by Dixit (2000).

Dixit started from the assumption that it is desirable for central banks to formulate policy rules and then stick to them. A central bank that does not do that may quickly lose its credibility, which may after a while lead to higher inflation. This is the most important reason why the Maastricht Treaty has charged the ECB with, first and foremost, maintaining price stability.

An individual country that is hit by a large asymmetric shock, however, may in certain circumstances find it advantageous for the central bank to deviate temporarily from its policy rules and attune its policy to eliminating the consequences of the shock, even though it may thereby lose some of its credibility. An individual country may therefore be tempted to put political pressure on the ECB to deviate from its policy rules. According to Dixit, such political pressure is bound to be successful from time to time, and so in the long run the credibility of the ECB will be undermined.

An easy way to avoid all this is to set up the policy rules in such a way that countries are never tempted to lobby against the ECB. This requires that the policy rules are flexible enough such that a country that is hit by a strong asymmetric shock can be partly accommodated. Policy rules that totally neglect asymmetric shocks are, according to Dixit, too rigid, and may provoke lobbying from countries that are adversely hit by these shocks and therefore undermine the credibility of the ECB.

## Do clusters and asymmetric shocks in the euro area constitute an argument against it as an optimal currency area?

To conclude this section, we pose the question whether the euro area is an optimum currency area given the extent of clustering and the size of the asymmetric shocks that we observe.

Eichengreen (1991) showed that the regional real exchange rates in Europe are substantially more volatile than those in the USA. This is confirmed by Bayoumi and Eichengreen (1993): there are clearly more demand and supply shocks at the national level in Europe than at the state level in the USA. Furthermore, shocks in Europe tend to be more persistent than in the USA. This would suggest that the euro area, compared with the USA, may perhaps not be an optimal currency area.

This is not necessarily a correct conclusion, however. It is not because it is hard, and sometimes even impossible, for the ECB to cushion the asymmetric shocks in the euro countries that national central banks would do a better job. Indeed, asymmetric shocks seem to be especially prevalent not at the national level, but at subnational level (see Forni and Reichlin 2001; De Grauwe and Vanhaverbeke 1993; De Nardis *et al.* 1996), such that national central banks would also be confronted with asymmetric shocks, just like the ECB. Furthermore, absorbing asymmetric shocks requires a degree of 'fine-tuning' that is not achievable given the limited information (and the limited economic knowledge!) available to the monetary authorities (Mélitz 1996). Finally, there are also other ways in which the effects of asymmetric shocks can be absorbed. This is the topic of the next section.

## THE ROLE OF FISCAL POLICY IN STABILISING ASYMMETRIC SHOCKS

We discussed above the implications of asymmetric shocks for common monetary policy. On the one hand we explored to what extent monetary policy is insulated from the temptation to react to asymmetric shocks. On the other hand, we explained that monetary policy should not be completely passive in the presence of large asymmetric shocks. Even so, asymmetric shocks, small or large, primarily demand a fiscal policy reaction because factor mobility can only absorb asymmetric shocks to a limited extent. There are several ways in which fiscal policy can contribute to the stabilisation of these shocks. We discuss these possibilities in this section.

### Automatic stabilisers

Macroeconomic stabilisation at the national level is the responsibility of the national government. Stabilisation at this level is partly achieved by the automatic stabilisers. When the business cycle deteriorates, tax revenues fall and transfers by the government rise, in particular those for unemployment. As a result, fluctuations of private-sector disposable income become smaller and the economy is (partly) stabilised. When the government sector, as a share of the total economy, is large (taxes and government expenditures are high), the automatic stabilisers are more effective. Empirical research by Fatas and Mihov (2001a; 2001b) for the US states and the OECD countries reveals a strong and robust negative correlation between the size of the government and the volatility of economic activity. However, we do not argue that a larger government is better for the economy. Higher taxes also affect the supply side of the economy and may lead to lower natural (i.e. business-cycle corrected) GDP.

Many economists view the automatic stabilisers as the ideal mechanism for absorbing shocks. They do their job automatically and do not require any explicit policy intervention. However, because they lead to higher deficits during downturns, there is a danger of violating the 3 per cent deficit criterion enshrined in the Maastricht Treaty and the Stability and Growth Pact.[8] However, some researchers, such as Buti *et al.* (1998) and Buti and Suardi (2000) do not agree that this is a danger. They argue that when countries stick to their commitment to a medium-term budget balance or budget surplus, there should be sufficient room to exploit fully the automatic stabilisers to absorb asymmetric shocks. A purely cyclically driven increase in the deficit by at least 3 per cent of GDP has rarely occurred in the past. This seems to be confirmed by the analysis of Eichengreen and Wyplosz (1998), who used historical data. Moreover, in such a situation, the economic decline is likely to be so large that the escape clauses of the pact can be successfully invoked.[9] Buti and Sapir (1998) provide estimates for several countries of the sensitivity of the deficit for changes in GDP. For the Netherlands, for example, a fall of GDP by 1 per cent leads to a fall in government revenues by 0.5 per cent of GDP and a rise in government expenditures by 0.2 per cent of GDP. The sum of the two numbers is approximately 0.8 per cent. With a structural deficit of zero, GDP should fall by at least 3.75 per cent for the 3 per cent deficit ceiling to be violated. The Dutch economy is relatively sensitive to changes in GDP due to the relatively large public sector. The largest sensitivity is estimated for Sweden, where the government balance deteriorates by 0.9 per cent of GDP if GDP falls by 1 per cent. Over the period under consideration (the 1960s up to the mid-1990s) Sweden was indeed characterised by its large public sector.

Fully exploiting the automatic stabilisers, as envisaged in the Stability and Growth Pact, requires that countries run surpluses during booms. This proved to be problematic in the past. During the high-growth period in the second half of the 1990s a number of countries (including Germany and the Netherlands) failed to eliminate their structural (i.e. corrected for the economic cycle) deficits. Some countries (Germany included) have already violated the 3 per cent deficit over the past years.

## A centralised fiscal system

The automatic stabilisers act like an insurance mechanism against the effects of asymmetric shocks on countries. To illustrate this, suppose that a country consists of two regions. The regions pay taxes to the government and receive certain transfers in return. When the business-cycle situation of one of the regions improves relative to that in the other region, the first region will then contribute more taxes to the government and will receive fewer transfers. The opposite is the case for the other region. This therefore means that resources flow from the region hit by the good shock to the region hit by the bad shock. In other words, the fiscal system acts like a regional-level insurance mechanism for the economies. One could imagine that such a centralised tax-transfer mechanism could also be implemented for a group of countries. However, such a mechanism also introduces a number of complications. Probably the main one is that such an implicit insurance mechanism inevitably leads to systematic redistribution. Because of their higher income levels, richer countries will on average contribute more tax revenues and receive fewer transfers than poorer countries. This makes richer countries reluctant to participate in a centralised tax-transfer system, despite the fact that both poorer and richer countries would benefit from a pure insurance mechanism.

As early as 1977, the MacDougall Report (European Commission 1977a; 1977b) studied to what extent a federal fiscal system compensates for regional income differences. The same question was posed by Sala-i-Martin and Sachs (1992). Both the MacDougall Report and Sala-i-Martin and Sachs found substantial effects: according to the MacDougall Report, 28 per cent of the income differences between US states will be compensated by federal transfers from the federal government. Sala-i-Martin and Sachs provide an even higher estimate, of 33 to 40 per cent.

Von Hagen (1992) notes that these estimates measure the joint effect of, on the one hand, insurance and, on the other hand, redistribution out of solidarity considerations. Even if we neglect the shocks, a lower-than-average income leads to disproportionately lower tax contributions and disproportionately higher transfer receipts, and hence to redistribution among regions. Subsequent work following Sala-i-Martin and Sachs tries to solve this problem in a variety of ways. Von Hagen (1992) computed to what extent business-cycle fluctuations in the various states are damped by transfers from the federal government, and interpreted this as the extent to which these transfers operate as an insurance mechanism. Based on this, Von Hagen concluded that transfers from the federal government insure away about 10 per cent of the regional business-cycle fluctuations. Related work by Fatas (1998), Athanasoulis and Van Wincoop (1998) and Obstfeld and Peri (1998) confirmed this figure. Mélitz and Zumer (2002) found a somewhat larger degree of insurance. Asdrubali, Sørensen and Yosha (1996) and Pisani-Ferry, Italianer and Lescure (1993) found estimates of similar magnitude for the insurance provided by the federal government. However, these authors used a different methodology: the study by Asdrubali *et al.* is based on a variance-decomposition method, while Pisani-Ferry *et al.* obtained their results from a macroeconomic model simulation.

Table 5.1 provides a summary of the results of these studies. From it, we can conclude that the extent of insurance provided by federal transfers is probably slightly over 10 per cent. However, as explained earlier, it is important to distinguish between federal transfers as an insurance mechanism and federal transfers as a solidarity system. Failure to make a sharp distinction between the two, as in Bayoumi and Masson (1995), leads to inaccurate estimates.

Similar studies have also been conducted for countries other than the USA. Table 5.2 summarises the results of the most important studies. Federal transfers to the provinces in Canada provide roughly the same degree of insurance as in the USA; the insurance mechanism in the UK is slightly larger. Other countries vary widely: in both France and Germany fiscal transfers play an important role in insuring the various regions against income shocks. The insurance role in Italy is negligible. However, Italy aside, we can conclude that any monetary union under consideration should feature a centralised fiscal system that insures regions (at least partly) against income shocks.

## Fiscal discretion

Discretionary fiscal policy assumes an 'active' government in the sense that it reacts with policy changes to new economic developments. This contrasts with the case of the automatic stabilisers that do not require any policy intervention to fulfil their role. An example of fiscal discretion is a reduction of the tax rate in response to an economic recession. An excellent and recent example concerns the shift to 2004 of the German tax reduction originally planned for 2005 so as to give the ailing German economy a boost (see, for example, *The Economist* 2003).

*Table 5.1* Estimates of federal transfers (redistribution and insurance) within the USA

| | *Federal transfer*[a] | | |
|---|---|---|---|
| *Author* | *Redistribution* | | *Insurance* |
| MacDougall Report (1977) | | 28% | |
| Sala-i-Martin and Sachs (1992) | | 33–40% | |
| Von Hagen (1992) | 47% | | 10% |
| Pisani-Ferry *et al.* (1993) | – | | 17% |
| Bayoumi and Masson (1995) | 7–22% | | 7–30% |
| Mélitz and Zumer (2002) | 16% | | 15–20% |
| Asdrubali *et al.* (1996) | – | | 13% |
| Fatas (1998) | – | | 11% |
| Obstfeld and Peri (1998) | 19% | | 10% |
| Athanasoulis and Van Wincoop (1998) | 20% | | 10% |

Source: Von Hagen (1999), after minor adjustments.

Notes

a The numbers provide the *net* federal transfer to a region as a result of a 1 dollar difference in the level or the change of income of the region relative to the average income in the USA.

*Table 5.2* Estimates of federal transfers (redistribution and insurance) in countries other than the USA

| | *Federal transfer*[a] | | |
|---|---|---|---|
| *Country/author* | *Redistribution* | | *Insurance* |
| Canada | | | |
| MacDougall Report (1977) | | 32% | |
| Bayoumi and Masson (1995) | 39% | 14% | |
| Mélitz and Zumer (2002) | 16% | | 10–14% |
| Obstfeld and Peri (1998) | 53% | | 13% |
| France | | | |
| MacDougall Report (1977) | | 54% | |
| Pisani-Ferry *et al.* (1993) | – | | 37% |
| Mélitz and Zumer (2002) | 38% | | 15–20% |
| Germany | | | |
| MacDougall Report (1977) | | 29% | |
| Pisani-Ferry *et al.* (1993) | – | | 34–42% |
| Italy | | | |
| MacDougall Report (1977) | | 47% | |
| Obstfeld and Peri (1998) | 8% | | 3% |
| United Kingdom | | | |
| Mélitz and Zumer (2002) | 26% | | 21–26% |

Source: Von Hagen (1999), after minor adjustments.

Notes

a Explanation: the numbers provide the estimated *net* federal transfer to a region as a result of a 1 dollar difference in the level or change of income of a region relative to the average in the country.

Many economists are sceptical about the scope for discretionary fiscal policy to stabilise the economy. Fiscal policy is not suitable for 'fine tuning' because relatively little is known about the size of the effects of a fiscal expansion or contraction and because the time lag between the observation of a downturn and the implementation of a fiscal policy change is often rather long. Measures have to be worked out and then be approved by the legislature. After that, they have to be implemented. The economy may well find itself in a different phase of the business cycle by the time that the fiscal policy change takes effect. This way, an anticyclical fiscal policy may work out procyclically and destabilise the economy.[10]

A recent strand of the empirical literature estimates the economic effects of discretionary fiscal policy. Fatas and Mihov (2001c) found that an increase in government expenditures has a large and persistent effect on consumption and employment. In particular, this is the case for an increase in the wages in the public sector. Blanchard and Perotti (2002) distinguish between the effects of changes in government expenditures and changes in taxes and conclude that a fiscal expansion in both cases has a positive effect on production. However, both an increase in government expenditure and an increase in taxes affect investment negatively. An extensive empirical investigation covering over 90 countries led Fatas and Mihov (2003) to conclude that frequent use of discretionary fiscal policy leads to macroeconomic instability, which in turn is costly in terms of economic growth.

## FISCAL TRANSFERS TO ABSORB ASYMMETRIC SHOCKS[11]

In the previous section we explained how existing adjustment mechanisms, which operate via government policy, can cushion asymmetric shocks. The automatic stabilisers operate exclusively at the national level and stabilise disposable income and the demand for products. The tax-transfer system in a country insures regions against region-specific shocks. Given that by far the largest shares of the governments' revenues and expenditures are concentrated at the national level (the budget of the EU is relatively small), there is hardly any insurance of country-specific risks through 'Brussels'. However, the degree of insurance provided by the tax-transfer system in existing monetary unions could give an indication about the need for such a system at the European level. In the previous section it became clear that the estimates of insurance of region-specific shocks vary rather widely, but are on average in the order of 10 to 15 per cent. This is a significant, but not terribly substantial, degree of insurance.

Despite the fact that in the two decades preceding monetary unification the monetary autonomy of the countries in Europe gradually shrunk, the switch to the euro proved to be a large step. This step is so large that some countries have decided to not participate (yet). However, a substantial centralisation of the tax-transfer system would constitute an even larger decrease in national policy autonomy and cannot be expected to materialise in the near future. A number of experts have therefore investigated the possibility of setting up an insurance scheme by means of direct fiscal transfers among countries hit by asymmetric shocks. Such a scheme differs from the structural and cohesion funds, which are primarily intended to raise the welfare level of the poorer regions to the same level as that of the richer regions. However, the Maastricht Treaty in principle leaves open the possibility of an international fiscal transfer scheme (FTS). Article 103A.2 of the treaty allows for the possibility of 'community financial assistance', comprising both transfers and loans against favourable conditions – see Metten (1999).

Von Hagen and Hammond (1998) mention a number of conditions that a well-functioning FTS needs to fulfil. First, it should only provide insurance against temporary and asymmetric shocks because this is the type of shock for which the loss of monetary autonomy is most problematic. Second, the scheme should be simple and automatic. This is particularly important when some countries fear that other countries might abuse the system in order to receive more transfers. A third condition is that the net transfers must on average be zero over time to avoid systematic redistribution among countries. Fourth, the scheme should be balanced on a period-by-period basis (that is, in each period the sum of the net transfers over all countries should be zero). A fifth condition is that the shocks that the scheme is supposed to provide insurance against are uncorrelated over time. Transfers resulting from persistent shocks may weaken the incentive for governments to take away the source of the persistence of the shocks. A final condition is that the scheme cushions a substantial part of the shocks, otherwise the costs are too large to make the scheme worthwhile.

The disadvantage of a large coverage is that it may enhance the danger of moral hazard that is typically present in such schemes.[12] Moral hazard may arise because the country-specific shocks are not perfectly observable. As a result, the cross-border transfers cannot be conditioned explicitly on the exogenous shocks, but need to be conditioned on observables (such as the change in unemployment or economic growth). However, these observables are also affected by government policies. Knowing that the transfers (precisely because they are based on these observables) will at least partly compensate for the consequences of weak policy, the incentive for governments to implement structural reforms is weaker, especially when these reforms are politically costly. Particular examples are labour market reform (such as easing dismissal restrictions) and pushing back the welfare state. These types of measure are politically sensitive and may easily lead to social unrest.[13]

Beetsma and Bovenberg (2001) constructed a model in which countries can form a monetary union and in which country-specific shocks can be (partly) absorbed by an FTS. The transfers resulting from the FTS are based on a combination of exogenous shocks and a variable termed 'discipline'. Discipline is a catch-all term, capturing among other things the efficiency of the public sector, the monitoring of the handing out of benefits and the limitation of privileges of specific groups, and, more generally, the structural reform and deregulation of the economy. More discipline, on the one hand, leads to more resources, which can be used to serve the general interest. On the other hand, more discipline is costly from a political perspective. To authorities other than a country's government, the exogenous economic shocks and discipline are only observable in a combination, but not separately.[14] Hence the transfers can only be based on this observed combination, but not separately on the shocks or on discipline. For this reason, the FTS weakens a government's incentive to increase discipline. After all, the government knows that the resulting loss of resources will be partly compensated by transfers from other countries. The analysis by Beetsma and Bovenberg (2001) shows that in the presence of serious distortions in labour and product markets or a large public sector (which in turn leads to more distortions due to the large required tax revenues) it is optimal not to set up an FTS. In these circumstances, the danger of moral hazard is particularly serious. Most countries in the euro area are indeed characterised (still) by substantial distortions, despite the attempts (often half-hearted) at structural reform. In addition, public budgets are often not transparent. Therefore, the danger of moral hazard is serious for the euro area members, and so an FTS (as modelled by Beetsma and Bovenberg 2001) would be a dangerous option for Europe.

To limit the danger of moral hazard, transfers in the context of the FTS need to be based on observable variables that are as much as possible beyond the influence of the governments. Beetsma (2000) analysed a scheme that largely fulfils this condition.[15] The idea is to base transfers on exogenous sectoral shocks caused by developments in the world market for products in which the export sectors are active. The scheme is devised in such a way that the net transfers to each country are zero when all countries have an identical sectoral structure. Countries may still show differences in economic developments, but these will be caused by domestic circumstances (e.g. differences in policy and in the quality and priorities of the government) and provide no reason for international transfers.

Suppose that the world market (the market for tradables) consists of $j = 1, \ldots, s$ sectors. We denote by $x_{ijt}$ gross value added (in euro) of the exports by sector $j$ in country $i$ to the rest of the world (RoW) in period $t$. The RoW consists of all countries minus the euro area. We can write:

$$x_{ijt} = w_{ijt} X_{jt} \tag{5.1}$$

where $X_{jt}$ is the total export from the euro area to the RoW of products from sector $j$, while $w_{ijt}$ is the share of country $i$ in this total. We can now make the following decomposition:

$$\begin{aligned} x_{ijt} - x_{ijt-1} &= w_{ijt} X_{jt} - w_{ijt-1} X_{jt-1} \\ &= (\Delta w_{ijt}) X_{jt-1} + (\Delta w_{ijt})(\Delta X_{jt}) + w_{ijt-1}(\Delta X_{jt}) \end{aligned} \tag{5.2}$$

($\Delta$ denotes the change in a variable.) The component $(\Delta w_{ijt})X_{jt-1}$ is negative when the productivity of country $i$ in this sector increases at a slower pace than the average productivity in entire euro area in this sector. The difference will most likely be the result of differences in government policy, investment climate, investment behaviour, etc.; in other words, these are all factors that do not justify international transfers because they are determined by national choices. The same holds for the term $(\Delta w_{ijt})(\Delta X_{jt})$, which is of second-order magnitude and therefore likely to be small. The term $y_{ijt} \equiv w_{ijt-1}(\Delta X_{jt})$ is largely beyond the control of the policymakers in individual countries and therefore justifies intra-European cross-border transfers.[16]

Because a value of $y_{ijt}$ different from zero consists of compensation for capital providers and a compensation for workers, the question is: which part of $y_{ijt}$ should be compensated by the FTS? To keep the analysis as simple as possible, suppose that all individual securities holdings (stocks and bonds issued by companies) are perfectly spread over all individuals in the euro area.[17] It would then be reasonable to assume that the FTS should only cover independent shifts in labour income. Let $p_{jt}$ denote the average productivity in sector $j$ in the euro area. We express this as the value-added production per worker. The change in employment in sector $j$ in country $i$ associated with $y_{ijt}$ therefore equals $w_{ijt-1}(\Delta X_{jt})/p_{jt}$. Suppose further that $s_{jt}$ is the average salary in sector $j$ in the euro area. The increase in labour income in euros associated with $y_{ijt}$ is $w_{ijt-1}(\Delta X_{jt})(s_{jt}/p_{jt})$. Therefore, full coverage of an unexpected change in labour income implies a *gross* transfer to country $j$ of:[18]

$$gtr_{ijt} = -w_{ijt-1}(\Delta X_{jt})(s_{jt}/p_{jt}) \qquad (5.3)$$

The sum of gross transfers across all countries and all sectors will only in very special cases be exactly equal to zero. Therefore, the sum of these gross transfers needs to be financed (or rebated in case it is negative).

The question of what proportions countries should contribute is not trivial if countries differ from each other in dimensions other than just their sectoral structure. Take as an example the case where a small country, S, and a large country, L, set up a joint FTS. For simplicity, suppose that the sectoral structure in both countries is the same, so that L is a 'blown up' version of S. Moreover, suppose that for the first sector $\Delta X_{1t} < 0$, while for all other sectors $\Delta X_{jt} = 0$ ($j > 1$), hence the gross transfer flowing to L is larger than the gross transfer to S. If both countries contribute equally to the scheme, income in country S could therefore even be further destabilised. One possibility would be to make the contributions proportional to GDP, in which case L contributes a share $\text{GDP}_{\text{L}t-1}/(\text{GDP}_{\text{L}t-1} + \text{GDP}_{\text{S}t-1})$ of the sum of the gross transfers. Because both countries are characterised by the same sectoral structure in this case, the net contributions will be zero. Country L would only receive a net transfer as a result of the bad shock to export sector 1 if $w_{\text{L}t-1} > \text{GDP}_{\text{L}t-1}/(\text{GDP}_{\text{L}t-1} + \text{GDP}_{\text{S}t-1})$.

Another complication is the potential differences in the variances of the sectoral shocks on the world market. Some sectors, such as the production of natural resources or the chemical sector, are characterised by larger fluctuations in prices and production than other sectors, such as the food industry. Standard theory says that countries whose economic structures are relatively skewed towards risky sectors should pay a risk premium to persuade other countries to participate in the FTS. It is quite clear that it may be politically difficult to agree on the contributions, especially when they need to be differentiated across the participating countries.

The preceding analysis suggests that the proposed scheme is less vulnerable to moral hazard than other schemes proposed in the literature. Because our scheme is based on *changes* in $X_{jt}$, a permanent decline of sector $j$ will *not* lead to a permanent stream of transfers to countries that have a relatively high proportion of their economic activity in sector $j$. When a systematic decline of this sector is foreseen, a temporary stream of transfers can be used to restructure the economy towards other activities.

## CONCLUSION

The presence of asymmetric shocks is one of the main obstacles to a well-functioning monetary union. In this chapter we provide an overview of the relevance of asymmetric shocks in the euro area and shown how disequilibria resulting from asymmetric shocks can be reduced. Geographical concentration of economic activity affects the vulnerability of regions to asymmetric shocks. Given the limited role of factor mobility in cushioning such shocks, this has potential policy implications, both for the regional policies when regional disequilibria arise within a country and for macroeconomic policy when the resulting regional effects are so large that they affect the economy as a whole.

In this chapter we discuss extensively the various macroeconomic policy options available to handle asymmetric shocks. We should, however, emphasise that clustering is not the only source of asymmetric shocks. Asymmetric shocks could also arise from changes in producer or consumer confidence and could even be caused by economic policy changes.

We argue that the degree of shock asymmetry in Europe is not given, but will be affected by the process of economic and monetary unification itself. Asymmetric shocks arising from policymaking itself will become less important. This is not only the case for monetary policymaking, but also for fiscal policy, where a progressively tighter monitoring of individual policies (among others by means of the stability programmes under the Stability and Growth Pact) will reduce idiosyncratic policy deviations. As for the asymmetric shocks that relate to the geographic concentration of economic activities, the main questions are whether we can expect further clustering in Europe and what form this clustering will take: are we dealing with the concentration of ever more specialised firms that depend on each other (such as in Silicon Valley in the USA) or are we dealing with a clustering of a large set of different activities in certain geographic areas? After all, more specialisation implies a large burden on the channels that could restore equilibrium in the case of asymmetric shocks. On top of all this, it is crucial to what extent the economy at the country level is affected. It is likely that this influence is largest for the smaller economies that are less diversified.

The empirical research discussed above suggests that the sum of the various effects results in a slowly increasing correlation among the business cycles. On top of this, we expect that international labour mobility will increase for various reasons (such as diminishing language, cultural and institutional barriers).

We therefore expect that in the longer run the asymmetry of the shocks at the country level will decline, while the stabilisation of these shocks will become easier. As this is a process that proceeds only slowly, the role of fiscal policy in the near future will be important. Countries need to provide as much room as possible to the automatic stabilisers and need to avoid measures that can have procyclical effects. In particular, they should avoid the temptation to relax fiscal policy during an economic upswing. One cannot exclude the possibility of an increasing pressure to set up a system of fiscal transfers for asymmetric shocks or the possibility of a further centralisation of the tax-transfer system at the European level. Should this happen, then it is important that such institutional adjustments will be properly designed and will be robust against abuse.

## ACKNOWLEDGEMENTS

We thank Peter van Els for his helpful comments on an earlier version of this paper.

## NOTES

1 The starting point of this literature is the classical article by Mundell (1961), who received for this contribution, among others commendations, the Nobel prize in 1999.
2 A reason could be the presence of economies of scale or a faster technological progress in these activitites as a result of a concentration of knowledge.
3 This does not necessarily mean that the effects of a change in the common monetary policy are symmetric. The transmission of a change in the common monetary policy may differ across the countries in the union. For extensive empirical research on the monetary transmission mechanism in the euro area, see Angeloni *et al.* (2003) and the references therein.
4 An earlier review of this literature is found in Italianer and De Haan (1997). The ensuing overview also discusses some of the more recent contributions.
5 The real exchange rate between two economies with the same currency is defined as the relative labour cost.
6 Both goods and labour markets need to be flexible. A relative decrease of the price of the export goods needs to be accompanied by a reduction of the labour cost per unit of product. Otherwise, unemployment will not disappear despite the fall of the price of the export product.
7 The negative consequences of an expansive fiscal policy are perceived as relatively mild, while they receive the benefits in the form of higher expenses.
8 The contributions in Brunila *et al.* (2001) provide details about the operation of the Stability and Growth Pact. For an overview of the economic reasons and the effectiveness of the pact, see Beetsma (2001).
9 A fall of GDP by 2 per cent on an annual basis will in general lead to a waiver of the sanctions. In case of a slowdown of between 0.75 and 2 per cent an exception can be made, provided the country concerned can justify the violation of the 3 per cent norm by factors that were beyond its control. See Brunila *et al.* (2001).
10 An example of a fiscal measure that worked out procyclically is the tax relief that accompanied the introduction of the 'Tax Plan for the 21st century' in The Netherlands. The tax relief was intended to increase the acceptability of the plan (and not as a measure to influence the cycle). However, the relief took effect when the Dutch economy was on the verge of overheating and thus worked out procyclically.
11 A substantial part of this section is based on ideas that have earlier been discussed in Beetsma (2000).
12 By 'moral hazard' we mean that the scheme can adversely affect the behaviour of the authorities.
13 Recent plans in France to raise the pension contribution period of civil servants to that for market employees led to large-scale strikes.

14 Take for instance an observed increase in unemployment. This can be the result of a slowdown in world trade, which is an exogenous shock to the country under consideration. The *extent* to which the shock affects unemployment, however, depends on the structural labour reforms conducted by the government ('discipline').

15 The ensuing discussion is to a large extent based on Beetsma (2000), whose results in turn are based on ideas he worked out jointly with Eric Bartelsman.

16 One may expect that $\Delta X_{jt}$ is largely determined by the situation on the world market, although this variable is not insulated from the policies in the euro area. The ECB could, for example, reduce the external value of the euro in order to stimulate exports to the RoW. However, the influence of an *individual* government on $\Delta X_{jt}$ is limited. If the negative value of $\Delta X_{jt}$ is the consequence of policy choices at the European level, then the FTS that is discussed provides insurance against the asymmetric effects of weak policies at the supranational level.

17 It is easy to work out a case where asset holdings are unequally distributed. However, in practice it is difficult to properly measure the degree of diversification of investments.

18 The net transfers are obtained by subtracting the contributions of the individual countries from the gross contributions – see equation (5.3).

## REFERENCES


Aksoy, Y., De Grauwe, P. and Dewachter, H. (2002) 'Do asymmetries matter for European monetary policy?', *European Economic Review*, 46/3: 443–69.

Angeloni, I., Kashyap, A. and Mojon, B. (eds) (2003) *Monetary Policy Transmission in the Euro Area*, Cambridge: Cambridge University Press.

Arreaza, A., Sorensen, B.E. and Yosha, O. (1997) 'Consumption smoothing through fiscal policy in OECD and EU Countries', in J. Poterba and J. von Hagen (eds) *Fiscal Institutions and Fiscal Policy*, Chicago, IL: Chicago University Press.

Artis, M.J. (1999) 'Asymmetric shocks in Europe: Measurement and significance', in R.M.W.J. Beetsma and C. Oudshoorn (eds) 'Tools for Regional Stabilisation', Discussion Paper no. 9903, Dutch Ministry of Economic Affairs.

Artis, M.J. and Zhang, W. (1997) 'International business cycles and the ERM: is there a European business cycle?', *International Journal of Finance and Economics*, 2: 1–16.

Asdrubali, P., Sørensen, B.E. and Yosha, O. (1996) 'Channels of interstate risk sharing: United States 1963-1990', *Quarterly Journal of Economics*, 111: 1081–110.

Athanasoulis, S. and Van Wincoop, E. (1998) 'Risk-Sharing within the United States: what have financial markets and fiscal federalism accomplished?', Research Paper no. 9808, Federal Reserve Bank of New York.

Bayoumi, T. and Eichengreen, B. (1993) 'Shocking aspects of European monetary unification', in F. Torres and F. Giavazzi (eds) *Adjustment and Growth in the European Monetary Union*, Cambridge: Cambridge University Press.

Bayoumi, T. and Eichengreen, B. (1997) 'Optimum currency areas and exchange rate variability: theory and evidence compared', in B.J. Cohen (ed.) *International Trade and Finance: New frontiers for research: Essays in honour of Peter B. Kenen*, Cambridge: Cambridge University Press.

Bayoumi, T. and Masson, P.R. (1995) 'Fiscal flows in the United States and Canada: lessons for monetary union in Europe', *European Economic Review*, 39: 253–74.

Beetsma, R.M.W.J. (2000) 'How to deal with asymmetric shocks under European monetary union', *Revue de la Banque*, 2/3: 173–6.

Beetsma, R.M.W.J. (2001) 'Does EMU need a stability pact?', in A. Brunila, M. Buti and D. Franco (eds) *The Stability and Growth Pact: The architecture of fiscal policy in EMU*, Basingstoke: Palgrave.

Beetsma, R.M.W.J. and Bovenberg, A.L. (1998) 'Monetary union without fiscal coordination may discipline policymakers', *Journal of International Economics*, 45: 239–58.

Beetsma, R.M.W.J. and Bovenberg, A.L. (2001) 'The optimality of a monetary union without a fiscal union', *Journal of Money, Credit, and Banking*, 33/2; Part 1:179–204.

Beetsma, R.M.W.J. and Oudshoorn, C. (eds) (1999) 'Tools for Regional Stabilisation', Discussion Paper no. 9903, Dutch Ministry of Economic Affairs.

Blanchard, O.J. and Quah, D. (1989) 'The dynamic effects of aggregate demand and supply disturbances', *American Economic Review*, 79/4: 655–73.

Blanchard, O.J. and Perotti, R. (2002) 'An empirical characterization of the dynamic effects of changes in government spending and taxes on output', *Quarterly Journal of Economics*, 117/4: 1329–68.

Brunila, A., Buti, M. and Franco, D. (eds) (2001) *The Stability and Growth Pact: The architecture of fiscal policy in EMU*, Basingstoke: Palgrave.

Buti, M. and Sapir, A. (eds) (1998) *Economic Policy in EMU – a study by the European Commission Services*, Oxford: Clarendon Press.

Buti, M. and Suardi, M. (2000) 'Cyclical convergence or differentiation? Insights from the first year of EMU', *Revue de la Banque*, 2/3: 164–72.

Buti, M., Franco, D. and Ongena, H. (1998) 'Fiscal discipline and flexibility in EMU: the implementation of the Stability and Growth Pact', *Oxford Review of Economic Policy*, 14/3: 81–97.

Calmfors, L. (2001) 'Unemployment, labour-market reform and monetary union', *Journal of Labour Economics*, 19: 265–89.

Cohen, D. and Wyplosz, C. (1989) 'The European Monetary Union: An agnostic evaluation', CEPR Discussion Paper no. 306.

Cukierman, A. and Lippi, F. (2001) 'Labour markets and monetary union: a strategic analysis', *Economic Journal*, 111: 541–65.

De Grauwe, P. and Vanhaverbeke, W. (1993) 'Is Europe an optimum currency area? Evidence from regional data', in P.R. Masson and M.P. Taylor (eds) *Policy Issues in the Operation of Currency Unions*, Cambridge: Cambridge University Press.

De Nardis, S., Goglio, A. and Malgarini, M. (1996) 'Regional specialization and shocks in Europe: some evidence from regional data', *Weltwirtschaftliches Archiv*, 132/2: 197–214.

Dixit, A. (2000) 'A repeated game model of monetary union', *Economic Journal*, 110: 759–80.

*Economist, The* (2003) 'The French and German economies', 5–11 July: 28–29.

Eichengreen, B. (1991) 'Is Europe an Optimum Currency Area?', NBER Working Paper no. 3579.

Eichengreen, B. (1993) 'European monetary unification', *Journal of Economic Literature*, 31: 1321–57.

Eichengreen, B. and Wyplosz, C. (1998) 'The Stability Pact: More than a minor nuisance?', *Economic Policy*, 13: 65–113.

Erkel-Rousse, H. and Mélitz, J. (1995) 'New Empirical Evidence on the Costs of European Monetary Union', CEPR Discussion Paper no. 1169.

European Commission (1977a) *Report of the Study Group on the Role of Public Finance in European Integration*, Vol. I, Studies: Economic and Financial Series A13, Brussels.

European Commission (1977b) *Report of the Study Group on the Role of Public Finance in European Integration*, Vol. II, Studies: Economic and Financial Series B13, Brussels.

Fatas, A. (1998) 'Does Europe need a fiscal federation?', *Economic Policy*, 13/26: 163–203.

Fatas, A. and Mihov, I. (2001a) 'Government size and automatic stabilizers: international and intranational evidence', *Journal of International Economics*, 55/1: 3–28.

Fatas, A. and Mihov, I. (2001b) 'Fiscal policy and business cycles: an empirical investigation', *Moneda y Credito,* 0/212: 167–205.

Fatas, A. and Mihov, I. (2001c) 'The Effects of Fiscal Policy on Consumption and Employment: Theory and evidence', CEPR Discussion Paper no. 2760.

Fatas, A. and Mihov, I. (2003) 'The case for restricting fiscal policy discretion', *Quarterly Journal of Economics*, 118/4: 1419–48.

Forni, M. and Reichlin, L. (2001) 'Federal policies and local economies: Europe and the US', *European Economic Review*, 45/1: 109–34.

Frankel, J.A. (1997) *Regional Trading Blocks in the World Economic System*, Institute for International Economics, Washington, DC.

Frankel, J.A. and Rose, A.K. (1997) 'Is EMU more justifiable ex post than ex ante?', *European Economic Review*, 41/3–5: 753–60.

Frankel, J.A. and Rose, A.K. (1998) 'The endogeneity of the optimum currency area criteria', *Economic Journal*, 108/449: 1009–25.

Funke, M. (1997) 'The nature of shocks in Europe and in Germany', *Economica*, 64/255: 461–69.

Gordon, R.H. and Bovenberg, A.L. (1996) 'Why is capital so immobile internationally? Possible explanations and implications for capital income taxation', *American Economic Review*, 86/5: 1057–75.

Helg, R., Manasse, P., Monacelli. T. and Rovelli, R. (1995) 'How much (a)symmetry in Europe? Evidence from industrial sectors', *European Economic Review*, 39/5: 1017–41.

Italianer, A. and De Haan, J. (1997) 'Werkgelegenheid en groei in de EMU', in H. Jager (ed.) (1997) *De EMU in Breed Perspectief: Preadviezen van de Koninklijke Vereniging voor de Staathuishoudkunde*, Utrecht: Lemma.

Krugman, P.R. (1991) 'Increasing returns and economic geography', *Journal of Political Economy*, 99: 483–99.

Krugman, P.R. (1993) 'Lessons of Massachusetts for EMU', in F. Torres and F. Giavazzi (eds) *Adjustment and growth in the European Monetary Union*, Cambridge: Cambridge University Press.

Mélitz, J. (1996) 'Assessing the costs of European Monetary Union', *Atlantic Economic Journal*, 24/4: 269–80.

Mélitz, J. and Zumer, F. (2002) 'Regional redistribution and stabilization by the centre in Canada, France, the UK, and the US: a reassessment and new tests', *Journal of Public Economics*, 86/2: 263–86.

Metten, A. (1999) 'Comment on 'European fiscal stabilisation: an operational concept?', in R.M.W.J. Beetsma and C. Oudshoorn (eds) 'Tools for Regional Stabilisation', Discussion Paper no. 9903, Dutch Ministry of Economic Affairs.

Midelfart-Knarvik, K.H. and Overman, H.G. (2002) 'Delocation and European integration: is structural spending justified?', *Economic Policy*, 17/35: 322–59.

Mundell, R.A. (1961) 'A theory of optimum currency areas', *American Economic Review*, 51: 657–65.

Neumann, M. and Von Hagen, J. (1994) 'Real exchange rates within and between monetary unions: how far away is EMU?', *Review of Economics and Statistics*, 76: 236–44.

Obstfeld, M. and Peri, G. (1998) 'Regional non-adjustment and fiscal policy', *Economic Policy*, 13/26: 205–59.

Pisani-Ferry, J., Italianer, A. and Lescure, R. (1993) 'Stabilization properties of budgetary systems: a simulation analysis', in European Commission, *The Economics of Community Public Finance*, European Economy, Reports and Studies 5: 417–55.

Puga, D. (1999) 'The rise and fall of regional inequalities', *European Economic Review*, 43/2: 303–34.

Sala-i-Martin, X. and Sachs, J. (1992) 'Fiscal federalism and optimum currency areas: evidence for Europe from the United States', in M. Canzoneri, V. Grilli and P. Masson (eds) *Establishing a Central Bank: Issues in Europe and lessons from the US*, Cambridge: Cambridge University Press.

Sibert, A. (1999) 'Monetary integration and economic convergence', *Economic Journal*, 109: 78–92.

Sibert, A. and Sutherland, A. (2000) 'Monetary Union and Labour Market Reform', *Journal of International Economics*, 51: 421–35.

Sørensen, B.E. and Yosha, O. (1998) 'International risk sharing and European Monetary Unification', *Journal of International Economics*, 45/2: 211–38.

Svensson, L.E.O. (2000) 'Open-economy inflation targeting', *Journal of International Economics*, 50/1: 155–83.

Von Hagen, J. (1992) 'Fiscal arrangements in a monetary union – some evidence from the US', in D. Fair and C. de Boissieux (eds) *Fiscal Policy, Taxes and the Financial System in an Increasingly Integrated Europe*, Deventer: Kluwer Academic Publishers.

Von Hagen, J. (1999) 'A fiscal insurance for the EMU?', in R.M.W.J. Beetsma and C. Oudshoorn (eds) 'Tools for Regional Stabilisation', Discussion Paper no. 9903, Dutch Ministry of Economic Affairs.

Von Hagen, J. and Hammond, G.W. (1998) 'Regional insurance against asymmetric shocks: an empirical study for the European Community', *The Manchester School*, 66: 331–53.

Weber, A. (1990) 'EMU and Asymmetries and Adjustment Problems in the EMS: Some empirical evidence', CEPR Discussion Paper no. 448.

# Index

Page numbers for figures have suffix **f**, those for tables have suffix **t**

For Product Safety Concerns and Information please contact our EU
representative GPSR@taylorandfrancis.com
Taylor & Francis Verlag GmbH, Kaufingerstraße 24, 80331 München, Germany

www.ingramcontent.com/pod-product-compliance
Ingram Content Group UK Ltd.
Pitfield, Milton Keynes, MK11 3LW, UK
UKHW011018180926
475701UK00004B/817

* 9 7 8 0 4 1 5 6 5 5 4 7 7 *